What People Are Saying About
Sacred Mysticism of Egypt

Fotoula Adrimi has had powerful initiations into the ancient world of Egypt. It is clearly her destiny to bring through the ancient teachings she has been shown. The Egyptian Goddess Isis brought Fotoula into a world where spiritual awakening was possible and whose paradigms can be accessed to help all of life now. And we are now gifted by what she learned in *Sacred Mysticism of Egypt*. *Sacred Mysticism of Egypt* is filled with wonder and leads us home to the embodiment of the Divine Self. This brilliantly written book opens our perception, deepens our understanding of spiritual truths, and leads us to a path of self-realization. In *Sacred Mysticism of Egypt*, Fotoula Adrimi guides us to finding the diamond within us all. She exquisitely followed a path of mysteries that have been found hidden beyond the monuments, statues, pyramids, and hieroglyphs. This book is really about the extraordinary changes we can make in our lives and for the planet through embracing the power of unconditional love and understanding that we are beings of Divine Light. This book will uncover ancient teachings that will amaze you!
Sandra Ingerman, world-renowned shamanic teacher and award-winning author of twelve books, including *Walking in Light* and *Soul Retrieval*

Fotoula is a deeply spiritual and wise teacher. Her work is grounded in love and reaches into the sacred caverns of the heart. If you are ready to deepen your soul's journey, you could not find a better guide.
Michael Stone, founder of *Well of Light*

This is the book we all need to be reading in these times we are in today. Fotoula's new book, *Sacred Mysticism of Egypt*, magically and cleverly invites the readers onto the bridge to access the heart-centered Light and unconditional love from these ancient teachings of Egypt. She creates a path to these teachings with simple tools, to access ancient spiritual messages that we can tap into and use today. Fotoula, from her own experience and exquisite writing style, takes us on an unforgettable healing journey for ourselves and those whom we touch.
Terry Morgan, shamanic astrologer

I grew up with a Dutch mother who knew her true spiritual home on Earth was Egypt. Ancient Egypt was a common topic of conversation in our living room in the Netherlands. Fotoula Adrimi's new book takes us on a journey of initiation into the Living Light. Did you know that the veil separating Present and Past can be lifted? That ancient mystery teachings can still be accessed and retrieved as paradigms for our time?
Imelda Almqvist, forest witch, painter, international teacher, and author of *Sacred Art* and *North Sea Water in My Veins*

In this book, Fotoula Adrimi is our guide as she takes us on a journey of initiation into the HEKA teachings of ancient Egypt that will inspire and inform our own spiritual path. Through her remembrances of past lives, Fotoula provides incredible insights into this rich spiritual tradition of the Living Light. And the beautiful spiritual practices she offers will support readers to access their inherent power and love. Truly, this is a book of service.
Fi Sutherland, author of *Coming Home: Awakening through the Stillness into the Living Light*

This book reveals previously unknown secrets and spiritual truths found within the era of Ancient Egypt. From the perspective of a gifted seer and shaman who's accessed wisdom and insights through her current past-life experiences, this manuscript provides powerful lessons and teachings, allowing the reader to dive deeply into mystical ways of being that enlighten individuals and the entire cosmos.

Dory Cote, shamanic practitioner and shamanic teacher

Sacred Mysticism of Egypt

The Ancient Path of HEKA Initiation

Also by Fotoula Adrimi
The Golden Book of Wisdom
Ancient Spirituality and Shamanism for Modern Times
ISBN: 9781999641009

Also by The ISIS School of Holistic Health
Fi Sutherland, *Coming Home: Awakening through the Stillness into the Living Light*
ISBN: 9781999641023

Sacred Mysticism of Egypt

The Ancient Path of HEKA Initiation

Fotoula Foteini Adrimi

BOOKS

London, UK
Washington, DC, USA

CollectiveInk

First published by O-Books, 2025
O-Books is an imprint of Collective Ink Ltd.,
Unit 11, Shepperton House, 89 Shepperton Road, London, N1 3DF
office@collectiveinkbooks.com
www.collectiveinkbooks.com
www.o-books.com

For distributor details and how to order, please visit the 'Ordering' section on our website.

Text copyright: Fotoula Foteini Adrimi, 2024

ISBN: 978 1 80341 712 7
978 1 80341 926 8 (ebook)
Library of Congress Control Number: 2024943071

All rights reserved. Except for brief quotations in critical articles or reviews, no part of this book may be reproduced in any manner without prior written permission from the publishers.

The rights of Fotoula Foteini Adrimi as author have been asserted in accordance with the Copyright, Designs and Patents Act, 1988.

A CIP catalogue record for this book is available from the British Library.

Design: Lapiz Digital Services

UK: Printed and bound by CPI Group (UK) Ltd, Croydon, CR0 4YY
Printed in North America by CPI GPS partners

The author of this book does not dispense medical advice or prescribe the use of any technique as a form of treatment for physical, emotional, or medical problems without the advice of a physician, either directly or indirectly. The intent of the author is only to offer information of a general nature to help you in your quest for emotional and spiritual well-being. In the event you use any of the information in this book for yourself, which is your constitutional right, the author and the publisher assume no responsibility for your actions.

We operate a distinctive and ethical publishing philosophy in all areas of our business, from our global network of authors to production and worldwide distribution.

To Fi Sutherland, my dearest friend and co-teacher in the ISIS School of Holistic Health Ltd.

To Akis, my precious nephew and godson.

Disclaimer

Many of the ancient Egyptian myths were written on papyrus and on the walls of the tombs in precise code, with little embellishment. As a good story-teller, I tuned into the material and allowed it to re-emerge so that it is captivating for the reader. I stayed true to the original story but brought life into it, to make it accessible. I see myself as a transmitter of truth, instead of a translator.

The content of this book is for personal use. You are not authorized to teach or reproduce any of this material, which is copyrighted.

The case studies in this book are true, but names were changed to protect the identities of those involved.

The author does not offer medical advice or advocate the use of any techniques as a form of medical treatment for physical or mental illness without the advice of a physician. The intent of the author is to offer information of a general nature to help people in their spiritual journey. In the event you use any of the information or exercises in this book, which is your right, the author and publisher assume no responsibility for any outcomes.

None of these concepts has been scientifically proven, and no claims are made as to their effectiveness and authenticity.

The porphyry sarcophagus [...] was the baptismal font, upon emerging from which, the neophyte was "born again," and became an adept.

— **H.P. Blavatski**

Contents

Preface	xv
Foreword	xix
Acknowledgements	xxii
Introduction	xxiii

Part 1:	The Golden Times Foundation Teachings	1
Chapter 1	From Atlantis to the Land of KHEM (Egypt): A Portal of the Living Light	5
Chapter 2	A Spiritual Heaven on Earth	16
Chapter 3	The Living Light: The Essence of Divine Consciousness	29
Chapter 4	We Are Multi-dimensional Etheric, Physical Beings	38
Chapter 5	Creation Story: From Spirit to Matter and Back	52
Chapter 6	Monads-Neteru: The Cosmic Archetypes of Existence	63
Chapter 7	The Enlightened Ones	74
Chapter 8	The Great Pyramid and Initiation	88
Chapter 9	Horus of the East	107
Chapter 10	Etheric Keys in Sacred Sites	116
Chapter 11	The Divine Mother Speaks	128
Part 2:	Initiation as a Channel of HEKA	137
Chapter 12	The Goddess Iset and the Seven Gates of Awareness Initiation	141
Chapter 13	The Light of Atum Initiation	148
Chapter 14	The Wisdom of Thoth Initiation	155

Part 3: Mystical Esoteric Practices of Ancient
       Egyptian Spirituality   165

Chapter 15 Activation through Iset   168
Chapter 16 May I Pass in Peace: Death and
              Eternal Life   181
Chapter 17 The Universal Law of Ma'at: Divine
              Truth and Justice   190
Chapter 18 The Universal Law of Ma'at: Divine
              Order and Manifestation   200
Chapter 19 Death, Resurrection, Reincarnation   212
Chapter 20 Releasing the Dead and Healing the
              Living   225
Chapter 21 Initiation into HEKA: Walking the
              Path of the Living Light   236

Afterword   247
Author Biography   249
Previous Titles   250
Note to the Reader: Where Do I Go from Here?   251
References   254
Glossary of Terms   256

Preface

In 2006, unexpectedly, the Goddess Isis, known as Iset in ancient Egypt, came to me in a meditation and asked me to be her teacher. At the time, I had little understanding of what was being asked of me. I had no idea that the Path of Isis would become the foundation stone of my spiritual life and help me expand into new multi-dimensional spheres of awareness.[1]

Before birthing into this life, I was a being of Light consciousness in the cosmos. Iset, as the Divine Mother, asked me to incarnate on Earth. As a being of Light consciousness, choice, as it is understood on Earth, does not exist, nor does one say no to the Divine, as this would be nonsensical. There were two options. Either, I could be born into a human life from conception, or enter at the age of 30 as a walk-in. The walk-in scenario would allow another soul, the original being destined to be Fotoula, to experience human life until 30. Then this soul would move into the spirit realms, and I would inhabit their body.

A walk-in comes into a body that already carries the karma, knowledge, habits, and patterns of the previous soul and their ancestors. An analogy is choosing between building a new home or buying one from someone else; in the latter, it takes time to reconfigure the house to your personal expression. There is also a karmic link between you and the first occupant. And, whilst the spiritual Light that the new soul brings, together with an intention to serve life, can mitigate some of the karma of the original soul, other karma still has to be purified.

For these reasons, I chose to be birthed from the beginning. I was born in northern Greece and grew up in a house by the sea in the town of Kavala. As a child, I found life difficult. There was a sense of oppression within my family and in my community, with little opportunity for individual expression, free thinking, and spiritual expansion. My soul had never experienced such a restrictive environment. In previous incarnations, I had been cocooned and lived in loving, supportive surroundings, able to expand spiritually.

I would often gaze at the Aegean, knowing that across this sea lay the sacred land of Egypt, my spiritual home. I was naturally clairvoyant, and I would often find myself spontaneously in what I now know as shamanic journeys. On many of these journeys, I was accompanied by a shining woman with wings (Iset) to ancient Egyptian temples, and I would feel as if I was truly there.

In these alternative realities of the shamanic journeys, I knew that what was happening in the external world could not harm me; an imaginary wall of Light separated me from the dramas of everyday life. Within the safety of the Light, I found much to explore; as well as Iset, other luminous beings, such as Mother Mary, would help me negotiate life. I had a strong faith in Divine goodness, and Mother Mary would bathe me in unconditional love.

She answered my questions and showed me what to do. I disliked conflict. My soul had been very pure and innocent before incarnating, and Mother Mary taught me how to stand up for myself. Through these journeys and meditations, I became highly clairvoyant, seeing and hearing spirit, like my great uncle who died when I was 11.

In dreams and journeys, Iset spoke to me about the Golden Times of Egypt, the Path of Initiation, the Great Mysteries. Little did I know that one day I would again access the old wisdom that lay inside me and lead pilgrimages to the ancient places of power. My time with Iset awakened my fascination with the mysticism of ancient Egypt and Atlantis, but in provincial Greece in the '80s it was hard to find esoteric books, as any spiritual quest was frowned upon by organized religion. In response, I turned to the ancient Greek texts, such as those written by Herodotus and Plato, to discover more about ancient wisdom and Egypt.

When I was 13 years of age, my world upended. I became frightened of my clairvoyance. Adults told me that what I was doing was wrong; an insignificant girl should not speak to Mother Mary. For the first time, doubt, feelings of guilt, fear of spirits, and self-judgment arose within me. I abandoned the spirit realm and immersed myself in everyday life.

For a while, nothing significant happened until I had an awakening experience at the age of 30 and suddenly started to access my spiritual knowledge. When, in 2006, Iset asked me to be her teacher, one night shortly afterwards an alignment took place within me. In my first book, I share how this happened. In summary, I woke up in bed as a column of Light entered my body through the navel. The energy was so strong that the bed was moving from side to side. Iset told me later that this was when the beings of Light embedded in my body all the teachings that I was to channel, and the plan for my future life.

This was the turning point that transformed my life. I immersed myself in Iset's teachings that I channeled. And since that time, I have been consciously working daily with Iset, other beings of Light, and the energy of the Living Light — the Light of awareness and ascension that Iset teaches. I have been channeling a vast body of work consisting of rituals, ceremonies, Light language chants, meditations, and esoteric teachings that form what Iset calls, *The Path of the Living Light*. Iset says that this is the path to embodied ascension: instead of leaving our body behind at death, we transform it into the spiritual Light that is beyond the physical. We can become the Living Light: awaken into the enlightened Self, whilst living in the world. This path spans lifetimes and many spheres of existence. It is a path of awakening out of the Earth's social conditioning. Iset has shown me that I worked with and taught this path in ancient times, in Atlantis, Tibet, and the Golden Times of Egypt.

In February 2019, after teaching the 3-day course, *the Spiritual Path of Iset*, I had a significant dream. Iset asked me to write a second book: a book that presented fundamental principles of spiritual awakening that would be a stepping stone for increased awareness and esoteric learning. In the dream, we discussed the preface and first chapter. I awoke with a sense of purpose and wrote those chapters. Then I waited while continuing with my spiritual practices as my soul expanded. At the start of 2021, a new body of work based on the understanding of the multi-dimensional self and the process of awakening into the Living Sun we all are came through. I resumed writing, and this book is the result.

In the book, I reveal some of the teachings that Iset has offered me. I share experiences and rituals from my past lives in ancient times, and teachings on how to overcome different situations you may meet in your life and spiritual path. I talk about some of the ancient Egyptian myths and their esoteric meanings, what is hidden behind the symbols and stories. I explain the three main paths of the ancient initiate. I offer activations that may help you in your soul's journey.

Whatever this book is for you, my sincere hope is that you discover the path that leads you into the embodiment of your incredible spiritual essence.

Endnote

1. The sphere of existence we are mostly aware of when alive is the physical realm. Outside physical life, many other worlds exist. Sometimes we can astro-travel. For example, when we awake from a dream and we know we have been somewhere, but do not know where. Our consciousness exists in many planes at the same time, but we mostly consciously know the earthly realm.

Foreword

by Bhola Nath Banstola, Himalayan Nepalese Shaman

Fotoula and I first made contact in 2013. Lord Shiva came in a vision and invited her to travel to Tibet. He told her to find the Jhankri-shaman Bhola and how she could locate me. Since then, Fotoula has taken part in many of my courses and three pilgrimages to the Himalayas.

In getting to know Fotoula and the ISIS School of Holistic Health, there have been glimpses of the ancient spiritual tradition of Egypt and her work with Goddess Isis. Fotoula identifies Isis as her leading spirit guide, who looks after everything she does in her spiritual life and the material world. I am, therefore, grateful to this Goddess who has brought us together.

In her book, Fotoula opens a path for us to walk in the First Time when people lived on Earth fully aware of their spirit. The awakened human being is what she describes as the Living Light. She evokes memories of a time long gone when truth and justice reigned, rather than our age of corruption and greed. And the secret of that age was simple — awareness through the embodiment of our enlightened spirit.

In my Himalayan tradition, there are myths about how humans came to be. One of our myths of creation is that the human soul came as an intense Light orb, manifested like a Garuda-eagle floating in the Vayu wind, merged into the water and solidified into a physical form. We are now in this physical form, with little memory of the immensity and Light we came from. Remembering, awakening, and embodying our Light, becoming the Living Light as Fotoula describes, is to be truly alive and again "remember" who we are. This book is an invitation and a map towards self-discovery of our essential nature as a being of Light. Although our current Kaliyuga reality is far removed from the times described in the book, these ancient teachings offer a way to overcome our modern state of mind. I believe, as well as many fellow shamans and masters, that the fundamental cause for the difficulties we face in our world, including environmental destruction, wars, and physical and mental illness, is we have forgotten the source of our provenance, thus our roots.

The way out of this chaotic era is not by exclusively relying on our welfare, environmental policies, and technological advances; however, they have become our "comfort zone." Our human race has become passengers on a wrecked ship looking for rescue ropes to save ourselves from the infinite sea of Maya-illusion. We are missing a vital and intrinsic vibrant thread within us all: the power of our life essences — Atma.

People in the Satya Yuga-Golden Times are described in the ancient texts as embodied deities walking in the bosom of Mother Earth. They are our ancestors. Fotoula guides us through her memories of that time and considers the critical aspects of harmonious living that we can all adhere to — truth and justice allow us to flow with the Divine Order of the cosmos. This axiom, which the ancient Egyptians called the Rule of Ma'at, is the antidote to the suffering caused by the insatiable mind of the conditioned reality.

The book is a valuable resource for spiritual awakening and an essential guide for the practitioner of our times. Fotoula ascribes the Living Light to the ancient Egyptian word HEKA, meaning the power of creation; the other side is unconditional love. We shamans have tasted the fruits of such practices with this power and can attest to their efficacy in overcoming the issues humanity faces today.

This resource book is a "wake-up call" and an invitation to follow a spiritual path to enlightenment. Whilst focused on ancient Egypt, the spiritual practices offered are universal and relevant to whatever tradition you follow. The universal power of creation enhances every spiritual endeavor, whether a shamanic ceremony, a yoga practice, or a dynamic Mantra recitation. This secret ambrosia elevates everything else into an authentic state.

Fotoula leads us onto this ancient path by sharing authentic resources and practices to remember this forgotten link that can weave together old and new through her well-written book. She transmits the mysticism and spirituality of ancient Egypt, planting a seed of wisdom in each of us that can grow through our spiritual practice. This book is a wealth of knowledge, profoundly researched and tested, supporting your awakening.

We can only radiate the Living Light within ourselves through regular practice, expressing gratitude to our ancestors and teachers, and remembering our source.

My hearty congratulations to Fotoula for how she has been able to tap the ancient wisdom of the Egyptians.

May all be benefited!

Bhola Nath Banstola
President, Nepal Shaman Association
Executive Director, Academy for Tantra and Shamanic Studies
Kathmandu, Nepal
Date: April 16, 2024

Acknowledgements

I wish to thank Fi Sutherland, co-teacher in the Isis School of Holistic Health. Fi has been an incredible friend and pillar of support of the Temple of Light that Iset is reintroducing through these teachings. Fi has meditated daily since 1995. When she stepped onto this path, she discovered the missing link that these teachings re-establish. Fi has been a source of inspiration and encouragement as well as giving me valuable feedback. The book is a joint effort between the Goddess Isis, myself, and Fi.

I wish to thank Sandra Ingerman for her wonderful support over many years, her love, and friendship. Sandra has been a source of deep inspiration from my early days as a teacher.

I wish to thank my teacher and friend Bhola Banstola for his wisdom, working partnership, and teachings.

I would like to thank my beautiful friend and psychic medium Ian Shanes for our deep soul connection, and the lifetimes of friendship, including ancient Egypt. Similarly I thank the late Frank Babcock: my first mentor, who saw me in spirit as the ancient Egyptian High Priestess, although he had never met me.

Finally I would like to express my deepest gratitude to my students, readers, and seekers of truth on the path of the ancient Egyptian mysteries: the initiates of the Living Light beyond time. You have taught me more than I could ever teach you.

Introduction

Eons ago, a great civilization existed on Earth, in which human beings were aware of their spiritual nature. This civilization exists as a soul memory and initiates deep longing towards harmonious spiritual living in a supportive community. The foundations of this extraordinary civilization were built on the spirituality of the Living Light, which provided the fundamentals for the Golden Times of ancient Egypt, described with the term Zep Tepi, "The Initial Time."

Since 2006, I have been remembering my past life and spiritual work during Zep Tepi, working with, teaching, and embodying the Living Light frequencies. In this book, I share the spiritual heritage of the Living Light. I include aspects of history, teachings, and personal experiences from communing with the monuments of ancient Egypt. Throughout, you will find historical descriptions as well as rich explanations of the ancient Egyptian spirituality as taught to the initiates and adepts of the temples. I will lead you through ceremonies, journeys, and spiritual practices that help you access the etheric energy and spiritual path of the Living Light.

Ancient Egypt was created as a sanctuary, a holy place where the Living Light teachings were accessible to all who wished to become an awakened spiritual being whilst living in a human body. My aim in writing this book is the same: to familiarize you with the teachings and spiritual tradition of the Living Light for the purposes of spiritual expansion and awakening.

For the ancient Egyptians, to be alive meant to live spiritually aware, walking a spiritual path to ascension. This was the most important purpose of human life: to awaken and become the Living Light. They would describe our conventional Western lives as "dead," people living with no spiritual awareness. A life devoid of spirit was seen as one of suffering. It is only the awakened soul that can embody the state of contentment and grace.

My accounts may differ from those of Egyptologists who view ancient Egyptians as a primitive people and believe that the Great Pyramid was constructed in 2490 BC using archaic tools. The spelling and interpretation of some of the ancient words may also deviate from academics. I will lift the veil of time and show a different reality to that taught by historians, and I hope you will find it rewarding.

During Zep Tepi, people's lives focused on spiritual development and soul evolution, supported by the community. The prevailing culture honored the sacred. Nowadays, few of us live in spiritual sanctuaries. You may have multiple obligations and limited time for meditation. The practices in the book, whilst carrying the ancient wisdom, are designed to support you, a spiritual seeker in modern times.

Spiritual Transmissions of Sacred Knowledge

As you delve deeper into the teachings of the Living Light offered in the book, some of you may experience an etheric transmission of high frequency. Accordingly, you may feel tired or even sleepy and unable to read further. Do not push yourself to continue reading; allow the activation of sacred knowledge to take place and either fall asleep or meditate in silence. You may also experience physical sensations, sense pressure in different parts of your body, and feel some pain when energy blocks in your tissues are released. This is normal.

The energy of the Living Light is very strong, and your current body may not be used to high vibrations, even if you have had a spiritual practice for many years. Take care of yourself following the practices. If possible, avoid television and refrain from the harsh energies of our world, including draining relationships. Take time to integrate the energy into your body so that your vibrational frequency increases. Helpful ways include walks in nature, drinking water, relaxing, taking a bath, eating some nurturing food, or swimming, especially in nature. Insights and realizations may arise, either in your everyday life or during dreams.

Each chapter offers you etheric energy downloads, openings in awareness, and gates of initiation, where more of your spiritual power is activated. For this purpose, it is important to read the book in sequence. Afterwards, you can concentrate on specific chapters which attract your attention.

Psychic Awareness versus Inner Wisdom

People often ask, "Will I be able to engage with the path of the Living Light if I am not psychic? What if I do not see or hear spirit or have visions during the spiritual journeys?"

Since childhood, I have been naturally psychic. Enlightened spirit beings and those who have died are as close to me as people who are alive. My father jokes that I spend more time speaking to the dead than the living. I have been very fortunate to have a well-grounded sense of discernment and know which spirits to work with. I wish to thank Iset, who has been instrumental in my work, as well as other enlightened beings. They have helped me stay aligned with my soul's purpose, as being psychic can be a double-edged sword. I have seen people lose sight of their spiritual path as soon as they develop psychic gifts, renouncing soul evolution in favor of communicating with spirits.

The basic psychic gifts can be divided into four categories. You may have one main gift or more than one. Clairvoyant people see images, colors, and spirits. Sometimes this happens with their eyes open, but mostly it is through an inner third-eye connection, the spiritual eye. People see images in their head, and this is why it is easy to confuse a clairvoyant image with imagination, especially for the beginner. With clairaudience, some people hear spirit as thoughts, speaking in their own voice. At other times, they hear a distinctly different voice in their ear, as if someone is talking to them. Clairsentience is generally a more accurate form of communication. There are no images or sounds; you feel physical sensations in your body that point you to the essence of the message. For example, in a guided meditation to a temple, you may not see any images, but you have a felt sense of being there. The fourth psychic gift is claircognizance (inner knowing). You know something, although you do not know how you know. I remember one of my power animals appearing to me in this way. I knew there was a panther beside me, even though I could not see, hear, or feel it.

We all have psychic gifts, and given time and practice, we can develop them. However, most people equate psychic ability with either clairvoyance or clairaudience and dismiss other forms of spirit communication. For some, clairvoyance and clairaudience are not possible, even though there is a deep desire to see and hear spirit. This desire can be a mind trap. The mind wants what it cannot have and blocks further spiritual progress. "If only I could hear my spirit helpers, I would know what to do." This is not the case. Helping spirits are not here to live our lives and tell us what to do. This is our job. We have to go through the process of grinding the coarse diamond to develop the inner shine and evolve.

Whether we are psychic or not, when we are on a spiritual path, and we have an important choice to make, we will be guided to the right decision. Life will bring us to that point where we know what to do. This inner knowing may be the result of an intervention from a spirit guide or the voice of our wise self.

Sometimes people think that unless they see or hear spirits, they will not be able to progress on their spiritual path. A lack of natural psychic ability does not prevent anyone advancing. Psychic work can be over-emphasized and a trap in itself. Excited about seeing and hearing spirit, we may spend hours in spirit communication. Then, instead of developing spiritually, we develop psychically, which does not help our soul's evolution.

Thus, psychic development and spiritual development are not the same, although the two can coexist. Spiritual development is the inner transformation into the enlightened spirit, and this takes dedicated practice with high vibrational Light frequencies.

Some of my students work deeply with their body and inner connection instead of opening psychically. In investigating this, I was told that their soul had chosen not to be distracted by psychic gifts so that it could focus on spiritual awakening, overcome the social programing, and reach enlightenment.

There is another truth that I have observed in many students who were naturally psychic. As they evolved spiritually, their psychic gifts, especially clairvoyance, diminished. If we identify spirituality with psychic seeing, we may think that these people have regressed. The opposite is true. When you develop spiritually, your psychic gifts may appear to diminish, when actually they become more selective. You may not see spirits as clearly as before, but you are more centered, and your spiritual Light grows. This means that your inner awareness expands, rather than relying on spirits outside of you for answers. When you need to see or channel, the spirits will come, but you will see less details than before. The details are not important. Instead, you receive the essence of the communication in a quick and effective manner.

In walking the path of the Living Light, I invite you to release expectations, develop acceptance, and surrender. Know that the path that opens for you will be personal and completely aligned with your higher purpose and the wishes of your soul.

***

Try not to compare your experience with that of someone else's; yet allow yourself to learn from them.

In spiritual work, we all have a little piece of the puzzle; no one has the full picture, and whatever you bring can change someone else's understanding. Do not judge yourself or what you receive. Many people regard what others experience as more noteworthy, dismiss what comes to them, and give up. Walk your path with humility and purpose, and adopt a beginner's mind which remains open to new learning.

Remembering

Throughout the book, I include journeys to the time of Zep Tepi, where we commune with the sacred sites, and beings of Light, and anchor the energy in the body. Stepping onto this path may lead you to remember your past lives, when you mastered the egoic conditioned mind and worked in service for the highest good of all.

Etherically, the Golden Times of ancient Egypt are spiritually protected, for good reason. Journeys and meditations that take us to this time need to have a pure intention. As I have learned through my practice, curiosity about these times is not a good enough reason to allow us to engage with them. These times were characterized by a strong intention to help humanity to evolve and will repel discordant energies. I invite you to adopt a similar intention: "May I travel to these times in service to the highest good. May I receive what can help me and humanity at this time in our history."

My Earliest Experience of Zep Tepi

In 2006, I took part in a healing course. From the first hour, the outline of a well-built man appeared in front of me. When I had my eyes open, the outline appeared luminous yellow. When I closed my eyes, I saw it as emerald green, one of the vibrational colors that Iset comes with. This man never said anything, and I assumed he was a helping spirit assisting in the course.

During the morning, the teacher was trying to remove a spirit attachment from one of the participants but was unsuccessful. She emailed her friend Frank Babcock, an experienced healer who specialized in removing spirit attachments and worked distantly. Frank replied that, guided by his spirit helpers, his etheric body had been in the room, not to remove the spirit attachment but to pay his respects to a high priestess from ancient Egypt: me. He was the well-built man I saw.

The teacher suggested I email Frank, who lived in the USA. He encouraged me to share my spiritual experiences with him. In those early years of my development, Frank became a trusted mentor. He suggested I do a past-life regression journey to the Golden Times of ancient Egypt and find out more about myself.

My Journey to Zep Tepi
As I started the journey, I felt apprehensive. This is such a sacred time, and the task felt daunting. I called my guardian angel to be with me, and immediately an angel, dressed in a cyan blue mantle, appeared. Never had my spirit guides manifested so quickly. The angel said he would accompany me in the journey and follow my lead. I then asked to access my past life in ancient Egypt.

I saw myself standing in a desert, and before I could go anywhere, a voice asked, "Why do you wish to go there?" I replied that I was following my friend Frank's suggestion, and I was curious to discover my past life. Suddenly, I was back in my room, and the whole vision disappeared.

Then, I reflected on why I wanted to go there. I could feel there was a higher purpose behind the journey. I tried again. This time when I was asked why I wished to go there, I said that I wanted to remember the spiritual truths that could help myself and the world in our current times. This was a good intention. In the next instance I experienced myself in a different body, the one I lived in during those times. Since then I have maintained the same intention: "May I access the Golden Times to remember how to serve the highest good and help myself and others awaken."

An Invitation

We access the Golden Times to remember, and remembering is a process that opens from within, through the quietening of the egoic mind. We allow the high vibrational energy to work through us, and we may experience insights. When these realizations come, it is as if they were always within us, even if we had no previous knowledge of them. We connect to these distant ancestors to create a link through time and space, like a cable that enables a transmission of the Living Light, which can be felt as love, become knowledge, or be experienced as etheric energy.

It is conceivable that you had past incarnations during those times, and something deeper is trying to awaken you to that fact. One of the teachers of those times, called Im-Hot-Tep,[2] meaning "He Who Comes in Peace," invites us to participate in this very important spiritual work with a pure intention and open heart. Below is a channeling from him:

***

"I am your ancestor, and you are the descendants. I know you; you have incarnated many times. I recognize you, for I recognize the vibration of your soul. This is why you are here, and why you are connecting with these times. We created ancient Egypt so you can remember. Many incarnations have passed between the Golden Times and your time, and you have lived many lives since you were here. You can receive what has been anchored there. It is there to be accessed by those who seek the Light and the path towards awakening, the path that will carry you back to Source.

Even in the Golden Times, people could forget who they were: beings of Light incarnated in the physical world. The material world can consume one so easily. You know how much spiritual practice you can do in one moment, and then so easily forget (who you are) in the next. This is part of the Earth experience; it takes effort to walk the path of Light. Your heart knows this path and brings you back to it. No matter how many hours, years, and lifetimes pass, we meet you again. Thank you for engaging with this work. It is a great honor to know that our work has value to you and continues to do so after all this time."

The Three Parts of the Book: Foundation-Initiation-Esoterica

The ancient Egyptians loved the number three, creating many trinities that represented the Divine Father, Divine Mother, and the Divine Child. The most famous of these trinities is Osiris as the Father, Isis as the Mother, and Horus as the child.

Ausir (Osiris) is the first king, the ruler who is in his heart. The heart is the foundation of the Living Light teachings. The teachings are based on a twofold energy principle of Divine power and Divine love, which are the same. In the first part of the book, I talk about Creation and Un-creation, the journey of incarnation and the journey back to spirit after death, which is a mirror for another journey, that of incarnation into a physical self and ascension into the infinite spirit. As we study the ancient Egyptian ways, I share the complexity and the simplicity and beauty of these teachings and take you to meet the Neteru. The beings of Light, known as the gods and goddesses of ancient Egypt, embody Divine principles, universal laws, and energy fields that support our awakening. We go to the pyramids and the temples, travel down the river of life, and become the rising sun of the east, the bringer of the new day.

In the second part, we meet the Teacher of the Living Light, the ancient Egyptian Goddess Isis or Iset (pronounced *eeset*), as she was known in ancient times. Iset opens a path for us to reclaim ourselves from Set, the forces of chaos. I introduce the three main spiritual paths of initiation that were practiced in those times, namely the Seven Gates of Awareness, the Nine Primordial Neteru, and the Path of Djehuti (Thoth). We build our altar as a mirror of the universe, and we open our sacred space that becomes the holy of holies. In the spiritual practices, I offer you a taste of the teachings of each initiatory path, so you can connect with them.

Finally, Horan (Horus) is the spiritual warrior, who meets and overcomes the forces of chaos that keep him stuck. In Part 3, we encounter Horan as the falcon who has mastered its flight in the physical and spiritual realms. We journey into the necropolis to experience a double death. We access the halls of Ma'at and take part in the mysteries of resurrection of his father Ausir (Osiris).

In this book, we journey back in time and discover we are journeying deep inside. I wish you a fruitful and rich journey.

Endnote

2   Im-Hot-Tep was the chief architect and engineer of key sacred sites in Egypt. We will meet him in various parts of the book.

Part 1

The Golden Times Foundation Teachings

In the first part of the book, we lift the veil of time and space to remember an era of peace, truth, and justice, when humankind lived in harmony with each other and the world. Life supported the spiritual awakening of the soul. Aware of their spiritual nature, and assisted by the community to develop their individual inherent gifts, human beings thrived. They created an incredible civilization whose testaments, such as the pyramids and the ancient sites, can bring us into a state of wonder and awe.

In this section, we explore the ancients' way of defining and working with the multi-dimensional self, and we make contact with our "double," our Ka, the etheric counterpart of our physical self. We find hidden truths in myths and legends about the process of creation and the manifestation of the Divine Consciousness that we are all part of into matter. We invite the activation of hidden abilities that enable us to work with etheric Light.

The foundation teachings focus on two processes. First, to bring eternity and everlastingness into the now, as the current moment is where transformation can occur. Second, to increase our vibration through engaging with the Neteru, what we now call the gods and goddesses of ancient Egypt. Our aim is twofold: the spiritualization of our body and the embodiment of our spirit.

***

Invocation of the ancient initiate of the Living Light at the time of initiation:

"*O my mother Nut, the infinite sky, stretch your wings over me. Let me become like the imperishable stars, like the untiring stars.*"

Response from the teacher representing Osiris:

"*May Nut extend her arms over you, in her name of She Who Extends Her Arms, chasing away any shadows, opening this Path of Sacred Knowledge, and enabling your Light to shine everywhere.*[3]"

The Spirituality of the Path of the Living Light

During the Golden Times of ancient Egypt, people held different perspectives about themselves and their lives:

- They saw themselves as a Divine being, what they called a Neter, that walked the Earth. Life on Earth was finite, but they were not. They lived life with the awareness of the eternity of the soul.
- The soul was regarded as the Living Light that was placed in the body. At death, the soul, called Ka, reunited with the infinite spirit, and the luminosity of the soul was revealed. This was why it was important for each person to die well and not get stuck, like ghosts, in the earthly realm.
- Each person who incarnated had an etheric counterpart, also called the Ka. This etheric self was multi-dimensional. It could access the alternative realities beyond physical life.

- They adhered to the principle of oneness. The whole of the cosmos was seen as one being, whose cells are the different cosmic bodies. Everything that existed was viewed as part of this cosmic body of creation. This was called the body of Ausir (Osiris).
- Life on Earth was an opportunity for spiritual expansion. The aim was to become "the ocean," infinity.
- While studying the spiritual path of Truth (called Ma'at), they may discover they already are the shining spirit, known as Sahu. They could shine the Light of their soul while living rather than wait for death. Unlike the physical body, this luminous awakened state was not ephemeral. The person who ascended in their spiritual Light, conquered death and became one with the cosmos for all eternity.

The teachings of the Living Light mapped the relationship between the human being and the cosmos, and between the physical and spirit self. They provided a framework for a deeper understanding of human life and eternal spiritual life.

These teachings are ancient, but they meet us beyond space and time. Their medium of transference is an etheric energy of high vibration, which we may describe today as a form of spiritual Light. I share foundation teachings on these perspectives in this first part of the book.

Endnote

3 Source: I included parts of the ancient texts as described by Almond, J. & Seddon, K. (2002). However, I have re-written them so that the meaning becomes more obvious.

Chapter 1

From Atlantis to the Land of KHEM (Egypt): A Portal of the Living Light

Channeling from Iset:
See yourself as the body of creation, the whole of the cosmos.
See yourself as the consciousness that flows into all life.
See yourself as the consciousness that manifests itself in every single being, whether this is a star, celestial body, or blade of grass.
See the same consciousness, which manifests in trillions of beings, in your current body.
See yourself as the Living Light that radiates from your heart-center and throughout your body, and have the intention, "May I manifest myself into the state of the Living Light that I am."
As you speak this intention, imagine every being in front of you manifesting their inner Light. They are all radiant beings like you.
In this space, give thanks for your physical life and for the journey of awareness that you are on, even though you are eternity and the always and already enlightened.
See in front of you the sacred Ankh — eternal life, that is now being given to you.

The Atlantean Connection

In this first section, I explain how Egypt came to be one of the key centers of the Living Light. In order to talk about the Golden Times of ancient Egypt, we need to go further back, to another time and place: the islands of Atlantis. The ancient Egyptian mystery school was birthed by the Atlantean sages who looked for places to download their sacred knowledge outside Atlantis.

In its golden era, Atlantis was an important spiritual school for souls who incarnated on Earth. A place of Light and beauty, a marvel to behold. People enjoyed long lives in a natural environment with a semi-tropical climate. Many spiritual teachers helped people manifest their soul gifts and ascend. For many years, these same teachers oversaw the ruling of the Atlantic nation, an enlightened government.

In my first book, I describe the fall of Atlantis and the repercussions of that karma for our times. In this book, I include a few key events that relate to the birth of Egypt. The Atlanteans used etheric energy for communication, electricity production, crystal technology, medicine and healing, connection with the higher realms and other dimensions, and with the extraterrestrial worlds we originate from. Wishing to expand their influence and connect the whole of the Earth through etheric energy, the Atlanteans undertook an extensive building project. Numerous sacred sites, pyramids, temple complexes, and standing stone circles were erected on power points around the world. Natural formations where the etheric energy of the Earth was strong were chosen. This enabled them to create a stable climate over their world. At a central point, on one of the Atlantean islands, they constructed a huge tower, the "control room" for the entire system.

Many of these sacred sites were built in places populated by other nations. In the main, these indigenous people regarded the Atlanteans as gods, due to their amazing technology and spiritual gifts, and they allowed the Atlanteans to settle and erect the structures on the land they occupied.

In the beginning, the Atlanteans respected the indigenous people. Although they focused on their plans and did not fraternize with the local tribes, they accepted their hospitality and help with building projects. In exchange, the Atlanteans offered gifts of knowledge to the people.

In Egypt, and elsewhere, they erected their astounding edifices, largely undisturbed. Once built, a small contingent of Atlanteans remained on site in modest settlements to maintain them. In Egypt, the Atlantean people lived mostly around the pyramids of Giza, in a city called Iunu, the city of the sun of creation. Later, a second phase of construction was initiated in Egypt, and structures that emanated the Living Light were created along the Nile. These temples were collectively known as the Band of Peace. Many of the subsequent temples that we see today were built over Atlantean sites.

The Downfall of Atlantis

In the Atlantean civilization, the priesthood and the more advanced students lived apart from the community on a beautiful mountain, and enjoyed a privileged lifestyle. However, as their spiritual development took precedence over the people they served, their temple complexes became more ostentatious, and a division evolved between them and their students.

Traditionally, students only gained privileges by following a rigorous spiritual path for many years that offered no guarantees of outcome. As an increasing number of less advanced souls incarnated, the dissension between the priesthood and these souls grew. These students became resentful of the amount of spiritual practice they had to do, and angry about the lack of rewards. In response, the priesthood withdrew further to protect their vibration.

At some point, a popular leader emerged amongst the people and demanded that the priesthood relinquish their governing powers. Negotiations between this leader, his acolytes, and the priesthood continued for many years, but nothing satisfied this leader's thirst for power. Eventually the priesthood withdrew completely; if the people did not want them to govern, they could rule themselves. This was a mistake. It was like parents acceding to the demands of young children, allowing them to control powerful Light technologies of which they had little understanding.

Some of the priesthood also succumbed to the persuasive oratory of the new leader, who promised his followers easy access to privileges and powers. These priests and priestesses shared sacred knowledge inappropriately, and the misuse of etheric energy commenced. Accordingly, the collective energy of Atlantis started to fall. Dark rituals, sacrifices, and secret ceremonies in hidden underground chambers, offering power and control to participants, flourished. These dark practices invited onto the planet dark spirit entities from the cosmos, which were not human. The entities attached to people and fed off any negativity and egoic desire for power. These entities are still around the Earth today.

The spiritual program in the temples was now run by inexperienced priests, hungry for power. The initiations into the Living Light that these priests performed were harmful. The priests did not have the specific knowledge, training, and energy vibration to invoke and hold the true activations. Consequently, many who were initiated in those times received incomplete and altered attunements that damaged their Light bodies. In some cases, people died during the initiation process.

These injuries have remained with people over lifetimes. Some people who are currently incarnated are still carrying trauma from the dark times of Atlantis. As the Path of Living Light opens again on Earth, the damages can be healed.

Sheila's Story

Prior to facilitating an Isis School pilgrimage, I travelled to Egypt before the group to revisit some of the sacred sites. As I entered a chamber in an important temple complex, I became aware that this was a place where dark rituals had occurred, in ancient times and more recently. The helping spirits guided me from wall to wall to realign the energy imprints and free peoples' soul fragments trapped in the walls by dark rituals.

During the pilgrimage, our group visited this same chamber to do a ceremony. Sheila had joined the pilgrimage at the last minute. Throughout the ceremony, Sheila could feel an incredible blue light surrounding her. I could see psychically that the blue light was realigning symbols misdrawn on her body during an initiation in Atlantis, bringing the correct symbols through in the right sequence. Then a strong and loving presence, in the form of an emerald green light, enveloped her, restoring her etheric body and aura. Sheila became emotional. Her helping spirits suggested rest and no spiritual work for the next few days.

That night, as she lay in her hotel bed, a beautiful presence, one of the masters of Atlantis, came to her. The man held her with love and respect and explained about her past life — she had been born in Atlantis during the dark times, and was drawn to spiritual work. Full of innocence and Light, she agreed to take part in an initiation, believing she would be able to help others. Unfortunately, the initiation went wrong, and she died. Sheila saw psychically the young priest who was forced to perform the initiation and who was blamed for her death. The older priests, who knew the initiation could go wrong, were "holding space," drawing her energy and stealing her power.

The master apologized to Sheila for what happened. He was in the mountains with other teachers and had left Atlantis to its fate. They knew chaos would reign after their withdrawal but did not consider the immense human suffering to innocent souls. He regretted his actions. He now works in the spirit realms in high vibrational places of power and helps those who carry etheric trauma from Atlantis.

In the following days, Sheila went through a crucial transformation and healing. Although she was vomiting and had a high fever, she was unconcerned. She knew her current physical and etheric bodies had to be purified from the unskillful energies of the Atlantean life. Afterwards, she felt newly born.

Later in the pilgrimage, we visited another temple, and I performed an initiation into the Living Light for the participants. Sheila was radiating and felt emotional. She was told that she had received the initiation she should have been given in Atlantis. Sheila was ready to enter the next chapter of her life.

Colonization and Creation of the Atlantean Empire

As the collective consciousness of the people lowered, the Atlantean empire became increasingly power-hungry. Those in charge had advanced technology at their disposal. They decided to expand the key project of connecting the whole of the Earth through etheric energy, although the vibration of the energy was now discordant. Their aim was to conquer the whole world and plunder the natural resources of other lands. Previously, the Atlanteans had worked in harmony with the local people; now they regarded them as subservient. They saw themselves as a superior race who were offering ignorant people the gift of civilization. At the same time, they were conducting genetic experiments on their own people and the indigenous tribes, altering the human DNA to increase fertility.

Their plan was to expand the central tower so that it would become a symbol of power that all could admire. They also misused the etheric technology. From the control room, they broadcast etheric messages that reoriented people's brain waves towards fear so that it would be easier to control them.

Their pride was their downfall, and eventually their plan backfired. A war took place between the ruling Atlanteans and a small segment of the population who were resisting the totalitarian regime in Athens, Greece. When the rulers tried to use the tower as a weapon, a huge explosion took place, and the Atlantean lands sank under the ocean. The resulting tsunami created what we know as the great flood.

During the dark times, some enlightened teachers were appalled by the heavy karma that was being created. Working fully for the Light, they refused to fight with etheric energy, nor did they wish to contravene peoples' free will. Thus, they had no way to stop the descent into chaos. Instead, knowing that the Atlantean empire would fall, they chose to focus on safeguarding the path of the Living Light in other parts of the world. Telling people that they had decided to ascend with their students to other realms, they left Atlantis in secret, and moved to remote areas of the planet, such as the Himalayas, Peru, Latin America, and Egypt. The local people welcomed them. These teachers started teaching covertly, away from the prying eyes of the empire.

After the fall of Atlantis, some of the more aware souls who survived the flood also came to Egypt. They brought remnants of their technology with them, which was used sparingly in ceremonies and temple construction. In the texts, these people are described as the children of Horus who arrived from the west. Together with the Atlanteans, in situ they created a sophisticated civilization that was based on the principles of the rule of Ma'at: Divine justice and Divine order. The Golden Times of Egypt were birthed.

Leaving Atlantis and Arriving in Egypt — My Vision

In 2006, I attended a spiritual workshop on Atlantis. I took part in a meditation to travel back in time and see myself in Atlantis. My journey took me to the final days of Atlantis.

I saw myself sitting on top of a mountain knowing that all would be lost. The mountain city, with its beautiful stone inlaid streets, whitewashed houses, gardens filled with perfumed flowers, charming parks, and market squares, would soon disappear, engulfed by water. The waters had been rising steadily. For the last 3 days, we had felt the volcanic eruptions and earthquakes as the world around us shook.

As I sat, I reflected on what had happened. At the beginning of this dark time, many in the mountain community fled to other lands. I and a few other spiritual teachers and students withdrew to a cave. The remaining citizens in the mountain adobes knew we were there, but did not disturb us. Occasionally, they came to receive healing, as strange and unknown illnesses began to appear in a population that had been physically robust. The genetic manipulation and the misuse of etheric energy was creating abnormalities in the human race, which were difficult to cure.

In the early days, when a few people developed deformities — facial and body rashes, black spots on their stomach, and coughed up blood — they were ostracized. The Atlantean regime banned them; only healthy individuals could be citizens. They claimed this was to prevent the disease spreading and did not say how the deformities originated. Instead they blamed outside factors, yet the illnesses only affected those who had taken part in the medical experiments.

The majority of the population did not object to people being ostracized. They believed the given narrative that it protected them and their families. However, as the symptoms became widespread, an increasing number of people became unwell. When people in the ruling classes also fell ill, they hid the signs and wore masks in public and clothing that covered their bodies. Fear was rampant. Diseased people were arrested and killed to eradicate the problem. Such loss of human life. The disease, not fatal in itself, became a death sentence. The ruling class could not admit failure; they had sought to create a "perfect" race.

We watched from the mountain as the darkness covered one of the most beautiful and sophisticated civilizations that had ever existed. We were unharmed — protected by the Light, and ignored by the authorities. Some of our students wanted to join the resistance and urged us to retaliate using etheric energy. Some left and did so. I could not misuse the energy — direct the Light against people, even if they were harming others. My path had always been that of the observer — to work with the high vibrational energies of Light for the highest good, respect people's free will, and not interfere.

Sitting on the mountain top, I grieved for all that had come to pass. I was aware that people had died traumatically and their souls were not at peace. The last year of warfare had created a realm of lost souls in the astral plane that had never previously existed. All of my community were psychic: able to feel spirit beings and communicate with the invisible realms. We had to add layers of protection around our domain to shelter us from the heavy energy and incredible anguish of these lost souls. In doing so, we had closed down and withdrawn from the world into our small sanctuary of high frequencies.

There had been so many distressing changes in the last 100 years. Before, no one had witnessed or taken part in such blatant manipulation and destruction of the human body. People knew how to leave their body and move into the spirit realms. And after many years of spiritual practice, as many as one third of the population were able to ascend into their shining spirit. Now these ways were lost, wiped out in the space of a few generations.

During the years of chaos, heavy karma was created — karma that would play out many times, until humanity awoke from the disarray and chose another way. As long as division reigned, similar circumstances of fear-generating regimes would continue to appear and rule the Earth. Those who were the instigators of such karma would have to experience it from the other side. Those who preached superiority would incarnate as people considered inferior by the majority. Those who were the masters would experience life as a slave.

The only way out of the heavy karma is for souls to awaken collectively to what they are doing and allowing to happen, and choose love, kindness, and compassion, over fear, separation, dominion, and war. Only then will the Earth come out of the cycle of destruction. All of us in the sisterhood and brotherhood of the Light knew this, and we did what we could to help the people who came to us to access their Light and gifts. We understood that when these souls reincarnated, any Light work they did in the Atlantean life would benefit them, and the spiritual path would open for them at some point.

As I sat, I was filled with a new sense of purpose and joy for the Light work that would continue beyond Atlantis, and the beauty generated through it. At this point, a flying vehicle landed on the mountain top. It was in the shape of a flat tetrahedron and flew using etheric energy. The people manning it were outside the regime. They had saved as many as they could from the floods and now the energy reserves were running low; the generators and etheric Light convertors had been destroyed.

We flew to Africa and landed on the Nile. In the vision, I saw myself float down the Nile and arrive at the city of Iunu, near the pyramids. Members of the sisterhood and brotherhood of Light were waiting for me. They grasped my hands and lifted me out of the river. I had arrived in the land of Khem, Egypt. I was, once more, home.[4]

Summary

The history of Egypt starts in Atlantis. For thousands of years, Atlantis was a prosperous civilization whose main focus was spirituality and soul evolution. The Atlanteans developed advanced technology that utilized etheric energy that was far superior to our current electrical devices. At some point, they decided to connect the whole of the Earth with etheric energy and built pyramids and megalithic structures around the planet. Whilst, they were initially a peaceful nation living in harmony with the Earth and others, they succumbed to corruption and greed. They manipulated etheric energy for selfish purposes and introduced expansive policies that enslaved other nations. Such a civilization cannot sustain itself, as karma must be repaid. Eventually, the destruction of the Atlantean world took place through fire (explosions that caused volcanic eruptions) and water (the great flood). Some wise elders who escaped the destruction took the esoteric teachings of the path of ascension to other parts of the world, including Egypt, and created esoteric schools of wisdom teachings.

Endnote

4   The Living Light vibration, when anchored in a place, creates a distinct energy field that feels like home, no matter whether you are in your home or elsewhere. I have created this field in different countries and opened temporarily a spiritual sanctuary, so no matter where I was, I was at home. In that lifetime, when I arrived in Egypt, this energy field was already in place, and I felt instantly at home.

Chapter 2

A Spiritual Heaven on Earth

Channeling from Iset:
The sacred land of Egypt is a mirror reflecting the essence of the spiritual heaven onto the Earth.

By experiencing the reflection of heaven on the physical world, you can remember your origin as a being of Light.

You can see yourself as part of the cosmic network of Light.

In Egypt, the sacred sites were built to align with the universal truth of oneness.

People came together and worked with celestial beings to channel the high vibrational energies into the physical world, and shape the physical reality so that the energies of the Living Light would continuously flow to the land.

The network is aligned to the awakened consciousness of the human heart. It is waiting for you to come and meet it through this higher state.

The network of Light never sleeps. It is active and will respond to the wishes of your soul. It will recognize you as you connect with it through a pure intention.

When your feet touch the sacred land of Khem, the Light will flow to you.

Creating Heaven on Earth

The intention of the wise Atlanteans who came to Egypt, before and after the fall of the empire, was to actualize the hermetic axiom of "as above, so below," and recreate the harmony of heaven on Earth. They knew that living in a place of high vibrational energy was an incredible gift. Their intention was that Egypt would become a holy land, a sanctuary, a temple of the Living Light that would serve humanity, during the Golden Times and the dark times.

Egypt is a special land, a unique place. Egypt was designed as the perfect sacred place where the two opposites states — abundance and emptiness, life and death — come together, mirroring human nature. A place where duality can be transformed into oneness.

The River Nile, flowing from south to north, symbolizes the Milky Way and divides the world of the living (the east bank) from the spirit world of the dead (the west bank). The Nile is the life-giver, the bringer of abundance. Through its annual flooding, the soil was naturally fortified by nutrients from the hills and propagated rich and healthy crops. With rainfall limited to an average of 7 days a year, the Nile is the river of life. Beyond the Nile is the desert, the place of emptiness, the absence of life. This is an area of high vibrational energy, a place to discover oneself beyond distractions, a sacred place of pilgrimage. Mountains, hills, and other geographical formations in the Sahara desert are aligned to celestial bodies that sustain the high vibration.

In building sacred Egypt, the wise Atlanteans aimed to support the continuous awakening and spiritual expansion of the human race. Aware of the evolutionary Divine plan, they knew that at some point the world would fall into another era of the ego, when the connection with the Divine self would be lost. Then, after thousands of years of domination by the conditioning, the human race would find its way back to its Divine expression and embody the Living Light once again. And the Golden Times, Zep Tepi, would return.

Even during the dark times, the wise Atlanteans understood that there would be sparks of Light, periods when spiritual expansion was possible and the Living Light would support people who sought spiritual awakening. These times are like gateways to a higher level of consciousness. Many such gateways have opened in the Earth's history.

For instance, Armstrong (2007) writes about the Axial Age, the period from the ninth century to the second century BCE, when figures such as the Buddha, Socrates, Confucius, Jeremiah, Ezekiel, the mystics of the Upanishads, Mencius, and Euripides emerged. In response to the violence of the time, these sages advocated the abandonment of selfishness and the development of compassion, empathy, and respect for others.

These periods of potential spiritual expansion are steps towards the re-emergence of the Golden Times. Each one adds something to our collective understanding, gives us the opportunity to re-evaluate the way we live, and creates a different inner and external reality. And while each one also provides humanity with an opportunity to exit the spiritual underworld of the mind, nothing is lost if the door closes. Every one of these gateways becomes part of our collective path that meanders in spiraling circles and gradually takes us towards the awakened era of the enlightened heart.

The Aims of the Wise Atlanteans of Egypt

The Atlantean people embraced a bigger perspective of human life on Earth. To achieve this, they did the following:

- Created a spiritual school where the teachings of the Living Light supported peoples' soul expansion.
- Created a civilization based on the principles of Divine justice and Divine order, later described as the Rule of Ma'at.
- Provided a place for holistic healing of the mind, body, and spirit that helped people overcome the trauma of Atlantis and its karmic implications, and encouraged them to make different choices for themselves and their lives.

- Created a place where high vibrational energies of Light were available at all times, where the energy of the Living Light was anchored in the land and flowed and supported people for centuries to come. Even today, the Living Light responds to the open heart of those who visit the sacred sites, whether people are aware of it or not.
- Safeguarded the teachings and energy of the Living Light for future generations. They foresaw a time when initiates (students of the path of the Living Light) and teachers from other times would reincarnate and live normal lives until a spiritual awakening took place. These people would be drawn to Egypt to rediscover their inherent spiritual gifts and share them for the highest good of all life.

Thus, ancient Egypt was built as a portal of the Living Light to serve humanity and hold the key of eternal life (Ankh) — spiritual ascension — for current and future generations. Egypt is one of the keys for manifesting ourselves as the Ankh on Earth. Every aspect of the creative plan for Egypt was designed to radiate the timeless quality of eternity that Ankh represents. Even the morphology of the land, the shaping of the River Nile and its delta, express the symbol of the Ankh, as does the human form: a human being with their arms outstretched.

The Astral Connection — Sirius Star

In birthing Egypt, the wise Atlanteans created structures and monuments in the shape of pyramids and obelisks that gathered and distributed the high vibrational frequencies of the cosmic energies of the Living Light. Temple complexes were built to support the sacred sites and the people who wished to engage in spiritual work.

Different star constellations supported the flow of the Living Light towards the Earth. The Atlanteans created the monuments in a way that harnessed the Light of creation in its purest form, by aligning the sites to different frequencies emitted by particular stars: the suns in the night sky. These frequencies were accessed with etheric symbols, taught to the initiates. The hieroglyphs found in the ancient temples still emit distinct frequencies of the Living Light. These frequencies come under a specific band of etheric energy for which the main key portal is located on the Sirius star: our spiritual sun.

Sirius star is the brightest star visible from the Earth with the naked eye. The energy it emits enables spiritual awakening, should we choose to align with it. We can access the energy by engaging in spiritual and personal development work, with a pure heart and intention. The frequency emitted to each of us will match the level of our consciousness. As we grow spiritually — individually and collectively — a larger part of the bandwidth of the Living Light flows to us, at increasingly higher frequencies.

The Atlanteans, even with their high awareness, recognized that what they and their community had achieved spiritually could easily be lost. The wisest person can succumb to the ego and lose their way, and many years and lifetimes of awareness and spiritual work can be forfeited very quickly. The high frequencies, anchored in the sacred sites, are an antidote against the forces of chaos, the forces of the conditioned mind, that we all experience.

Sacred Construction

Every aspect of the construction of the temples and pyramids followed the Rule of Ma'at and respected all life. This included deference to the unseen world and the spirits of the land where the quarries were situated. Before construction, the priesthood would make offerings and ask for help from the land spirits. They explained that the stone would be used in a sacred temple. Stone was used mainly in the temples; palaces and homes were built of mudbrick or other materials that did not need to last.

Because the temple stones had to be flawless to allow the energy to flow through the monuments evenly and unimpeded, the spirits would tell the priest exactly where the stone should be extracted. Sound technology verified the spirits' suggestion and the stone's integrity. The pharaoh, as the ruler of the land, or his representative priest, would make a commitment to respect the land and honor its gift.

When I visited the ancient stone quarry at Gebel el Silsila, on the west bank of the Nile, I was struck by the feeling of peace and harmony that emanated from the site. Despite the continuous extraction of stone over hundreds of years, the land was serene. The Egyptologist showed me the chambers of people who had been buried there, as this was a place of high vibration. In contrast, when I once visited a modern quarry, I found the energy to be discordant, and the spirits of the land were sad and angry.

Energy Technology

In constructing these magnificent structures, the engineers of Zep Tepi used advanced technology that worked harmoniously with the etheric energy of the cosmos, the prana or chi flowing to Earth. Prana can be transformed into electrical power, and laser technology was used to cut the stones with precision accuracy. This Light and mind technology was combined with sacred sounds that raised the huge stones into the air and positioned them in exactly the right place.

Modern engineers, such as R. Bauval (1994), demonstrate that the pyramids and temples of Egypt could not have been constructed by unskilled slave labor. These monuments, especially the pyramids, have been built with such refinement that defies current standards of engineering. Modern attempts to recreate the Great Pyramid using ancient and modern tools have failed. In the excavation of a later workmen's village, located near the pyramids, detailed records were found outlining the payments to workers, their days of work, accidents, akin to the records of a modern construction site. These workmen were not unskilled slaves in fear for their life, pulling stones along trestles.

The Miracle of Giza

The pyramid complex of Giza is a remarkable example of sacred engineering involving mathematics, geo-astronomy, and spiritual energy. It is an expression of the sacred science that was known and practiced in those times. The chief engineer had the title of Im-Hot-Tep, meaning "He Who Comes in Peace." This was not someone's name, but our equivalent of a job title. He who comes in peace, is one who carries a high vibration of peace and brings peace on Earth. Thus, Im-Hot-Tep is a high adept. Everyone who worked in the construction of the sacred sites was an initiate. They engaged in daily spiritual practices to harness and develop the enlightened qualities of harmony, peace, and unconditional love that the sacred sites emanated.

Spirituality was a way of life, and came before learning a trade. Each person's work was viewed as sacred and an expression of their inner Light in the material world. In subsequent centuries, such as the New Kingdom, and especially when the Greek Macedonians took over Egypt during the period of the Ptolemies, Im-Hot-Tep was identified as a person and elevated to a deity. It is important to realize that the Greek conquerors had a different culture and understanding of the Divine. They saw God as a being outside of themselves, and it was easy to imagine that an engineer who built the pyramids could be a semi-god, like the plethora of semi-gods in their own religion. Whereas the ancient Egyptian adepts sought the Divine within themselves.

The Sanctuary of Absolute Peace

I have facilitated ceremonies and initiations in sacred sites in Egypt and in prehistoric sites around the world. During the ceremonial work, some people who are psychic see the Living Light emanating in different colors, as well as the beings of Light who are working with us. Even people who are not clairvoyant experience an overwhelming sense of peace when they meditate there. For some, there is a feeling of coming home, of lightness, of being surrounded by love. This is what the ancient Light engineers wished to achieve: places on Earth where the high vibrational energies could quieten the conditioned mind and allow the sacred heart to open and share its inner wisdom.

The sacred heart is not the heart we understand in our everyday life, a seat of passion and romance. The sacred heart is our heart chakra, the seat of the Divine and of inner wisdom in the body. This sacred heart is all-knowing, recognizes right from wrong, and has the power to keep us centered within the body and aligned with the cosmos at the same time. Consequently, when we engage in spiritual practice in sacred sites, we may receive insights about our personal life and life in general, and experience deep healing.

All Are Welcome in the Priesthood of the Living Light

Ancient Egypt was conceived as an esoteric school, a place where spiritual learning was available to all. The wise Atlanteans were very humble and respected the cultural differences between themselves and the local tribes. To the Atlanteans, everyone was a being of Light who had incarnated to evolve through the human experience. They envisaged the birth of a new nation, one where the legacy of the Living Light would be shared with everyone. The Atlanteans knew that sharing the teachings was one way of purifying the heavy karma of the Atlantean empire. They were grateful to the indigenous population for giving them this opportunity for Light work.

Alongside the sacred buildings, the Atlanteans created a rich and sophisticated spiritual tradition based on the principles and teachings of the Living Light. The Seven Gates of Awareness courses that we teach in the Isis School derive from the same esoteric tradition.

In ancient Egypt, the teachings were taught on two levels:

- For those uninterested in pursuing spiritual learning in depth, the teachings provided a foundation, spiritual principles that formed part of the culture and way of life. These principles were summarized in the Rule of Divine justice — treat everyone and everything with respect, honesty, humility, and truth. No matter a person's profession or place in society, all were encouraged to adhere to the Rule and respect the sacred. A harmonious society and way of life could be maintained, and chaos averted.
- For those who wished to pursue spiritual teachings, numerous temples and temple complexes were created as part of the esoteric school. Initiations into the Living Light and teachings of the path of ascension were shared over many years. People could live in the temples as priests or priestesses, known as "The Servants of the Place of Truth." Or, they could live in their community and attend the temple several times per week for spiritual instruction. For those who progressed on this path, the main initiations were held inside the Great Pyramid. This path was long and arduous. In taking spiritual initiation, initiates came face to face with all that needed to be healed within them.

The path of the Living Light spans lifetimes; it is not an instant fix. It will meet us repeatedly in different lives. We may have begun the path in ancient Egypt and find it again in this or another life. We may walk away from it and return to it in a different incarnation. In the bigger picture, there is no time; we incarnate in different eras, in what we call the past or future, to evolve spiritually. Based on our vibration at the time of death and our karma and spiritual understanding, a lifetime in a place where the path of the Living Light exists may open for us.

Summary

Egypt was created by wise Atlanteans as a temple of the Living Light. The land and the magnificent structures, pyramids, and temples, many still standing today, were erected to emphasize Divine connection for the people of those times and future generations. The whole of Egypt was built as a spiritual sanctuary for soul evolution through the flow of high vibrational etheric energy from Sirius star and other celestial bodies. Spiritual work was open to all, but, similar to today, few sought spiritual truth in depth. The key foundation of the teachings was Divine justice and Divine order, or the Rule of Ma'at, which permeated every aspect of human life. Thus, spirituality was not something separate, but a way of life.

Spiritual Practice to Connect with an Ancient Sacred Site

Imagine that you are standing on the desert floor, in a circle of people. Everyone is here to access Zep Tepi (the Golden Times) with a pure intention from their sacred heart. Feel the Earth beneath your feet and the energy of Mother Earth flowing around and through you.

Join hands with everyone in the circle. The energy of the Living Light flows to all. In this space say: "May all the Light, energy, and beauty I access during this journey be brought into my current body and life. May it help me realign with my

Divine purpose of awakening into the Light that I am. I ask that the energy of the Living Light emanate from my heart-center, for the highest good of myself and all beings."

Invite your helping spirits who work for the highest good and the Light to assist you and create a safe and protected space around you, even if you do not know who they are. Then call in "The Opener of the Ways," the guardian between this current time and Zep Tepi. Reaffirm your intention to work for the highest good and the Light.

Imagine a veil in front of you. Beyond the veil is Egypt, as it was in the Golden Times. As the veil lifts, see yourself walking on a path in the desert. Beyond the desert is a river surrounded by reeds, bird life, and lush green nature. There is such a contrast between the desert path and the green riverside ahead. Birds fly above you, and as you raise your eyes upwards, you see the brilliant sun shining in the cloudless sky. Feel the warmth of the sun on your body.

Then a guide comes and takes you to the place you need to access right now, in your spiritual work. When you arrive there, make an offering of Light. Connect with your heart and ask that the Living Light that you are radiates from you, in all directions. Let it flow everywhere in gratitude for the gifts you will receive. The more it shines, the more it grows within you.[5]

The spirit guide takes you inside one of the temples, where the Masters of Light wait for you. They welcome you and offer guidance about your life and your path with the Living Light. They transmit energy and Light to you as you remain in this quiet space and receive. You may ask them questions such as, "Why am I here?" They usually answer with another question, for instance, "What brought you here?" Look inwards and find the deeper reasons that brought you to this holy place to feel the Living Light.

Stay in this place of self-enquiry for a minimum of 21 minutes[6] while the Masters of Light transmit the Living Light energy to you. When they have finished, they ask, "What have you learned from being here?" Let your heart speak for you and reveal what your mind does not know but your wise self guided you to discover.[7]

When you feel the practice is complete, thank the Masters of Light. Ask them to close you down and put protection around you.

Now leave the room and exit the temple. Step into the brilliant sunshine and find the desert path that takes you away from this site. As you walk, the veil lowers and you return to the present time. Now see yourself standing in a beautiful meadow of lush green grass. You join hands once again with the others. Intend that the energy of the Living Light flow around the circle and into the Earth. Imagine a column of Light coming down from the Heart of Creation into the middle of the circle. The energy of unconditional love flows all around the planet. Stay in this space for a little while sharing this Light.

Then slowly bring yourself back from the journey. Give thanks to all your helping spirits, the guide, the Masters of Light, to everyone who joined you in this sacred practice, and yourself.

Release your helping spirits. Ask that, before they go, they completely seal and protect you, your room, and the place where you are.

Endnotes

5   People ask, "If I use my own energy to send Light, will I be drained?" As a result they rely exclusively on channeling outside frequencies. These frequencies are helpful, but it is also important to enable ourselves to be the Light that we are. This is actually the secret. We are infinite. And the more we work to radiate our Light, the more it grows. We are the channel, and we are Source.

6. Many of the spiritual practices include a 21-minute meditation. The energy comes in increasingly strong waves so that your body adjusts to each wave. Sometimes you may feel an energy blast followed by a quiet space, the latter being an integration space, giving your body time to absorb the Light.

7. The ancient Egyptians worked with the sacred heart-center, Ib, to reveal the absolute truth. The ego-mind thinks it knows the truth, but only makes assumptions from its limited experience of life. To let your heart speak is to become the observer. This is easier to do in sacred spaces. Start speaking, even if you say — I do not know what I have received, and then pause. Let words slowly arise from within, and speak them out. Keep your mind quiet and let your heart speak. The more you do this, the more you will access the Ib. Caution: it is important to differentiate between your mind and your heart. To do this, forgo all desire. Do not fall into the trap of listening to your mind and saying it was the sacred heart that spoke.

Chapter 3

The Living Light: The Essence of Divine Consciousness

Channeling from Iset:
Connect with the Light of the World until you become that Light, the Light that you have always been. This is a journey of awakening into the Divine consciousness that you already are.

The Divine consciousness is multifaceted. As you walk the spiritual path, you meet each facet and gradually embody them in your life.

Opportunities to awaken into the spiritual self will always be offered to the seekers of Truth. Yet, no one can carry you through a Gateway of Light; the road is there, but you must choose to walk it.

The Path of the Living Light — A Gateway towards Ascension

I have been walking and teaching the path of the Living Light in many incarnations. In this life, Iset, in her role as the teacher of awakening and ascension, helped me channel and remember the sacred teachings. Iset has made the path relevant to our times and way of life, and although I refer to ancient Egypt, which is the last time this path was practiced in its entirety, this is not a history course. The essence of the path, its Light and wisdom knowledge, is transferred to us in ways that we can relate to now.

The Living Light spiritual teachings are one of the main gateways towards enlightenment and ascension on Earth. Other spiritual traditions contain parts of this path. Following the fall of Atlantis, some wise teachers brought the teachings to Egypt, whilst others took the Living Light to different parts of the world and created their own mystical esoteric schools.

What is the Living Light, and how can we become it? One definition is that it is a very high vibrational spiritual energy emanating from the Divine consciousness that created the whole of the cosmos, the physical and spiritual realms. We, and everything we see in our world, are a manifestation of this energy that runs through and connects the whole of creation. Different vibrations of Light create different realities: the higher vibrations, unseen with the physical eye, are etheric; whilst the denser frequencies express themselves as matter.

By aligning with the higher frequencies, we can access this Light in its purer form, gradually transform ourselves into the spirit being that we are, and bring the physical and spiritual aspects of our being into oneness. In its higher frequencies, this Light is spiritual energy that is all-knowing. Existing outside the body, outside form, it can heal and transform form. However, to access these higher frequencies and bring them through the physical body, we must raise our vibration and resonate with them. This is why the initiates of ancient Egypt devoted many years to spiritual practice.

Conversely, without a spiritual practice that accesses high vibrational energy, we will continue to resonate with the denser frequencies of energy, and be affected by the dramas of everyday life. The higher perspectives will elude us. The conditioned egoic mind and the social programming will keep us separate from our inner awakened consciousness.

The Living Light — Three Key Themes

- **The Living Light Is Unconditional Love**. Awakening, we gradually become a being of unconditional love. This transformation takes place through a feeling of grace that is self-generated by the continual opening and activation of our heart-center: the sacred heart that brings deep healing and inner transformation over time. To describe this state, the ancient Egyptians used the analogy of a mother feeding her newborn baby. This feeling is not exclusive to nursing women; everyone has the potential to experience unconditional love. When we awaken from the conditioning, we embody this state and become a being that expresses unconditional love for all.

- **The Living Light Is Wisdom Knowledge** that is born from within. It is through the awakening of the heart-center that enlightenment and ascension are possible. The sacred heart-center is defined as the center of our inner wisdom, rather than of passion and romance. We experience these awakenings as "aha" moments — instances of deep realization that emerge from within. Gradually, we reach a place where we truly know an aspect of spiritual truth, not through hearing it from a teacher or reading it in a book, but through self-discovery. Again this is not a one-off experience. These awakening moments continue to be generated the more we walk the path.
- **The Living Light Is Etheric Cosmic Energy** transmitted to Earth from celestial portals of Light. Different constellations support the transference of the energy to Earth. Aware of this, the ancient people orientated their monuments to particular stars and built the structures on sites that were conducive to the channeling of the high frequency of etheric Light. Even though most cannot see these Light frequencies with the naked eye, our spiritual work helps us perceive and feel them in our body. These harmonic vibrations instigate an inner awakening process. They create a sense of calmness and peace, and aim to restore homeostasis in our body and mind. Increasingly, we stay more centered and aligned with our Divine Self.

The Path of the Living Light Is Not a Religion

The modern interpretation of "gods and goddesses" of ancient Egypt is based on the current concept of religion and has no basis in ancient Egyptian spirituality. These "gods and goddesses" are beings of Light, described in the ancient Egyptian language as Neteru. The Neteru do not ask us to worship them or give our power to them. Each Neter (singular) embodies a different Divine principle in total perfection, and when we align with them and manifest their vibration in our life, we access a state of grace and beauty; hence, they are also known as "The Beautiful Ones."

These beings of Light hold key vibrations of the Divine consciousness and oneness that invite us to overcome the duality of the physical world. The Neteru have never incarnated, never taken physical form, yet their attributes exist within us.

Neither was this ancient spiritual tradition enforced upon anyone in the way that cultural conditioning may impose religion on people. Instead, the teachings are an invitation to the spiritual path of the Light, and it is our choice to accept the invitation, or not. Through the teachings and the high vibrational energy we channel, we gain our personal experience of the Light rather than following a prescribed dogma.

After the Golden Times, the Age of Corruption

The legacy of Atlantis, the corruption that came into the political systems, spiritual institutions, and society, as well as peoples' minds, is still alive today. This corruption also ended Zep Tepi. Corruption begins through the violation of the Rule of Ma'at. The egoic mind does not value this rule and sees no harm in breaking it. It only thinks about what it can gain at an individual level. It does not consider the karmic consequences of its actions or their impact on others. Moreover, one of the most damaging forms of corruption that precipitated the fall of Atlantis and ancient Egypt is the distortion of spiritual teachings and the misuse of etheric energy.

The further back we go in ancient Egypt, the purer the teachings and way of life. As we come closer to our times, corruption of the teachings took place, primarily by the priesthood who were tasked to safeguard them. The priesthood, "The Servants of Truth," forgot their purpose to serve the community, and hungered for wealth and political power. They opened the tombs of the deceased rulers which they had been sworn to protect, stole precious items, and justified the tomb looting as "restoration projects." During those times, the dark spirituality of Atlantis raised its ugly head. Sacrifice and the misuse of etheric energy to control peoples' lives and minds became rife. The vibration of Egypt lowered, and the ability to work with the Living Light was withdrawn from many. The Living Light only works for the highest good; it cannot be used unethically. Without this Light, the whole of Egypt went into decline. Eventually, the country was conquered by different people, and one of the longest lasting civilizations ended.

The karmic implications of the misuse of etheric energy are immense and affect people over many lifetimes. In Egypt, the portal of the Living Light co-exists with a portal of darkness, held in place by the heavy karma caused by this misuse. In this portal of darkness, there are trapped soul parts belonging to the perpetrators of the unethical spiritual work, even though these people may have reincarnated. Moreover, their victims may also be carrying trauma from that life into subsequent lives. This is why people sometimes have an instinctive fear of Egypt. In working with the Living Light, we can heal these lifetimes of darkness. We can release and bring closure to old traumas that we perhaps knew were there but did not wish to see. We can free parts of us held in past lives.

Helen's Story

Helen had participated in one of my shamanic courses and was also drawn to the path of the Living Light. However, some things associated with Egypt frightened her, although she did not know why. By the time the shamanic course ended, Helen felt she could trust me. I explained the basis of the Living Light path and she decided to join the first introduction course: The Spiritual Path of Iset, Part 1. The course went well, and, despite her initial misgivings, Helen enjoyed it. After the course, she worked with the spiritual practices.

Six months later, Helen joined the second course. When I began introducing one of the symbols, a wave of fear arose in Helen. She wanted to leave the room. I said that, if she wished, we could all help her heal this deep fear and the underlying cause. The group was very supportive. Helen decided to accept the healing.

I took Helen into a past-life regression to Egypt, where the fear originated. Helen saw herself as an innocent 12-year-old girl, who had joined the priesthood. She felt a deep spiritual calling and was happy she had been accepted into the training. The high priest noticed her, and one of his acolytes told her she had been specially chosen to receive an important initiation. He asked her to tell no one. On the night of the dark moon, she walked alone to an unknown part of the temple. She wore a white dress and carried a lotus flower, the traditional offering.

A group of people she did not know were waiting. The acolyte approached her and showed her a symbol. At this point in the regression, Helen started to shake. She was afraid of this symbol. I asked her to check her vision of the symbol with the symbol in the manual. She confirmed that the symbol the acolyte showed her had been distorted. I then asked her to tell me the outcome of the initiation without going through it. Helen said that the acolyte was doing a ritual that had been banned by the temple authorities. He invoked dark energies, and she could see these standing behind him. The acolyte sacrificed her, and she died almost instantly. Since then, her soul has carried a deep fear of Egypt, and although she had always felt drawn to spiritual work, she was terrified to access it.

In the regression, I asked for the spirit of the acolyte to come. He appeared in chains, representing the heavy karma he carried. In that life, he was scapegoated by the high priest and died a horrible death. Yet the heavy karma had not been absolved, and in his subsequent incarnations, he had very difficult lives. (The misuse of etheric energy creates imprints on the aura that are carried from lifetime to lifetime until they are healed). The acolyte acknowledged his misuse of the spiritual teachings. He kneeled before Helen and asked for forgiveness. As he did so, other young people dressed in white joined Helen. They too had been killed by this man. The acolyte was overwhelmed with remorse. The young people, including Helen, forgave him completely. They said that what happened was done, and no one needed to carry the pain from that life any longer.

Part of the acolyte's soul had been trapped in the ancient temple, and a portal to the spiritual realms opened and it moved to the Light. The Light from the portal flowed to Helen and the other people killed, and then flooded the whole temple, healing everyone and the land. Helen felt the power of the Light in her body and at the base of her throat, where she had developed thyroid issues. This is where the acolyte had stabbed her. As the healing continued, she experienced unconditional love and her eyes filled with tears of gratitude.

Simultaneously, the Light flowed to all of us who were supporting the healing and out to the world. Throughout human history, many have experienced the trauma of sacrifice. Through Helen's healing, the collective consciousness we are all part of also received a healing.

Since then, Helen has travelled to Egypt numerous times on spiritual pilgrimages and has visited the temple from her past life. Through this work, Helen released her fear, healed deep past-life trauma, and reclaimed her spiritual path.

Summary

The Living Light is an energy vibration emanating from Source, which creates the manifested realms and the physical and spiritual worlds which are inhabited by trillions of beings. We can call it the Light of creation. It is an energy that is intelligent and enlightened, carrying Divine knowledge and wisdom and enabling us to experience heightened states of grace and unconditional love. The Living Light only works for the highest good of all. As with Atlantis, Egypt fell into the darkness of corruption and greed. The priesthood misused the etheric energy, creating heavy karma and trauma for themselves, the land, and the people they served. We can heal these past lives, which may help some people in their current incarnation.

A Spiritual Practice to Channel the Living Light Daily by Connecting with the Sun and Moon

Every day the ancient initiates brought the shining light of the sun and the silent power of the moon into their body. This was an act of service to themselves, humanity, and all life. As the etheric energy of the sun and moon flowed through them, it flowed to everyone.

In this practice, we connect to the sun during the day and the moon at night so that balance is maintained within. The sun's light is visible, powerful, and active. It is a power we can feel on our skin, and that enables life on Earth.

The moon is a silent power. We may or may not be able to see the moon, yet its etheric pool is strong and stirs the waters of our abyss, our unconscious self. Whilst the sun initiates action, the moon invites us towards a state of self-inquiry and peace.

- **Connecting with the Sun — Ra: The Shining One**
  In the daytime, see the sun as a being of Light consciousness and a physical manifestation of the Living Light. Ask the

sun to send you blessings in the form of etheric Light. Wait until you feel the etheric energy of the sun coming into your body.

Say the Affirmation: May I become aware that I too am the Living Sun, the Light of creation, the sacred fire.

- **Connecting with the Moon — Khonsu: The Traveler**
  At night, see the moon as a being of Light consciousness, and ask to receive its blessing. As with the sun, wait until you feel the etheric energy of the moon flowing into your body.

  Affirm: May I be the silent Light that stirs the dark waters of the abyss and holds the key to all life. May I live with the awareness of silent knowledge.

***

The practice has three stages:

The first stage is an activation. You connect with the celestial bodies to activate the Light that exists within you.

The second stage is the embodiment of the Light. You become the active Light of the sun and the silent knowledge of the moon.

The third stage is the sharing of this Light with all beings. You envisage yourself as the body of creation, and the Light you receive in your body is shared with every being.

In the Golden Times, there were specific Light language chants and movements for each stage. I share these practices and Light language chants in the *Spiritual Path of Iset* course.

Chapter 4

We Are Multi-dimensional Etheric, Physical Beings

Channeling from Iset:
The basis of physicality is etheric Light.
We invite you to see your world beyond form.
Start by focusing on yourself and then the world around you.
Imagine that all you breathe in and out is Light.
As you eat and taste your food, imagine all you eat is Light.
As you look at your body, imagine that beneath your skin is radiant Light.
As you look at everything around you, imagine that everything you see is Light and has a spiritual consciousness. See the plants, animals, people, and stones as beings of Light, covered by a form.
Imagine too that your man-made machines, plastic items, and the bricks of the buildings are Light.
See yourself as Light. Only Light energy exists, manifesting in form.
And if all there is in the physical world is Light, what is beyond it?
The answer is Enlightened Consciousness.

Incarnation

The journey of incarnation into form has an intention. We are here to experience the physical reality and the gifts of the physical senses, to live through various situations, and meet different people. In this journey of physicality, we forget our spiritual nature and focus externally, towards the world. We act and react to our environment and to life's circumstances. At some point, after many such lives, we refocus inside. We realize that there is a bigger perspective than the one we see with our eyes, and this may lead us onto a spiritual path of self-discovery.

During the Golden Times, we were aware of our spiritual nature. To counter the pull of the external world, we had teachings and practices that enabled us to integrate our physical and spiritual self. These teachings centered on awakening and enlightenment. The aim was to live in the body with full awareness of our spirit and embody the Living Light.

The Facets of the Multi-dimensional Self

The ancient Egyptians understood that we are multi-dimensional beings living in a physical body. They used different terms to understand the bigger, spiritual self:

Divine Consciousness, the Creator: The Ba
All life is an emanation of the Ba, of Divine consciousness, the eternal spirit, the All That Is, that we are all part of. The Ba exists beyond time and form. It dreams and creates the form, and then projects the form — in our case, onto the Earth. Physical life and all spiritual dimensions are a holographic creation of the Divine consciousness that we are. The Ba does not incarnate.

The Body: Khat
Khat is the physical structure, the flesh and bones. The term also describes people who are unaware of their spiritual nature, completely absorbed in physical life, and not consciously connected with their Divine essence. In ancient Egypt, these people were called "the living dead": people who are not animated by spirit, and who are predominantly materialistic. This state, which is common in our world, creates much suffering. Such a life cannot bring lasting happiness and contentment. Instead, the conditioned mind and social programming torment us with their fears, worries, and desires. They show us a limited

perspective and control our individual life experiences, and we assume this is the absolute truth.

During the Golden Times, most people were self-aware. The prevalent attitude towards those living as a Khat was sadness. It was considered a failing of society that people lived in this way. Moreover, if someone is too attached to material life and ignorant about their Divine nature, they may not accept their death and move on to the spirit realms of the Light. The personality may refuse to merge with the Living Light of the heart-center and remain stuck in the lower astral planes as a lost soul, a ghost that haunts their home and neighborhood. Lost souls often attach to the living, commonly a relative, to sustain their existence. Invariably the relative starts to feel tired and unwell, and may develop the same physical conditions as the person who died. Due to their confused mental state and emotional overwhelm (fear, non-acceptance of death, anger, and grief), lost souls have a heavy vibration. The Earth is currently beleaguered by the heavy vibration of people who have not passed to the Light, due to factors such as traumatic and sudden death, war, natural disasters, and the lack of spiritual awareness about the continuation of life after death.

The Personality: Khaibit

What is the social programing, the conditioning of the mind? We are born a shining spirit, in a state of inner luminosity. Then we learn how the world around us functions, and we gradually absorb and adopt the values, beliefs, and ideas prevalent in our culture. Life events, positive and negative, including traumatic experiences, shape our perspective and create the conditioned mind, and we acquire our own unique way of being and operating in the world. Through this, we form our personality, which has a limited outlook. Part of our personality is the shadow, the aspect that tries to protect us from what it perceives as a hostile world. Many of our life choices as adults are based on painful childhood experiences and cultural beliefs of what we think will bring happiness and avoid further pain. All this is described by the word Khaibit.

Our personality is focused on material life and looks externally for answers and joy. It does not understand the inner self, nor does it know what true contentment is. It appears to have free will, and controls the way we act and react based purely on its beliefs. Through spiritual practice and awakening, we educate our personality. We show our ego-mind that there is another way of thinking and being.

The Enlightened Heart: The Ib
Inside our heart-center lies the Ib, the enlightened heart. This is the Ba in the body, the seat of the Divine within. The Ib acts as the observer, noticing and remembering everything that happens. It is also our conscience — the inner voice that encourages us to act with integrity and authenticity. Most of the time, the Ib does not intervene in our life. It allows the personality to decide what to do. It is the personality, in its desire for easy, short-term solutions, that silences the voice of the enlightened heart, the voice of our conscience. When we become aware of our spiritual nature, we start to walk the path of the heart and find the way back to the Ib, the eternal spirit within.

Instead of trying to silence the voice of the sacred heart, we now find ways to quieten our conditioned personality.

Surrendering the personality to the enlightened heart can be explained through a metaphor. It is like the individual drop of water surrendering to the expansiveness of the ocean. Both the drop and the ocean are water. The drop is unique, singular, and can be acknowledged as such. As a drop, it only has access to what a droplet can do. When the drop becomes the ocean, it yields its individuality to the whole, and its capability expands exponentially.

The drop, the Khaibit, the conditioning, holds itself back through fear and its attachment to being an individual drop. Its fear, born out of ignorance, is that it will lose itself in the vast body of water. What the drop does not realize is that, by merging with the ocean, it will not lose itself; it will become the whole ocean.

As is written in the ancient *Egyptian Book of the Dead*, the initiate of the Living Light asserts future generations to follow the spiritual path and become the whole ocean. "I achieved purification of my body (Khat) and soul (Ka) in the time of my youth, when other people were busy with the dazzling illusion of life [...] the essence of it is the one mighty ocean." (Seleem, 2001, p. 88).

In ancient times, beautiful rituals and initiations were performed in sacred sites of high etheric energy, in which people invoked the eternal spirit, the Ba, to inhabit their body. The intention was to walk a spiritual path and become the eternal spirit incarnated, and think, speak, and act from that premise, rather than obey the dictates of the personality-mind. An example of this is found in the Mysteries of Osiris ritual, where participants said, "O grant thou unto me a path whereon I may pass in peace, for I am just and true; I have not spoken lies wittingly, nor have I done aught with deceit." (Almond & Seddon, 2002, p. 126).

During life, immersed in the Khaibit, we can ignore the voice of the enlightened heart, our conscience. However, at death, our heart shows us exactly what happened and what we did or did not do.

After the Golden Times, the teachings of the Living Light were practiced for some time, and then the period of corruption infected the priesthood and society. Many turned away from spiritual practice, and people, including the priesthood, became less self-aware. Some tried to overcome their karma using unscrupulous methods. For example, members of the priesthood sold papyrus texts that claimed the person's Ib would remain silent after death, and not reveal unskillful actions by the personality. To encourage people to buy these documents, the priests said that without this papyrus the person would be devoured by a monster after death.

Did the priests forget that no one can escape their karma? Either knowingly or unconsciously, by selling these texts, the priests created heavy karma for themselves and their descendants.

Becoming the Shining Spirit: The Ankh
Enlightenment was described as Ankh — eternal life. In that state of being, we embody our sacred heart, Ib. We are fully alive, instead of being the living dead, the Khat. We are fully aware and awake, and express our inner radiance.

Ascension: Transformation of the Physical Body into the Ascension Body: Sahu
As the Ankh, we have the ability to transform our body into its inner nature of Light. Everything around us is Light, even the physical form can be described as condensed Light. The body transcends through the Light of the heart. Through this transcendence, we no longer inhabit a physical body that is bound by time and space, and subject to wear and tear from the elements. Instead, as we fully embody our spiritual nature, our body is transformed into the ascension body, Sahu, the shining spirit. We bypass the process of death.

The Etheric Self: The Ka

Between the Eternal Spirit, Ba, and the physical body is the etheric self, the Ka. The Ka is also known as the dream or astral body. The Ka is the double of the physical body in the form of energy.

The Ka is aware and travels throughout the physical world, as it is not bound by matter. It also travels across the etheric planes and different dimensions. The Ka has access to all worlds and parallel realities. It carries the knowledge of everything that has happened to us in this and other lives as energy imprints.

In everyday life, the Ka-double may be around our physical body, or elsewhere. At night, when we sleep, the Ka detaches from the body and travels in this and other realities. If someone is a healer in this or another life, their Ka may visit people, including family members and friends, and perform healings. The physical self has no idea what the Ka is doing. It may have no intention to heal, and may not know how to. The double, the etheric self, remembers the person's skills and wisdom from other lives, and uses them for the highest good when called to do so. The seed of our Ka is in the eighth chakra, the chakra above the crown.

A few years ago, during the night, I had an experience of my Ka. At the invitation of one of my spirit guides, I merged my everyday consciousness with my Ka and travelled with my spirit helpers to South America. I saw myself as a spirit guide for someone there. Time in this dimension is flexible. I spent months as a spirit guide for this person, during two hours of normal sleep.

The ancient Egyptians placed great importance in connecting with the Ka. They had practices that helped people experience and strengthen their connection to the Ka. They could heal energy imprints in the Ka from painful experiences in this and other incarnations.

The Ka in Life
The Ka/dream body is not external to us. It is an energy field that permeates the whole physical body, shielding and protecting it. When we are asleep, we are most vulnerable, as our Ka releases itself from the physical body and accesses other realms.

The Ka is a vehicle for the consciousness to access other dimensions and realities.

In our world, we may believe that it is our brain that thinks and decides what to do. For example, we assume our brain thinks, "lift the arm," and, almost immediately, our arm lifts. This is not accurate. The thought was not birthed in the brain. The brain is the computer that responds to the Ka. The Ka thinks and sends signals to the body and brain. The Ka body may have already raised its arm before the physical body performs the same movement.

The Ka is aware of the future, what is going to happen, for it carries this knowledge. One of the Ka's tasks is to protect the physical body from external influences, physical and etheric. The Ka knows beforehand if an accident will transpire, and may come close to the body to protect it and receive any fragments of the consciousness that dissociate. The Ka may also intercede on behalf of the physical self and influence it to act and prevent a mishap.

Our Ka may also intervene to help someone. I was meditating in a spiritual center with a group of people. Other people entered the meditation room to receive spiritual healing from those present. As the people passed by us, I saw my etheric arm lift and strike the back of my friend. My physical arm never moved. As I wondered, "Why did I hit my friend?" My friend started coughing. Later, she said that a heavy energy had come over her. Then, she felt a hand strike her back and she coughed and released the energy. It was my Ka body that took action, without any awareness or action by my personality.

We may also have premonitions of events before they occur, positive and negative. This is because the events are known to the Ka — in the etheric realm, they have already taken place. Everything first manifests etherically, then physically. Occasionally, when I pray for something, the enlightened spirits say that what I am asking has already happened.

The Ka is not interested in what the personality, the Khaibit, wants. Rather, the Ka tries to influence the personality positively and expand its viewpoints, and we may experience a sudden moment of awareness, an "aha" moment. The personality, stuck in the mindsets of its adopted belief system, may discard these precious moments of awareness.

The Ka — The Intermediary Between Spirit and Matter
The Ka communicates with the eternal spirit, the Ba, and the multi-dimensional worlds. This is the more spiritual aspect of the Ka that connects with the higher realms. This aspect is called the higher etheric Ka, and provides the Ba with information about the physical world and the spiritual realities it accesses. The eternal spirit observes the workings of the Ka and Khaibit.

At the same time, the Ka communicates with the body, the environment, and the physical world. This part of the Ka is closer to the physical body, has a denser energy field, and is more vulnerable than the higher etheric Ka. This is called the physical etheric Ka.

The conditioned self, Khaibit, is usually unaware of what the Ka does. However, through spiritual development, the personality can connect with and work more consciously with the Ka. And spiritual practices, such as those of the Living Light, also help the Khaibit connect with the eternal spirit, the Ba. The more we engage in spiritual work, the more we transcend the personality and connect with our higher purpose. The higher aim is to manifest the Ba state, the Divine consciousness while living in the body, and become the Ankh.

Death: The Ka Becomes the Vehicle of Transcendence
At death, there is the potential to integrate the spiritual and physical states. This is possible for most, unless someone does not move on and becomes a lost soul.

During death, the personality starts to experience a clear Light. This is the Light of the enlightened heart Ib. Attracted to this Light, the personality joins with the Ib and they journey through a tunnel — the central channel that lies within the body. Then, the personality and Ib lift into the Ka in the eighth chakra.

At this stage, the personality reviews and reevaluates its life through the eyes of the enlightened heart. The personality gains more awareness of the life lessons and circumstances it experienced, and its vibration gradually raises to that of the Ib, the enlightened state. The Ib accepts the personality without judgment, enabling deep healing of the Khaibit.

Once the review and healing is complete, the Khaibit and Ib merge into a united consciousness that travels within the Ka, the etheric self, into the higher states of the spiritual realms. At this point, the Ka's role is complete, and it dissolves.

At reincarnation, the Ib creates a new body and a new Ka, the double of that body. As the consciousness enters into the physical existence, it separates once again into the Ib and Khaibit, and lives another life.

Summary: The Etheric Self: A Multi-dimensional Existence

Every incarnated being is multi-dimensional and experiences three states of existence:

- The eternal spirit, the Ba, whose seat in the body is the heart-center, called Ib. This state can never be harmed, no matter what happens in our individual lives.
- The etheric self, the Ka, which engages with all dimensions, spiritual and physical. It is the intermediary state between the Ba and the physical consciousness or personality. It holds all the knowledge from the current life and other lives. The Ka connects to the eighth chakra and, while we are awake during the day, is also around

the physical body. Part of the Ka is linked with the physical body and is more vulnerable than the other part associated with the Ba.
- The physical self, Khat, and the personality, Khaibit, are the most vulnerable states, affected by the environment, the elements, and exigencies of physical life. The physical body perishes after death. An energetic imprint/memory of it remains in the Ka/etheric self, until the Ka dissolves.

Every being is simultaneously the eternal spirit, Ba; the etheric double, Ka; and the physical self, Khat. The Earth too is multi-dimensional and has an etheric self and a consciousness that is fully aware. The Earth is a physical, living organism, as we all are. From the tiny blade of grass, the smallest insect, the stars in the cosmos to human beings, we are all physical, etheric, and spiritual beings.

The purpose of life is to embody the awakened enlightened consciousness, where there is no death. We are the Ankh — eternal life. Our body transcends into the ascension body, Sahu.

Spiritual Practice: Ka Activation

We travel to the Golden Times of ancient Egypt, to the sacred site now known as the Temple of Karnak, or as it was once called: "Ipet-Sut" — "The Most Selected of Places." There is another interpretation of this ancient name. Ipet represents the energy of the Divine Mother Goddess, also called the Mother of Osiris, meaning mother of all creation. Sut is a plant, a reed found abundantly in the Nile. The reed was used to create baskets, beds, and other necessary items. Thus, Ipet-Sut is the mother of all who provides everything for the people.

Inside the complex lies a temple called the Temple of the Ka, which we will access in the meditation. The current temple is built on top of an ancient site that was destroyed. In the meditation, we will go to the ancient predecessor.

1. First, invite your spirit guides and teachers of the Light, the wise ancestors who worked with the Living Light for the highest good and the Light, and the enlightened Neteru to support you and create a sacred, protected space around you.
2. Intend to receive an activation and healing of your Ka. Ask to receive a transmission of Light for your highest good and soul evolution to the degree that you are able.
3. Ask for permission to travel beyond space to this ancient temple. Proceed only if you receive permission. If permission is not granted, try this practice another time.
4. Follow the journey below:

Imagine yourself outside a beautiful temple of white stone. The temple is bathed in sunlight. As you pass through the temple gate, some women wearing elegant, vividly colored garments welcome you. They carry bunches of flowers and bowls containing perfumed water and petals. As they dip the flowers into the bowl and sprinkle the water over your body and aura, they say, "Welcome. May the water element wash away all that you wish to clear from your life." Then they place the flowers on top of your heart-center for a few seconds.

They look directly into your heart-center and acknowledge the Light that you are beyond your current form. They see you as a radiant spirit. They bow to you and guide you inside the temple complex.

An old man dressed in white enters the courtyard. He is supported by two people, as he is lame. He is the teacher. Another helper hands him his staff of power. As he takes the staff, he transforms, becoming younger and taller. His presence and radiance fills the courtyard.

He asks you to follow him. Imagine crossing the courtyard and turning left into a chamber with no windows. This is the Temple of the Ka. The only light is from a ray of sunlight that enters through a small opening in the ceiling. As you look at the ray of light, you may see symbols and sacred geometrical patterns. These are the codes of power through which all life manifests.

The teacher invites you to stand in the ray of sunlight. As you do, the Light energy flows into your aura, and through your crown, into your body and chakras. Raise your hands up, palms facing the sky. Take your awareness into the tips of your fingers, and ask to connect with your Ka.

Your Ka, your double, appears in front of you in total perfection, without any illnesses or physical issues. Even though you may have aged, your Ka never has.

Your Ka sees you as your Ba, the radiant spirit. A bridge of Light is created between the Ka and yourself. Through this link, energy flows from you to your Ka and from your Ka to your sacred heart-center. This is an important link.

Meditate in this space for a minimum of 21 minutes. As you meditate, if you wish, you can make a commitment to live your life in accordance with the wishes of the infinite spirit and you can ask your Ka to assist you in aligning with this new reality.

After the meditation, a priestess who has merged with the cosmic energy field and consciousness of the Divine Mother comes to you. She offers you the Ankh, eternal life. The Ankh symbolizes someone who has fully manifested the enlightened state, someone embodying the Living Light.

Now, place your left hand on your right shoulder and your right hand on your left shoulder. The Light flows from your hands into the meridian channels of the body and down into the Earth. In this way, you share the Light with the Earth and all beings.

Slowly bring your hands into a comfortable position. It is now time to come back from the journey. Give thanks to all the people who supported you, the women who blessed you with water and chanted for you, the teacher, and the priestess embodying the Divine Mother. Also thank yourself.

Follow the man outside the chamber. As you return to the courtyard, the people smile and congratulate you. They are so happy you received this activation. Wave goodbye and walk back through the temple gate.

Your practice is complete. Slowly bring your awareness back to the room around you.

Give thanks to all the helping spirits, the enlightened Neteru, and yourself. Say that your practice is finished. Ask them to completely close and seal you, your space, and the building before they leave.

Write down any insights, experiences, and dreams you may have after the activation.

Chapter 5

Creation Story: From Spirit to Matter and Back

Channeling from Iset:
Creation is an act of unconditional love.

Like a mother who gives birth to a child, the whole of creation is birthed from the Creator's Divine body.

The cosmos is the child of Divine consciousness.

Every aspect, every being, whether a star, planet, or human carries the potential of the original essence, the Light of All.

Matter is solidified Light.

Light is the manifestation of Divine will.

And behind the intention, Light, and physical world is Divine consciousness, expressing itself and its power through unconditional love.

You and I and all beings, whether in spirit or matter, are created through the love and power of the Divine consciousness that we carry within.

Alternative Planes of Existence

During the Golden Times of Egypt, we had teachings about the multi-dimensional self and other spiritual dimensions. The physical reality is only one of the dimensions we inhabit. While we are in physical form, this is the realm we consciously engage with through the five senses: touching, smelling, seeing, tasting, and hearing.

In contrast to what our five senses tell us, the physical dimension is less real and more insubstantial than the spiritual planes. The physical dimension is a projection, a thought of manifestation, a concept that is dreamed into substance by the eternal spirit, the Ba, the Divine all-knowing essence. The spiritual planes, because of their closer proximity to the Ba, the ultimate truth of who we are, are more substantial.

Through spiritual practice and our sixth sense, we can develop our connection to the alternative realities. In the beginning, these realities may feel imaginary, as we cannot experience them with our five senses, and we have been taught that anything outside the material world is not real. Yet, something within may motivate us to practice spiritual teachings, and through perseverance, we open up to a whole new understanding of ourselves and creation.

Myths and Legends: A Multi-layered Approach
Blessed Are Those Who Behold (Channeling from Iset)
During Zep Tepi, people were aware of a process of creation from the spiritual into the etheric and physical realm. They were also aware of past cosmological events and a cyclical cosmic pattern within the time and space conundrum, which enabled them to predict future events and eras to come.

In order to safeguard this knowledge of creation and cosmic phenomena, the enlightened priesthood invented myths and stories, which were orally passed down for the thousands of years of ancient Egyptian spirituality. By 5000 BCE, the Golden Times had ended. The complex and sophisticated temple tradition continued and became part of a culture which incorporated fragments of the stories and myths. These stories were then taught widely to everyone. Many of the myths remained relatively unchanged for a long time and were finally documented.

The Pyramid Texts
In the sixth dynasty (2613–2181 BCE) effort was made to preserve the myths for future generations. The stories were carved on the inside walls of pyramidal structures erected in a location now known as the necropolis of Sakkara, near Cairo. This is why the

myths were called the *pyramid texts*. As the priesthood carved the hieroglyphs, meaning sacred glyphs or sacred inscriptions, they chanted mantras and held ceremonies that activated and energized the writings. The aim was multipurpose:

- To preserve the texts as a guide for humanity to overcome the chaotic states of the mind.
- To radiate etheric Light. The hieroglyphs emit etheric energy that can still be experienced today.
- To create an energy field. These pyramidal structures emit healing energy to help humanity overcome the inherent forces of chaos within themselves and in the world. When meditating inside these pyramids, a healing of our personality Khaibit can take place.

The Pyramid of Unas: A Living Textbook of Ancient Wisdom
This is one of the pyramids that house the myths. On one of the walls inside the pyramid there is a hidden etching of Horan (Horus), the spiritual warrior, that is only revealed in subtle light. Under the normal fluorescent lighting, the wall shows a decorative pattern. The Egyptologists have no idea what these particular symbols and patterns mean and surmise they are for decoration. But in sacred Egyptian sites everything has meaning and a purpose: to bring in etheric energy.

The discovery of the Horan engraving happened by accident. A local Egyptologist was in the Pyramid of Unas during a power cut. As he switched on his small electric torch, he noticed the wall with the colored patterns had changed. The subtle light of his flashlight revealed an etching of the pharaoh holding a spear, killing an animal.

The engraving depicts one of the most well-known spiritual teachings of ancient Egypt: the story of human awakening. The pharaoh, representing the human race, is shown as Horan, who overcomes Set, the forces of chaos (the animal symbolizing the base nature). Having triumphed over the conditioned forces during his life, at death the pharaoh (we) becomes Ausir (Osiris), the enlightened heart, whose Light shines like a star in the night sky.

The Hidden Truths of the Myths

Similar to this discovery, the myths and stories are also multi-layered. What is seen in bright light is different from what is revealed in subtle or spiritual light.

For the seekers of sacred knowledge, the initiates of the Living Light, hidden behind the myths were universal truths, which they could access through meditation. The spiritual teachers of the time would narrate a story. The initiates would take time to quieten their mind in meditation and contemplate what they had heard.

As the initiates meditated, they accessed their inner wisdom and discovered hidden teachings within the myth. They would then meet with their teacher to share and discuss the insights that had been unveiled.

Divine Plays

Since the Golden Times, the priesthood developed a way of sharing the Light energy from the myths with the community. They incorporated Divine plays, theo-dramas, into the temple festivals, attended by all, that re-enacted the myths.

During the play, the priests and priestesses would merge with the cosmic powers, the Neteru. The priesthood wore headdresses and masks representing the qualities of the enlightened beings they embodied. For example, the priest representing the spiritual warrior, Horan, wore the falcon headdress; a priestess of Iset had wings attached to her arms; a priestess of the Divine Mother, Hat-Hor, wore a headdress with cow horns surrounding the central sun, the point of creation. These theo-dramas invoked the etheric energies in a ceremonial yet lighthearted way, and it was easy for everyone to interact and receive the high vibrational Light.

In 2009, Iset asked me to introduce the ancient theo-dramas into our courses, with students playing the parts of the Neteru. During these Divine plays, we are joined by spirit beings, initiates of the Living Light from the Golden Times, who come and offer etheric support. The students who take part feel as if they are channeling the energies of the Neteru, instead of simply reading a text. As we continue to re-enact the plays, the energy vibration coming through the sacred Neteru strengthens.

One of the Key Myths of Creation: From the Awakened Spirit to Matter and Back

In the times of Zep Tepi, the process of creation was explained through a simple myth. Out of the waters, a mound appeared. Out of the mound, a lotus flower grew. As the lotus opened its petals, it revealed a baby sitting under the sun.

The myth describes the journey of the soul from the spirit state, before incarnation, to the material state. And then, through the path of the Living Light, the return —from the physical back into the Living Light, Ankh.

The creation myth talks about the state of the abyss, Nu — the primordial ocean or waters. This refers to the non-manifested state, the spirit state, pre-incarnation. Out of the abyss, a mound of earth emerges. This signifies the manifestation into the physical reality. The first thing created is the primordial lotus flower, also known as the Living Lotus. The lotus symbolizes unconditional love and is carried by the female Neteru in the images on the temple walls. In essence this means that the vibration of unconditional love gave birth to the physical world. You and all beings are birthed through unconditional love.

On top of the lotus flower is the human being, portrayed as a baby, sucking its thumb. The baby represents innocence. It is full of Light, untouched by the conditioning, with the sun above its head. This state is described as Ra-Horakti. Horan rising on the horizon like the sun. The being is radiating the state of the Living Light, awakening.

Creation is a process that repeats itself. Each time we incarnate on Earth, we arrive in the state of the innocent baby, the pure state of unconditional love. It is the same for all beings who incarnate into a body — animals, fish, birds, and trees too. Many of us are moved by the cuteness of a baby, human or otherwise. We may smile as our heart opens, perhaps unaware that when we look at the young ones, we are being bathed in the pure essence of the Living Light.

As we grow up, we become increasingly absorbed by the conditioning. The world grasps our attention, and we stop being aware of the Living Light. We lose contact with the Divine intelligence that flows through the physical world in the form of etheric energy, the etheric grid which connects everything in the cosmos. Gradually, the world consumes us, and we attend to what is happening externally.

The Myth Works Backwards: From the Physical Being We Journey to the Infinity of the Spiritual Self

Our spiritual work is the path that leads us home back to the beginning.

While we are absorbed by the physical world, our etheric body, our Ka is still connected to everything. Consequently, opportunities keep coming to take us into a spiritual experience. Our soul tries to bring us back to spirituality. Through spiritual practice, we retrace our steps to awaken into the Light of our Ib; we remember our luminosity and reveal our spiritual essence to ourselves. We reclaim our innocence and experience ourselves as the Living Sun, Ra-Horakti. We develop the state of unconditional love for all beings, becoming once more the primordial lotus, whose perfume permeates the whole of the physical and spiritual worlds. We exit the manifested state, entering a state of emptiness, the Abyss Nu, the state of pure consciousness.

The myth of creation is therefore circular rather than linear.

Through spiritual awakening, we transcend the ego and return to the emptiness of the void; we become the abyss Nu, the non-manifested state, the state of oneness.

Three Keys of Ascension

In the Golden Times, the aim of the School of Ascension was to help people rediscover the enlightened state and embody the creation myth. It was understood that the enlightened state is revealed from within. The person observes and learns from the mirrors that life holds, and the different experiences they encounter. They develop self-awareness and experience instances of self-realization that continue as long as the person remains engaged.

Through their spiritual practice and Divine connection, people could also understand deeper truths about the cosmos and the whole process of incarnation, reincarnation, and eternal life. People knew too, that no matter how many realizations they experienced or how long they had walked their spiritual path, it was easy to be re-absorbed into the conditioning. Accordingly, their intention was to keep experiencing the higher states of consciousness which create a feeling of being home. They purposefully sought to merge with the Light of their spirit.

Spiritual awakening is the transcendence of the physical reality through the manifestation of our essential nature of unconditional love.

We gradually transcend the conditioned mind as our Ib, the awakened heart within, manifests. We become the primordial lotus, and live on Earth as the Awakened Heart. This state of awakening is followed by enlightenment and ascension. Enlightened, we become the shining spirit, manifesting our essence of Ankh, eternal life. In ascension, we transcend the body. Our physical body no longer exists; our eternal body of Light, Sahu, is our vehicle to all realities and all dimensions. In this state, we are no longer subject to the wheel of reincarnation, and there is no death.

The three Keys to Ascension are:

- Embodying the awakened state in the physical reality by transcending the conditioned mind, the personality. We embody the sacred heart Ib, rather than the ego personality Khaibit.
- Awareness of the other dimensions and realities by engaging with the Ka, our etheric self.
- Realizing our potential as the Living Light, becoming the shining spirit in the ascended body.

Walking the Path in Life
In order to attain enlightenment, emphasis was placed on living an authentic spiritual life. All aspects of life were imbued by spiritual practice. At sunrise, people greeted and connected with the sun. At night, they greeted and connected with the moon. At meal times, they expressed their appreciation to all beings and the Earth for their contribution to the miracle of physical life. When they drank water, they connected to this sacred element, gave thanks, and blessed the water, imbuing it with the Living Light. Before they slept, they created a sacred space around their room. It was like sleeping inside the Holy of Holies of the temple. In everything they did, they invoked the support of the enlightened Neteru and asked the cosmic forces to ally with them. They aimed to live in an ethical way, according to the rule of Ma'at — Divine justice. Spirituality was a way of life.

They also had practices to increase their awareness of the Ka, connect with their spirit and dream body, and strengthen the connection between the Ka and the physical body. The physical etheric Ka, the more physical aspect of the Ka, was made stronger through etheric energy work. This bolstered the natural protection around the body and aura and offset accidents, misfortunes, and even physical illness, and reinforced the Ka's role as a shield against these forces.

The people were grounded and did not live in a spiritual cloud. The aim of spiritual work was to anchor everything in the physical body, where transformation is possible. And knowledge retrieved from the cosmic spheres was used to elevate physical life.

People who were ungrounded, who were not present, were described as having a "wandering Ka." Ungrounded people experienced the same problems as those with a weak Ka. As their awareness was not in their body, their Ka could not protect the Khat.

Illness was viewed primarily as a result of a person's disconnection from their spirit and their Ka. While receiving any necessary healing and spiritual interventions, someone who was ill was encouraged to increase their understanding of the deeper, spiritual, causes of illness.

The Keys for a Healthy Ka

These are some of the ways we practiced during Zep Tepi, to strengthen our Ka:

- *Live life in an ethical way.* Practice the rule of Ma'at and manifest Divine order instead of chaos.
- *Access the sacred heart Ib*, in the heart-center, through spiritual practices that invoke high vibrational energy, and create inner transformation. Teachings of the Living Light were practiced through meditations, sacred sounds, silence, time spent in sacred temples and sites of high etheric frequency, pilgrimages, rituals, and ceremonies.

- *Connect with nature and the four sacred elements* — earth, air, water, and fire, known as the four sons of Horan. Through connection with the etheric energy of the Earth, people experienced higher states of knowledge. They also connected with the Cosmic Winds (Shu), Celestial Waters (Tef-Nut), and Sacred Cosmic Fire (Sekhem).
- *Connect with the celestial body of origin and other portals.* People would connect with the star they originated from before incarnating, together with key portals in different star constellations, to open portals within the body.
- *Connect with the sun.* The sun of our solar system, and every star in the cosmos, was seen as the physical manifestation of the central sun, the point of creation, in the physical world.
- *Connect with the moon.* The moon represented the hidden power that lies in the unconscious. They understood that this power is in control of their lives.
- *Connect with the Sirius Star* (Sothis: mystical name of Sirius). This was a fundamental spiritual teaching on which the path of Ascension was built. Sirius emanates the Living Light. Sirius was known as the spiritual sun and was connected with Iset, who was identified as Isis of Sirius.
- *Connect to the Orion constellation, particularly the three stars of the Orion belt.* This is the Light of the enlightened heart Ib. Orion was connected with Ausir, and its spiritual name is Sahu, the same as that of the ascension body.
- *Connect with the cosmic forces*, the enlightened Neteru.

Summary

The ancient Egyptians share the spiritual teachings of the Living Light through practices that helped them remember their Divine nature. A key aspect of these practices was the connection with their Ka, also known as the double: the etheric multi-dimensional self. Those outside the priesthood could relate to the Living Light by practicing a conscious and just way of living through the rule of Ma'at and connecting with the cosmic forces-Neteru through myths and stories. These stories were re-enacted during festivals at key times of the year such as the solstices and equinoxes, when the etheric energies around the Earth are stronger.

For the adepts of the Temples, these stories had deeper meanings. They pointed towards a path of spiritual expansion. The myths were preserved in the *Pyramid Texts*, as a book of sacred knowledge, which can still speak to the seeker of our times.

***

"Read, children of the future, and learn the secrets of the best, which are so distant to you and in reality so near."

(Seleem, 2001, p. 10)

Chapter 6

Monads-Neteru: The Cosmic Archetypes of Existence

Channeling from Iset:
You are the children of the universe, the children of Divine Light.

Born out of the dark waters of the ocean of nothingness, you have been traveling the spiritual and physical worlds. Your Ba, your spirit, shows you the wonders of life, space, and time. And, after a while, it takes you back to where you started: the emptiness of the Divine Self.

Stages of Creation

There are infinite worlds, physical and spiritual, where the Ba, the infinite spirit, Source, manifests itself in trillions of beings. All beings are first conceived in perfect form. This first level of manifestation in this perfect, non-dual state, is comprised of beings of Light known as monads, or Neteru. It is through the monads that the Ba, the infinite spirit, manifests itself into all beings. Out of the monads, individual souls are created and inhabit the different realms/worlds, spiritual and physical. Collectively, all the realms inhabited by beings are called the dual or illusionary state. None of these worlds actually exist. They are a dream reality, a simulation game that we find ourselves in. The only thing that exists is the state of pure consciousness of the infinite Ba.

The Process of Manifestation of the Ba into the Individual Souls and Incarnated Beings on Earth

There are many monads, and each monad creates a plethora of master Kas, etheric beings. Each master Ka then multiplies into many individual Kas, individual souls, which together form the soul family. The master Kas and subsequent Kas bear the characteristics of the cosmic force — the monad that created them.

These Kas incarnate on Earth and other planets and worlds in whatever form these planets and worlds support. They also exist in spiritual realms. If incarnating on Earth, the individual soul (Ka) creates its image in an etheric (soul body, also called Ka) and a physical form (physical body) such as a mineral, plant, animal, or human being.

Monads are archetypes. Each Neter or archetype has key attributes and characteristics that are reflected in all of creation. For example, Ra is the archetype of the shining awakened spirit, and Horan is the archetype of the spiritual warrior. These archetypes are not mere concepts and ideas. They are beings of Light consciousness and we can communicate and work with them. The aim is for us to fully express the enlightened qualities these cosmic forces represent.

For instance, Goddess Hat-Hor, as the archetype of the cosmic Mother, is a force that expresses unconditional love for all beings, who are her children. A soul on Earth expressing this archetype may be someone who is naturally a motherly, nurturing person. However, on Earth, the energy of Hat-Hor that comes through the soul would not have the same purity as the Neter, unless the person is enlightened. Through our spiritual practice, and connection with Hat-Hor, we gradually transform the earthly state of love into the unconditional love of the enlightened state.

The Neteru in Ancient Egypt

In ancient Egypt, the Neteru were associated with different minerals, plants, and animals to define the characteristics and enlightened qualities of the archetype. Iset, the teacher of the Path of Ascension, is associated with the red carnelian stone, symbolizing the sacred menstrual blood, without which physical life would be impossible; the acacia tree, representing the tree of life that connects all realities; and the kite bird, known for its fast and focused flying. The kite also has a forked tail, denoting Iset's ability to access the lands of the living and dead.

Djehuti (Thoth) expresses the archetype of the wise elder and is symbolized by lapis lazuli, the myrrh tree, the ibis bird, and the baboon. Lapis lazuli is the stone of wisdom. Its indigo blue color and golden streaks matches the color of the third-eye chakra when open. Myrrh resin, made into incense and used in the temples during spiritual work, activates a heightened state of consciousness. When the sun rises, the baboon lifts its hands upwards as if honoring this physical manifestation of the Living Light. The ibis's beak is shaped like the moon, which is associated with the unconscious. The beak can detect vibrations, which allows the bird to find food underground — a metaphor for us finding hidden wisdom deep within.

When the ancient Egyptians wanted to invoke these cosmic forces in ceremonies, they used their representations from nature. For example, a priest who was channeling Djehuti would wear a headdress of an ibis and an amulet of lapis lazuli. A priestess channeling Iset would have wings made of multiple feathers, attached to her arms. In this way, people understood that it was one of the Neteru who was coming through the priesthood.

The ancients used this iconography to personify the Neteru when they inscribed and painted their ceremonies onto the temple walls. When we visit an ancient Egyptian temple, we can identify the cosmic forces, the Neteru, that were invoked in the different ceremonies.

The Egyptians decorated the temple walls not just for themselves, but also for future generations who would seek the Path of the Living Light. This is why they called their sacred spaces *"The Temples of Millions of Years."* They knew that these ceremonies, and the etheric energy they invoked, worked beyond time. As long as these temples are standing, the ceremonies inscribed on the walls are still taking place, and the power of the Neteru flows, even now. This is one of the key attributes of the Living Light: it works beyond time and space.

I have found this timeless quality when I facilitate pilgrimages to Egypt. The Neteru depicted on the temple walls bring forth the powerful etheric energy of the Living Light. As we connect with them with an open heart, the energy of the cosmic forces flows to us, even after thousands of years.

It is the same with the online courses for the ISIS School, whether these are live or pre-recorded. The high vibrational energy flows to each person who receives the activations and initiations for their highest good at the time they connect. There is no limitation for the Living Light and the Neteru. They meet you whenever and wherever you engage with them.

Neteru in Human Beings

In the human journey, a soul incarnates as a human being into a world of duality. The soul carries the qualities of all the Neteru as part of their Divine consciousness, although one key characteristic or archetype will prevail: that of their monad. We could say this archetype is the soul's nature. In the physical world, the soul's response to the environment, and the various life experiences it meets, will shape and determine the way it expresses the archetype. Through self-enquiry — awareness of our actions and reactions, our soul's deepest wishes, and what truly makes our heart sing — a soul may identify its predominant Neter archetype.

For instance, someone who has a thirst for learning, and develops unique ways to share their knowledge to help the community, carries the archetype of Djehuti. This person will incarnate in a specific family who may carry different or similar traits. There may be a family member from the same monad.

More commonly, family members express different Neteru. In coming to the Earth school, we meet people, particularly in our families, who are different from us. This gives us opportunities to experience contrasting ways of being. The challenge is to accept everyone in their uniqueness, rather than make them fit our perspective of how they should be. A person with the Djehuti archetype may find support in a family that values learning, or he may feel inadequate if his father expects him to become a footballer. Each soul's experience and expression of their Neter may be positive or negative, a gift or a burden.

Stages of Incarnation

A question arises — could we have more than one dominant archetype, or is there only one cosmic force we resonate with? The answer is not straightforward, as all of the statements below are true:

- The Divine consciousness gives birth to all the cosmic forces. As we are Divine consciousness, we have within us all the archetypes, Neteru.
- All cosmic forces, Neteru, are part of the Divine consciousness, and each is comprised of all the others.
- A unique cosmic force gives birth to our individual Ka and our soul family. This cosmic force archetype prevails within us.
- Although we are all one Divine being, we are also unique. We are the all and an individual. Therefore, nobody expresses their archetype in exactly the same way.
- In the material world, we express the monad in accordance with the wishes of our soul and the karma we are carrying.

It is also true that, because all monads are within us, we can develop other archetypes too. However, it will be our principal archetype that mostly resonates within us, and when we express it, we will find our life purpose. A metaphor explains this. We have a plethora of genes from our parents that determine our height, color of hair, eyes. There are many possibilities, yet only one will express itself in the physical.

This is another example from everyday life. Mary is a mother and teacher. She likes her job, but it is not what fuels her. She chose teaching because her parents encouraged her, saying it was a job for life. She is grateful for the stable salary and good holidays. In her later years, a colleague invited her on an environmental march. Mary was apprehensive, as this was new for her, and she knew her parents and husband would disapprove. The day she marched, she was exhilarated. Becoming an activist became her passion. She now describes herself as a peaceful warrior.

The archetype that invigorates Mary and gives her life meaning is not motherhood or teaching; it is the activist. Mary embodies the Neter of Horan, the spiritual warrior who fights to overcome the state of chaos and stands up against injustice and corruption.

In the physical world, the same archetype can be expressed positively or negatively. Consider the warrior Horan, fighting for justice. Some people express this peacefully, while others are filled with anger and hate, and may become violent. It depends on what motivates the person: love or unresolved inner trauma. We have all been molded by the conditioned world, and the mold obscures the pure expression of our Neter. Spiritual practice enables us to discover who we are beyond what has shaped us. It supports us to break the mold, remove the unhealthy pieces, and find a purer expression of ourselves, our archetype.

The Monads, Soul Families, and the Individual Soul

All the individual Kas of a soul family are similar. They share the same vibrational resonance. Some of these Kas remain as spirit beings, whilst others incarnate on Earth, or other worlds, in any form that is conducive for their and the collective soul's development. For instance, on Earth, they could incarnate in different cultures, genders, countries, and religions and have various experiences while expressing their archetype and unique vibration.

Kas from the same soul family do not usually meet each other. And, it is very rare for them to be together, in any type of relationship, as they are so alike. Each soul incarnates to have a different experience and then share the wisdom with its soul family. Engaging with a member of our soul family brings us little new.

We generally meet beings from different soul families who are our opposite or are complementary, to share our gifts. These beings are our kind and harsh mirrors to aid our soul evolution. When we attract the complementary type, we learn through joy, whilst our opposite teaches us through hardship.

All the Kas from the same family communicate etherically and support each other's evolution on Earth and beyond. The spiritual work we each do, and the evolution we go through, supports all the other Kas of our soul group. Sometimes, when one Ka has a big realization, this can fuel another Ka's awakening. This means that your individual spiritual work is helping the whole of your soul group. All of the learning, realizations, and awakenings are also shared with the Neter.

Channeling from Iset

"You are all individual beings, yet you are part of the whole. You are the brilliant sun and its rays of light. You are the rainbow and its individual colors. Through uniqueness, you grow and return to wholeness. From the state of individuality, you return to Source. You move between the two states, from non-duality and infinity to an individual with a purpose. This journey is beyond time, for you are eternity.

Your spirit is aware of what happens around you, beyond the physical world. All you have read about the monad, your Ka, and soul family, your spirit already knows. In awakening, you bring more of your spirit into your physical incarnation. The more spiritual work you do, the more inner transformation you accomplish. The more awareness and Light of spirit you bring into physical life, the more you become the Living Light. We give thanks to you for your journey and for incarnating at this time. Your life is precious and has so much to show you, even though your spirit is fully aware."

Summary

The ancient Egyptian gods and goddesses are cosmic forces and each expresses a Divine principle, an archetypal quality. These Neteru, or monads, are a creative force that gives birth to families of individual souls. The Neteru are the perfect expression of the Divine consciousness beyond duality, whilst the individual beings birthed through them express these Divine principles within duality, in a non-perfect state. A soul family is a group of souls who carry the same vibration and the same archetype, and come from the same master Ka within an individual Neter.

Spiritual Practice: Spiritual Protection

The Earth is a multi-dimensional place — different realities exist within the planet. On Earth, there are higher and lower frequency realities, inhabited by beings of higher and lower awareness. In every realm, you will find a mixture of everything. For instance, in the human realm, there are people with tremendous wisdom and spiritual power, and people whose life is a living hell because their mind lives in dark despair. Beings who are less aware do not wish to awaken, and actively discourage others from awakening. They frown upon alternative spiritual pursuits and ridicule spiritual knowledge. Why are they so offended by others pursuing something different? Is it because they cannot handle the Light?

As spiritual practitioners, we have full compassion for these beings. Some are human, whilst others exist in a different form. They may be lost souls of people who died and have not been able to pass through the veil, or beings who are non-human — what we call entities. These spirit beings attach to humans and control them through their vulnerabilities. The world is filled with them.

When we do any spiritual practice — whether it is a sound bath, drumming, meditation, healing — we open a door to the invisible realms. Consequently, we need to be aware of who and what can come through the door. This is why we always begin by creating a sacred space that is protected by the enlightened spirits we invoke. When we close the sacred space and release the spirits, we always ask them to place protection over us and our home. In this way, we close the door firmly to the invisible worlds.

The following practice is beautiful, powerful, and effective. I suggest you practice it whenever you feel you need protection.

In a beautiful space of connection, call the enlightened Neteru, your Ba, and Ka to support you in your sacred work. Ask three key Neteru: Wad-Jet, the cobra, a female spirit who protects the initiates and spiritual practitioners from earthly foes; Nekh-Bet, the vulture, a female spirit who protects from spiritual foes; Khepher-Ra, the scarab, the power of the rising sun, the infinite spirit in its enlightened state, to create a safe space around you for this practice, the intention of which is to rebuild your spiritual protection.

- Call Wad-Jet by chanting her sacred name three times.
  Chant: Wad-Jet An (An means divine essence).

  As a result, from deep within the Earth, the power of the sacred cobra rises within your body and through your central channel, emerging from your third eye. The eyes of the cobra are spitting fire that burns away all unskillful

energies in your aura. (Stay in this space for 5 minutes). Say, "May I now see my path clearly."

Affirm: "May the lady Wad-Jet be with me, for I am a sacred being, working for the highest good. The protection from the Earth for my earthly body and life is within me."

- Call the power of the vulture Nekh-Bet, one of the largest birds.
  Chant thrice: Nekh-Bet An.
  As a result, the vulture comes down from the sky and sits upon your head. Her wings shield either side of your head. She screeches and frightens away any unskillful spirits and entities in your aura. Light flows from her wings into your head and throughout your body and aura, cleansing you. Meditate for 5 minutes. Say, "May I now see my path clearly."

  Affirm: "May the lady Nekh-Bet be with me, shielding my crown from any unskillful spirits and entities, for I am a sacred being working for the highest good. The protection from the sky for my spiritual body and spiritual life is around me."

- Imagine that inside your heart-center is the scarab carrying the rising sun. Connect with the heart-center and affirm:
  "The power of the rising sun is brought to me by the sacred scarab Khepher-Ra. Like the sun, I rise from the night into the day as the Living Light that nurtures all life, for I am a sacred being in my heart, working for the highest good. The protection of the Divine Self is with me."

  Now chant thrice: Khepher-Ra.

Then, focusing on your heart-center, see yourself as the shining Light. Meditate for 5 minutes.

- Slowly bring yourself back. Give thanks to the Neteru, Wad-Jet, Nekh-Bet, Khepher-Ra, your Ba, and Ka. Release the enlightened ones, asking that, before they go, they completely protect and seal you, your room, and home.

Chapter 7

The Enlightened Ones

Channeling from Iset:
The Light is born out of the abyss, creating the physical realm of the illusionary dream. All you see with your eyes, including your own form, is imaginary. Only the pure consciousness of your enlightened state exists.

The consciousness creates the illusion so that it can know itself through the multiplication of trillions of beings, trillions of forms. When you find your way back to Divine consciousness, you will no longer experience the illusion of form. The way back is through the path of unconditional love.

The Neteru are around you, so close to you, for they are part of you. They support and fill you with the Divine love that created you. They hold you in your process of spiritual growth.

The Neteru

The ancient Egyptian spirituality is not a polytheistic religion that worships gods, goddesses, and animal idols. It is a sophisticated tradition which views the Divine holistically as a state of being that we are all part of. And, through the process of creation, this holistic aspect is individualized. The Neteru are cosmic forces embodying principles of the Divine consciousness — principles we all share. The Divine consciousness gives birth to the Neteru, and all the Neteru are part of the Divine Consciousness. Similarly, all colors are part of white light, and when white light is refracted through a piece of glass, the Light appears as distinct colors. This is also explained in the following quotation from the *Pyramid Texts*, which names some of the Neteru: "Ra, Tem, Utchatet, Shu, Geb, Osiris, Set, Horus, Mengt, Bah, Ra-er-Nehen, Tehuti, Nut, Isis,

Nephthys, Hathor, Mert, Ma'at, Anpu, are all the soul and body of Ra." (Almond & Seddon, 2002, p. 46)

There are numerous Neteru. Some of them are involved in the creation of the cosmos, and others work closer with the Earth and the human experience.

In the sky realm, the Neteru were identified with a celestial body, a star, or even a whole constellation. On these celestial bodies are portals of etheric energy that emanate towards the Earth the vibration of the specific cosmic force they relate to.

On Earth, the ancient Egyptians adopted countless ways to express the cosmic forces using animals, minerals, and plants. Depending on which area of Egypt they lived, different animals and plants were assigned to the same being, the same principle. Moreover, their civilization lasted thousands of years and saw many changes. Thus, identifying the different Neteru can be confusing. In this chapter, we will focus on the key Neteru found throughout Egypt, whose iconography and descriptions remained more or less the same.

We can work spiritually, beyond space and time, with these Light beings and the cosmic forces they emanate, and develop insights about the human predicament.

Cosmic Neteru of Creation

In the beginning, there was the non-manifested state of the abyss Nu. This is the state of the Great Mystery that can never be defined or known: both nothingness and all possibilities. Nu exists in darkness. All etheric energy is balanced, and there is no Living Light flowing.

Masculine Creators

Ptah and Khnum are expressions of the Divine masculine element. The creative force Ptah gathers the black soil from the lake of the abyss and creates form — takes the non-manifested state and brings it into manifestation. Out of that which cannot be defined emerges a new definable reality with form. As this is an unseen force, aligned to the abyss, Ptah is known as the Neter of darkness. In Egypt, in the temple of Abu Simbel, on February 22 and October 22, the sun rays light up the Holy of Holies. In that place are four statues, four manifestations of the Divine Creative force. Only three are lit by the rays of the sun. Ptah, remains in darkness, symbolizing that he cannot be known or seen. The other three are Amun-Ra, the Light of creation; Ramesses II, representing the people of the land; and Ra-Horakti, the human being at the point of enlightenment.

Similar to Ptah, Khnum is like the potter who finds the clay, places it on his wheel, and fashions living beings.

Amun-Ra is the Light of creation that constructs the physical world — the Living Light that is birthed from the abyss and creates all realms of existence and all beings inhabiting them. In a ceremony in the *Pyramid Texts*, Amun-Ra declares that he has created all aspects of the world out of his body.

Amun means the hidden one. The Living Light is a hidden light; we cannot see it with our physical eyes. However, through spiritual connection, we may feel the luminosity of the etheric energy. Hence the suffix Ra, meaning the shining one. Through the awakening process, our Divine Light which is hidden behind the veils of the conditioning, gradually becomes as visible as the light of the sun.

Atum is what we call Source, existing before creation and after dissolution of the world. Whilst the material dual world is finite, Atum is the infinite power that intends its creation and exists after its death.

Aten is the manifestation of the Living Light as the spiritual and physical sun. Akhet is the eternity aspect of the Living Light. It is symbolized as the endless horizon, which can never be reached, unless we embody the inner sun that then rises on the horizon.

Feminine Creators

Mut is the Divine womb that gives birth to the world — the physical and spiritual realms. Like Amun-Ra at mid-summer, in the spring Mut declares that all beings are created out of her body. The ancient Egyptian spiritual tradition is neither patriarchal nor matriarchal. Throughout the wheel of the year, aspects of the masculine or feminine may prevail, with neither as superior.

Mut is the great mother that brings the Living Light into matter. She has three aspects: the Creatrix that births the cosmos; Hat-Hor, the Nurturer of the world through her essence of life-giving unconditional love; and Sekhmet, the destroyer of chaos.

Hat-Hor is symbolized by the holy cow, an animal that gives everything to the people so that they thrive: her skin provides leather; her tendons are in musical instruments and bow strings; her flesh and milk feed the people; even her horns are used. Every part of the cow's body serves life. Hat-Hor is often portrayed as a woman with cow ears, or bare breasts from which Divine milk flows, pictured as Ankhs-eternal life. Hat-Hor means "House of Spirit." This refers to the physical body which houses our spirit.

In the temples are inscriptions showing the pharaoh, representing all humans, being fed by the milk of the Mother. During the Golden Times, the pharaoh was not the sole ruler of Egypt. There was a division of power and a working relationship between him and the high priestess of Hat-Hor. Neither the pharaoh, nor his council, could make certain decisions without the approval of the Hat-Hors, the priestesses. As the centuries passed and the patriarchy dominated, the role of the feminine as co-ruler was passed to the great royal wife, who carried the honorary title of the priestess of Hat-Hor. This was purely lip service. In reality, the carefully balanced leadership was lost.

The opposite aspect of Hat-Hor, as the nurturing mother, is Sekhmet, the destroyer of chaos. This is the Divine feminine force that protects order and destroys what does not serve the highest good. Sekhmet is portrayed as a fierce lioness, unhesitant in her protection of the young innocent cubs. When humanity repeatedly fails to respect the rule of Ma'at and creates turmoil, environmental destruction, and injustice, the destroyer Sekhmet awakens and oversees the destruction of the civilization. Sekhmet is a creatrix of a new way. The karmic forces activated by chaos always have to be balanced, and when her work is complete, Sekhmet transforms back to Hat-Hor, or the friendly cat Bastet.

Sekhmet was carefully invoked during healing, when illness was seen as a force that created mayhem in the body. She was also a protective power against injustice and corruption. In times of war, Sekhmet was summoned to protect the armies of Egypt and spread disorder in the enemy forces. However, Sekhmet is a primordial Divine force that cannot be controlled by the egoic mind. This force acts decisively, for the highest good. And, like the angry lion, it takes no prisoners. If invoked for selfish gains, this power may at best be ineffective, and at worst, it can turn against us.

There is a story about Sekhmet, which I have re-written so its meaning and teaching is more accessible.

***

A long time ago, a great civilization ruled the Earth. This civilization was located west of Egypt, in the middle of the Great Ocean. The people had fertile land, advanced technology, and abundance of everything. In the beginning, everyone gave thanks to the Divine, recognizing that their bountiful life was a gift from the Earth and the sky. They looked at the luminosity of the sun and bowed to the Light of the One. They respected all life-forms and each other.

In time, people became greedy. The more they had, the more they wanted. They forgot to express gratitude. "It's not the Divine that gives us all we have. It's not the Earth. We made it happen," they said. "There is no god or goddess. We are all-powerful and we can do whatever we want."

The temples were empty. No ceremonies were held to honor the Divine and thank the Earth. The people continued to plunder, and the more they took, the less the Earth gave. When their lands and animals failed to provide them with sufficient food, they went to war, enslaved their neighbors, and ransacked their lands. Corruption reigned. They built a huge tower to emit etheric energies to control peoples' minds, creating much suffering.

The Earth Mother petitioned the gods and goddesses. "Great beings of Light, sun and moon, the people are destroying the planet; many species are disappearing, the lands are full of poison, and humankind is enslaved by itself. Chaos is widespread. This cannot go on, nothing will remain."

Ra, the shining Light, the power that creates everything, saw that a new reality must be born out of the old one. He called all the Divine forces. One of them, Hat-Hor, spoke, "It is the role of a good mother to teach her children how to behave." Ra gave Hat-Hor his eye of fire. In taking his eye, Hat-Hor transformed into Sekhmet, the powerful lioness.

Looking at the Earth, Sekhmet saw chaos in every aspect of human life: in the priesthood and governments, and within each family. She released the fire of Ra, and an explosion took place that destroyed the tower and then engulfed the whole of the island. Rivers of human blood flowed through the land. After the fire, the water came. A great flood covered much of the Earth, purifying and cleansing all that had gone before.

The people who remained were frightened and realized they were powerless in front of such a destructive force. Their pride dissolved, and they kneeled on the altars of Mother Earth, asking for help. They vowed to live in harmony with the Earth, each other, and all beings, and honor the sacred. Ra called Sekhmet back, but such a force once unleashed is self-generating. One terrible destruction *followed another. Ra showed Sekhmet all the rivers of blood, but all Sekhmet could see was the chaos that still had to be cleared. So Ra intervened. He gave Sekhmet a sleeping potion of pomegranate juice and sang her a sweet lullaby. Sekhmet fell asleep, and when she awoke, she was filled with such sweetness that she transformed into Hat-Hor, the nurturing mother, or some say that from the fierce lioness, the cat Bastet emerged, and went to peoples' homes, purring. This domesticated side of Sekhmet was seen as a gentle healing power, one that was full of acceptance and no judgment.*

Some say it was wrong of Ra to have intervened, that he should have allowed Sekhmet to clear all the chaos and corruption, rather than leave some to fester. However, Ra said that this is part of humanity's growing process, and that human beings will eventually recognize what they are doing. In the meantime, no matter how soundly Sekhmet sleeps, she can always be brought back if things are once more out of control.

The Eight Primordial Neteru

In the Golden Times, the high initiates worked with eight primordial Neteru, eight principal aspects, which were both powers (masculine) and states of being (feminine), known as the Ogdoad, the numeral eight in Greek. This is an advanced teaching offered in the Book of Wisdom that Djehuti, commonly known as Thoth, gave to the people to help them awaken into their primordial essence of the Living Light. This book of knowledge was said to contain esoteric teachings that could only be understood as people developed their inner wisdom. If someone who was not an adept read the book, the teachings would go over their head.

The Ogdoad, with masculine and feminine representations, namely
    Eternity: Heh, Ha-u-het
    The hidden Light of Divine source: Amun, Amunet
    Primordial emptiness/night: Kuk, Kuaket

Abyss: Nun, Na-u-net
(and sometimes added) Creative Force: Gereh, Gerehet.

The Ennead: Principal Neteru Supporting the Human Experience

The nine Neteru below are cosmic forces that are accessible for us as we walk our spiritual path.

Out of Nu, the abyss or pure consciousness Atum, the creative Light, self-begotten and self-generated, created the cosmic winds Shu, that stirred the celestial waters Tef-Nut and manifested the cosmos, the female sky Nut, and the masculine Earth Geb. Once these were established, four other Neteru manifested: two brothers, Ausir and Set; and two sisters, Iset and Nebt-Het (Nephthys).

Iset brings the path of ascension through a portal in Sirius star. The hieroglyph on her crown is called the throne, pointing to the sky. She works through unconditional love. When we wish to walk the path with humility, dedication, and an open heart, Iset extends an invitation, and the path opens for us, lifetime after lifetime.

Ausir is the energy of the pure heart that is innocent and trusting.

The etheric portal that radiates the Ausirian energy to Earth is located in the Orion constellation, known as Sahu. For most of us, this portal is usually inactive when we are alive. When we die and leave the physical body, our etheric body receives an activation from this portal and our awareness increases exponentially. This enables us to see a bigger perspective, prevents us from getting stuck in the lower astral planes, and supports our journey to the spirit realms. It was said that at death, as we embody our spiritual nature, we become "like the undying stars that never tire of shining."

This is a metaphor that has been interpreted erroneously by some Egyptologists. They say the ancient Egyptians believed that when the pharaohs died, they became stars in the Orion constellation. The pharaoh symbolizes the people. At death, everyone becomes Ausir, returns to the state of the heart, and awakens into their bright Light, like an imperishable, eternal star. (Allen, 2015)

Set, also known as Seth, is the embodiment of the conditioned mind, the hurt human ego. Set experiences all the difficult human emotions: jealousy, pride, desire, and anger. He breaks the rule of Ma'at to get what he wants, regardless of the consequences and karmic implications to himself and others. Our world is currently governed by this Neter that is motivated by fear and a scarcity mentality. We may be tempted to label Set as evil, for he brings suffering; however, Set is neither good nor bad. He is a mirror so that we can see what our conditioning and fear creates. Set is symbolized by a grotesque animal that is constantly hungry, like the programed human mind. Alone, he roams the desert, isolated and unable to interact easily with others.

Nebt-Het is a quiet and silent Neter. She teaches us to withdraw from the world and discover the gift of knowledge through silence. In a deep state of peace, we connect with our wise self and, suddenly, a moment of awareness can arise, a "eureka" experience, that shifts our perspective. Nebt-Het heralds change after a period of stagnation. Her bird is "the screecher." Imagine sleeping in a dark, quiet space, and then the screecher bird comes unexpectedly and wakes you up. This is Nebt-Het's power. When Nebt-Het screeches, we cannot ignore the shrill sound that urges us to move out of our comfort zone.

Nebt-Het is the opposite of Iset. Whilst Iset is the active light of the day, Nebt-Het is the dark peace of the night. They come together to build stability, strength, and a strong foundation within us so that we can walk our spiritual path. This foundation was called the Djed pillar, symbolized by the backbone. Like a pillar holding the temple erect, the central meridian channel, located in the middle of the spine, enables connection with the Ka and the higher realms.

The Holy Trinities

The concept of the trinity exists throughout ancient Egyptian spirituality. This is based on the idea of a Divine masculine principle uniting with a Divine feminine principle to birth a new being. The new Neter is a distinct principle in itself. Below are some of the most common holy trinities:

Iset, the teacher of awakening, and Ausir, the open heart, give birth to Horan, the spiritual warrior, who awakens by prevailing over the internal conflicts generated by his egoic mind, Set. Horan is represented by the falcon or hawk. In the victorious battle with his conditioned mind, Horan loses an eye, his physical vision, and gains the all-seeing eye, the enlightened vision. The all-seeing eye, called the Utchat, was also a Neter and was invoked at the opening of the temple ceremonies to destroy illusion with its brilliant fire.

Set, as the forces of the conditioning, and Nebt-Het, the power that awakens us out of the darkness of the mind, come together and create Onpu (Anubis in Greek). Another name is Wapwawet, "The Opener of the Ways." Onpu opens the gate to the unseen worlds and protects the spiritual seeker. He is a protector of the sacred teachings and the psychopomp, the one who helps the souls of the dead pass to the spiritual realms (known as the Duat). Onpu is represented by the Egyptian dog, similar to the jackal. He is a guardian in the same way that a dog guards the home.

Ptah, the creator, and Sekhmet, the destroyer, come together to create Khonsu, the moon, the eternal traveler. This trinity represents the cycle of life, manifestation and destruction — everything that is created in form perishes eventually, like the moon that waxes and wanes and constantly changes. Khonsu destroys the illusion by making the unconscious conscious.

Other Key Neteru

Djehuti and Seshat are both Neteru of wisdom. Djehuti, a male form, symbolizes the peaceful wise elder who brings wisdom teachings to his community. Seshat, a female form, brings the wisdom of heaven to the Earth, creating perfect balance through sacred geometry and sacred architecture.

Ma-at is the Divine principle of justice and order that permeates all aspects of creation and holds the universe in perfect harmony. Anything that is out of alignment with Ma-at will eventually be destroyed by the chaotic forces that it generates.

There are countless Neteru. A whole book could be dedicated to them and their characteristics.

Anchoring the Light of the Neteru in the Temples

The ancient Egyptians spent thousands of years bringing the Light of the Neteru to their sacred temples and statues. Most of the main Neteru have a dedicated temple in different parts of Egypt. This was a room, or series of rooms, where the energy of the Neter was invoked and downloaded through daily rituals and practices. Still today, we can feel the energy of the Living Light and the Neteru in these temples.

There were also larger temple complexes dedicated to aspects of creation. For example, the Atum temple complex was located in Iunu, or Heliopolis, the city of the sun of creation, near present-day Cairo, and Amun-Ra in Waset, or modern-day Luxor.

The bigger temples and temple complexes were built in accordance with the myth of creation. They had a sacred lake that symbolized Nu, the primordial waters of the abyss. Out of Nu, the lotus flower emerged, representing the state of unconditional love, which then births the temple (the physical realm), and was a vehicle for the emergence of the enlightened state (the spiritual realm).

Summary

The Neteru, cosmic forces, archetypes, and monads are key to understanding the creative powers that manifest the physical and spiritual realms, including our own self as a physical and spiritual being. Some of the Neteru are cosmic forces describing genesis, whilst others are more relevant to the human journey of life and its potential for spiritual awakening.

Spiritual Practice with the Neteru

The spiritual practice takes you into an activation, and then into the embodiment of the Neter and the Light consciousness that you are.

Preparation: Becoming the Light Consciousness
Welcome all the enlightened beings you work with and Iset, Divine Mother, who has given these practices. Ask them to create a safe space all around you.

If you wish, you can light some incense. Allow the smoke to surround you and intend that you are cleansed from the energies of the world. Then sprinkle some water over yourself. You can light a candle and welcome this physical representation of the Light of creation into your practice.

State your intention to access your Light consciousness that becomes the vehicle that takes you to Zep Tepi and enables you to connect with the sacred Neteru.

Bring your awareness into your heart-center and visualize a brilliant sun, the Living Light that you are. Allow the luminous state that exists within to expand and encompass your body and aura. Imagine you are sitting within a luminous sphere.

Surrounded by your infinite Light, focus on the Earth. Your feet and the base of your spine are connected to the Earth, and the life-force energy of the Earth flows into your body, enabling you to further expand energetically. Become like the sky, Nut, which has no limits and permeates everything. You are a being of Light consciousness.

Spiritual Practice: Principal Neter Activation
In your Light consciousness, intend to journey to the Golden Times and remember yourself as the Divine Neter, for this state exists within you.

Imagine looking above and seeing the Milky Way, a celestial river filled with stars. Looking down you see the Nile River, flowing in the same direction as the Milky Way. As above, so below.

Along the river are temples. Now open your spiritual eyes and imagine or see these temples emanating Light. They are shining like stars.

As you look at the structures, you may feel a familiarity with one of them. Visualize yourself in your Ka, etheric body, standing in front of a temple. One of the temple servants welcomes you and takes you into the Holy of Holies, where a Neter waits for you. You and this Neter are aligned. If you wish, you can request that Light from the Neter flows into your etheric body and you receive an activation of this Neter to the degree that you are able.

You should also feel the energy flowing into your physical body. Even though you are linking to the Golden Times, this activation is offered to help you in your current life. Take time to quieten your mind and stay in silence until the activation is complete.

Once this activation of your principal Neter is complete, all the other Neteru appear and form a circle around you. They radiate rays of Light towards you and activate all the qualities of the Divine Consciousness within you, to the degree that you are able. Receive this second activation.

The purpose of working with the Neteru is to embody the being of Light that you are. Following the activations, see yourself once more as Light.

Finishing the Practice
Give thanks to the Neteru and the Neter you are, to the ancestors who built these temples, and to yourself. See yourself walking out of the temple. And then you rise into the sky as your Light consciousness: an expansive state of being.

Now, imagine looking down on the Earth and seeing again the temples, radiating the Living Light like stars. Imagine looking up into the night sky and seeing all the stars in the cosmos, radiating Light in all directions.

Then visualize yourself looking down at your body and flow back into it. From the sky, flow down into your crown, your third eye, throat, and down into your heart-center. Feel yourself expanding into your heart-center and into every part of you, down into your feet and the base of your spine.

Very gently, come back from the practice. And when you are ready, open your eyes.

Give thanks to yourself for this beautiful work and all the Neteru and helping spirits that assisted you. Give thanks to the Earth and the physical state. Say that you wish to close your sacred space, and ask the enlightened beings to completely protect and seal you, your room, and home before they go.

Chapter 8

The Great Pyramid and Initiation

Channeling from Iset
There are places of power in your world which are portals, gates through which the Living Light flows. These places create an incredible etheric field of their own. When you access these portals, a flow of intelligent frequencies can open you to your life purpose and raise your awareness.

The portals provide opportunities for you to merge with your infinite spirit, for as long as your physical body is able to work with the energy. Following the merging, there is an integration period that may instigate changes in your life.

The integration takes place between your egoic personality and your infinite spirit. You do not suddenly become the infinite spirit; your personality is still present. The more discordant aspects of your personality calm down, and your spiritual qualities flow more easily into your awareness and are more accepted by your mind. You then have the opportunity to make changes in your life, guided by the spiritual aspect of you.

This is the purpose of initiation — to bring more of your spiritual nature into your physical being and gradually transform yourself and your life.

The Pyramids

There are numerous pyramids in Egypt, beyond the more renowned ones in the north. The influence of the Atlantean and ancient Egyptian engineers of Zep Tepi expanded outside the Giza plateau, and they created many structures that are connected to the three main pyramids. Some of these structures are still visible today, whilst smaller ones have collapsed. In southern Egypt (upper Egypt), there are small pyramidal structures built from bricks that can still be found.

Each pyramid has its own characteristics, is aligned to different star portals, and offers access to a unique energy field. This can create energy shifts that raise our vibration and help us clear spiritual blocks from this and other lifetimes. Although the pyramids are portals in their own right, they work collectively to build a unified energy field that covers the whole of the ancient land of Khem. This network of the Living Light, channeled through sacred sites, is multipurpose:

- *Spiritual*: to enhance our state of consciousness, raise our awareness, and re-establish our inner connection with our spiritual self. Our inherent spiritual gifts also become more apparent. These gifts may be psychic gifts such as clairvoyance, telepathy, or astral communication. In ancient times, it was recognized that these gifts could become an ego trap. This is why access to the pyramids' initiation chambers and the rituals that took place therein was only open to those who had spent years in personal and spiritual development, worked from the heart, and upheld the rule of Ma'at.
- *Healing*: Healing energies flowed throughout the network and were concentrated in specific chambers in the pyramids. In ancient times, mental, emotional, and spiritual illness was often viewed as more debilitating than physical illness.
- *Electrical energy production*: The engineers of Zep Tepi could produce electricity with etheric energy that was harnessed through crystals and sound, and utilized throughout the temples. The energy was also used for travel, levitation of the large stone and granite blocks which formed the pyramids, and electrical light within windowless structures.

- *Climate control*: The etheric field also created a semi-tropical climate over the whole of the land it covered.
- *Communication*: The pyramids act as antennae that gather cosmic energies and emit and distribute these energies around the planet. They also send and receive messages from the cosmos and send and accept messages from different locations around the world. The ancient people communicated with different planets and worlds around the cosmos and fostered close relationships with other celestial beings. The language used for communication was a vibrational language that has been forgotten, but our soul remembers, for this is the sacred language of our multi-dimensional universe.

Notwithstanding the wonderful technology and energy production that the pyramids and other sacred sites enabled, their key purpose was spiritual connection and facilitation of the path to enlightenment and ascension for the individual.

The pyramids also help us align with our life purpose in a multi-dimensional way, beyond space and time. These are some of the alignments that these portals facilitate:

- Alignment of the physical body with its etheric counterpart.
- Alignment of the astral etheric bodies and chakras with the physical earthly bodies and earth chakras. As well as the seven main chakras in the body, we have chakras beneath our feet that connect us to the center of the Earth, and chakras above our head that connect us to Source.
- Alignment of our body's meridian system with the etheric meridians of the Earth, the ley lines, and the meridians of the web of Light that flow around the Earth and cosmos.

Sometimes, people who study the path of Isis cannot feel the energy even though their clients feel the Light channeled by them during healing sessions. Interestingly, these same people began to feel the etheric energy after our ceremonial work in the Great Pyramid, called Mner, the place of ascension. Following the initiation, their meridian channels opened, their awareness increased, and they could perceive the Living Light flowing into their body.

After receiving an initiation, we have a greater opportunity to experience states of bliss, which are self-generated. These blissful states can take place during meditation or even in our everyday life, and they are an indication of our heart-center opening. At some point, these expansive states of consciousness may be accompanied by a deeper understanding of ourselves, life, and spirituality. Truths that we knew only in theory become our wisdom knowledge.[8]

The pyramids have the physical form we see with our eyes and an etheric form. In the etheric, they are always in complete perfection. This is because the architects and builders of the pyramids first visualized them in the etheric in every detail and then built them in this realm.

Every day, throughout the times of ancient Egypt, and even after Zep Tepi, specific priests and priestesses, guardians of these sacred sites, would be at the pyramids to open sacred space and work with the energy. They would chant ancient mantras in Light language, even if, in later times, they no longer knew the meaning of the words.

When they died, some of these guardians chose to remain in spirit. They communicate with those of us called by the Neteru to work within the sacred sites.

The Pyramids of Giza

Most people know about the pyramids of Giza, one of the seven wonders of the ancient world. They are truly a miracle of science and sacred architecture, which, despite our current technology we cannot replicate. They are so well built that even when earthquakes and other natural disasters have taken place in Cairo, the pyramids remained unaffected. The only thing they have succumbed to is human interference — the white limestone casing and the golden pyramidions were removed by later rulers.

In the Golden Times, the three pyramids of Giza constituted an even more magnificent sight to behold.

***

Imagine traveling by boat to the site of the three pyramids. The River Nile is teeming with life, and the green, fertile river banks follow its course. As you look around, you hear palm trees swaying in the wind, see the ibis birds, and smell the heady perfumes of the flowers. And then, beyond the green land, the desert opens to welcome you. On a desert hill, in front of you, are three lights radiating so brightly it is as if three suns have descended on Earth.

Leaving the boat, you follow a straight causeway towards the hill and see that the three suns are the three pyramids. The rays of the sun touch the pyramids' white stone and their golden tops spread light everywhere. The light is so bright you can hardly look at the pyramids. At this place, you become the humble traveler. You kneel down and touch your forehead to the ground. You feel the Earth vibrating below you. The etheric energy flows into your body. The pyramids see you and acknowledge you. You have been blessed.

***

During the day, the pyramids radiated the visible light of the sun. On a clear day, they looked like suns floating on the horizon above the haze created by the desert sand. All who saw them were filled with awe.

At night, people went to the pyramids to feel an alignment that came from the cosmos. The pyramids gather the energies of specific star portals and have shafts pointing towards these portals. As in the whole of Egypt, the two main portals of Sirius (Iset) and Orion (Ausir) are present. Specifically, the three pyramids mirror the stars of the Orion belt and gather the energies of these star portals. In the Great Pyramid, narrow shafts from the main chambers, what we now call the King's and Queen's chambers, point towards Sirius.

The energy from the Sirius star supports our spiritual path while living in the body and has a healing effect. The Orion portal is significant at the time of death. For dedicated spiritual practitioners, who work for the highest good without an egoic agenda, a way exists to access this portal whist living. In Egypt, the way is created energetically in the numerous sacred sites dedicated to Ausir.

The three pyramids are part of the network that brings the Living Light to the Earth and raises the vibration of the whole of the North of Egypt. They connect with the web of etheric Light that flows throughout the cosmos, and gather and direct this Light to other sacred sites around the Earth via ley lines.

An Underground City and Tunnel Network

What we see in the Giza plateau and surrounding area, including the pyramids in Sakkara, Dashur, the Meidum pyramid, and those further afield, is only the tip of the iceberg. Underneath the desert plateau, there is a vast network of sacred sites that was hidden after Zep Tepi, covered by the shifting sands and lost in time. When humanity reaches a higher level of consciousness, some key parts of this network, including an underground city, will be revealed. For now, these sites are etherically protected, due to their sacredness.

The sites are connected by a plexus of underground tunnels that extend for miles. Some of the tunnels are now flooded by the Nile, others are dry and still functional. My understanding is that these tunnels are known to the local people and some Egyptologists, but they are closed to the public.

The tunnels act as ley lines for the whole of the sacred site, and even today carry a high vibration that maintains the frequency of this site. The tunnels were used by initiates to travel quickly from one site to another. The underground city at the center of the site, built during the time of Atlantis, was something akin to a control room where the etheric energy was transformed into various frequencies and used for different purposes, including to access parallel realities. Although we might compare this place to a modern electrical plant, it would be erroneous to think of the city only in material terms. As with everything in Zep Tepi, the ultimate intention of the city was spiritual evolution.

The Great Pyramid Mner: The Place of Ascension

The word, pyramid, describes the geometrical shape of the structure. It is derived from the Greek "pyramis" which means "vessel that receives the fire" (or the energy). The ancient Egyptians did not call them pyramids. For example, they called the Great Pyramid "Mner," meaning the place of Ascension.

The pyramids are not tombs. No one has ever been buried in Mner or in any of the Egyptian pyramids. And Mner was built much earlier than the time of Pharaoh Khufu, who claimed it for his own purposes. When it was constructed, and throughout Zep Tepi, the pyramid was a place of extremely high energy. This is because it was a temple of initiation and the activation of the Light bodies for initiates of the Living Light.

The initiates prepared for their initiation in Mner spiritually and physically through intensive purification processes that included fasting and meditation with high vibrational energies. Only initiates who had built a strong etheric field were allowed to enter the initiation chamber and receive the

Light. Afterwards, the initiates would share this Light with their community. Contrary to some modern beliefs, the initiates of the Living Light never used hallucinogenic substances to further their spiritual abilities. These substances were known to weaken and fragment a person's aura by opening the person too much, too quickly. This can create paranoia or worse, psychosis. In order for initiates to work with the high vibrational Light and transform their body, they needed to be well-grounded.

After Zep Tepi, the pyramid's visible opening was closed, and only one secret opening remained. The priesthood in the temple complex of Atum in Iunu was responsible for granting access. The remaining opening is still known to initiates of the Living Light. Apart from this physical access, there is also an etheric door and an etheric key that unlocks the door.

People who visit the pyramid today enter through an opening that was manually bored into the side of the pyramid. This is not the original entrance. Through this entrance, people climb up the Great Gallery to what is now called the King's Chamber. Most feel very little energy. Even psychic people sometimes go to the Great Pyramid and feel disappointed afterwards. This is because they walk through the physical structure, but the etheric door is not always open. To awaken the pyramid, the etheric door has to be opened.

If you have visited the Great Pyramid (or any of the pyramids), and did not feel very much energy, it is because the site was sleeping. Most of the time, due to the number of tourists, the site closes down. Your experience will be different when it becomes a ceremonial site. Then it will be fully functional and alive.

Initiation in the Great Pyramid: 2006CE
This was my first initiation in the Great Pyramid in this life. I was sitting in my hotel in Cairo, and through a window I could see the Great Pyramid. The previous day, I had booked a pyramid

tour with a travel agent, which consisted of a quick visit to the second pyramid of Khafre, a stop for a photo, and two hours of shopping. Not what I had hoped for. When I asked about the Great Pyramid, the tour guide insisted it was closed, but I discovered it was actually open. What should I do? I asked the spirit of the pyramid if it wanted me to visit. The spirit replied that it was my decision. I felt a foreboding presence. As I sat gazing at the pyramid, I decided to go.

I was apprehensive leaving the hotel, but as soon as I stepped out, a taxi man appeared. He asked if I wanted to go to the pyramids. I said I did, and he offered to take me for a small fee. Instinctively, I knew I could trust him, so I got into the taxi, and within 2 minutes we were there.

As soon as I exited the taxi, I was surrounded by men. Some of them pushed in front of me as I stood in the ticket queue. Overwhelmed, I started to leave. Then a strength came into me that said, "You can do this." Determined, I returned to the ticket office without any hassle from the men and bought a ticket.

When I entered the pyramid, I was alone. As I climbed the steep ramp in the Great Gallery towards the King's Chamber, I felt fearful. What if I fell? What if there was no one to find me? What if they forgot about me and closed the pyramid?

Although still afraid, I found myself at the top of a ramp on a ledge at the opening to the King's Chamber. The opening was low, and as I dropped to my knees and entered the room, I felt very humble.

I sat with my back against one of the chamber walls, as other people came and left. I found their presence reassuring, and my mind calmed. I asked my spirit guides for help and tried to sing some mantras, but I felt little connection. After an hour, I decided to leave.

As I walked down the ramp, alone, psychically I heard sounds repeating, over and over. Unconsciously, I started singing the sounds. Suddenly, a powerful rush of energy came from the pyramid and flowed into my body and aura. The pyramid had awakened. I felt as if I was walking in a living and breathing organism. With renewed purpose, I continued to sing and my heart-center opened. I felt elated. It was glorious.

Later, my helping spirit Iset said that these sounds unlocked the pyramid. And when the pyramid is opened etherically, the energy flows and meets us. Iset also said that I received an initiation that day. Overcoming the fear and breaking through limiting thoughts was part of the process that ancient initiates of the Living Light would also go through.

Walking the Path of the Living Light
In time, I recalled the initiations I received in the Great Pyramid in ancient times. These were a major aspect of the path of the Living Light. Even though, since December 21, 2012, I have been given permission to facilitate these initiations distantly, Iset invites current initiates to visit Egypt and receive an initiation inside the Great Pyramid.

In the Golden Times, the path of the Living Light was open to all. The first initiation took place in a local temple, following a foundation course. The initiation had to be approved by Ma'at, the principle of Divine Order. Afterwards, the neophytes opened the First Gate of Awareness. They practiced the teachings daily for 2 years. After 2 years, they participated in a ceremony in the temple of Amun Ra, Thebes (modern-day Luxor). During the ceremony, novices meditated from sunset to sunrise intending to commune with the Living Light.

In the morning, the neophytes would share their experiences, and for some a path opened to continue the mystical teachings of the Living Light. These students travelled to Iunu to receive an initiation inside Mner. Others studied a variety of spiritual disciplines and served their community in different ways.

Initiation in the Great Pyramid: Zep Tepi

As I meditated in the temple of Amun-Ra, I felt the unconditional love of the Divine consciousness. Peace descended over me. Light flowed into my body, and my spirit expanded. I felt formless and, at the same time, fully present in my body. Everything was held in a space of expansion, love, and peace.

In the morning, I shared my experiences with the circle of initiates. Then the ceremony was over. We ate some food and rested by the sacred lake. In the afternoon, one of the priests asked me to pack my belongings, as I would now continue my studies in Iunu.

In Iunu, I was met by initiates who were very serious and dedicated. Each day, we studied and worked together silently in the temple. I missed the lighter atmosphere of the south, the jokes and chatting between the initiates. The only thing that kept me there was the chanting; I had never heard such beautiful melodies. We would chant the sacred mantras for over two hours daily. Sometimes we would merge with a Neter and our voice would change. In the process, we became a pure vessel, the voice of the Divine Ones. During this time, I discovered one of my gifts, which has also become apparent in this lifetime. My voice can harmonize the sounds from others and bring them into something more beautiful.

After 2 weeks, the new initiates were asked if we wished to receive the Initiation of the Light Bodies inside the Great Pyramid. We had to make our own decision. My helping spirit Iset told me to accept the invitation. Yet, I was not sure.

In the end, I accepted and gave my answer to the priest. Later, in that life, when I was the priest, I learned how he spent the time holding space and praying that the initiates would find their calling and remain on the path their soul had chosen for them.

Then, unexpectedly, during the night of the full moon, I was woken by some of the senior priesthood and given a white gown to wear. They asked me to give them all my possessions, apart from my sacred objects. I was to wear no adornments or make-up. This initiation was a rebirthing, a letting go of my old life and a birthing into a new life.

We walked to the site of the pyramids. People were waiting for us, including the High Priestess and Priest. They were so encouraging. The High Priestess radiated love and beauty. She knew this initiation was important for me, and that it was also daunting, and she encouraged me energetically, without breaking the silence. She and I went into an underground tunnel (not the same entrance as now), and at the end of it she said I had to go into Mner alone. No one would be there until I arrived at the chamber of initiation at the top of the ramp. Once there, I was to sit quietly and wait.

Somehow, I found myself in the Great Gallery and knew instinctively I had to go up. An eerie blue light followed me as I walked, and I had to really concentrate where I stepped. As in my current life experience, I was frightened of falling and being left alone in this foreboding place. Many times I thought of giving up.

Finally, I arrived at the ledge. With my hands, I found the opening into the chamber, kneeled, and went inside. The chamber was in darkness. I sat alone for what seemed an eternity. Nothing happened. I called Iset, but could not feel her. Doubts and fears resurfaced. I pushed the thoughts away and chanted some mantras. Still I felt nothing.

Then, spontaneously, I connected to my heart and thought of the sound of creation that permeates everything. I chanted the sound and gradually felt safe. As I sat in the darkness chanting, I felt I was in the womb of the Divine Mother. I thought I saw different lights, or was it my imagination? I knew the initiation place, the sarcophagus, was somewhere in the chamber, and I got up and, feeling its energy, walked towards it. When I reached it, I climbed inside and lay down. Powerful energy flowed into my body. I closed my eyes and allowed the Light to pulsate through me. (Even today, many people may be able to feel this incredible Light when they lie in the sarcophagus.)

I heard the voices of the High Priestess and Priest speaking to me, calling my spirit to come into my body. I physically felt my spirit, my Ba, descend into me. I was then told to come out of the sarcophagus. I opened my eyes, and the whole room was illuminated. The High Priestess and Priest were standing beside the sarcophagus and helped me out. Other priests and priestesses were there too, and they all rejoiced when I stepped out.

In 2009, I had a dream. Iset came to me and invited me to lead a pilgrimage to Egypt. She said that we would go inside the Great Pyramid at the Equinox and receive the Initiation of the Light Bodies. Everything we did, Iset gave me. And what I channeled was based on this ancient initiation, adjusted for our current time. We booked private time in the Great Pyramid, and when we went there, I recognized the same fear and apprehension in many of our group. This is part of the experience. The programing tries to prevent us evolving and surfaces especially at the times we take important steps in our soul development. Inside the chamber of initiation, I saw the spirit, the Ba, of each person descend into their body as they lay in the sarcophagus.

Receiving such an initiation can become a turning point for us. However, the initiation is only a door, another beginning in the journey of the soul. It is a gift for us to work with as we walk our spiritual path.

The Great Pyramid Revealed

Inside Mner are spirit beings, some of whom were once human. These wise teachers remained in the Earth's etheric realm after death to guard this important structure in service to humanity. Other guardian spirits are highly evolved Light beings from different star constellations that support the Earth school. The pyramid is also a conscious being. It responds to our vibration. When we visit, it scans us, and it may offer us a gift of Light.

Inside the pyramid, there are three known chambers. Egyptologists have named these: the Well or Pit, which is at the bottom of the pyramid; the King's chamber, where the stone sarcophagus lies; and the Queen's chamber. In 2017, scientists using cosmic-ray muon radiography found a previously hidden large void (chamber) above the Great Gallery. As yet no access to this area has been discovered. In visions, I saw five chambers, and when I perceived the two hidden chambers psychically, they were as real as the three known rooms.

Three Main Known Chambers
currently, there is access to the three known chambers.

- The Well: located at the bottom of the pyramid and accessed through a narrow passage, is the place of alignment between the Earth and the galactic center.
- The Queen's chamber: a healing chamber aligned to the Sirius Star. This chamber, when activated, brings the Living Light from the Sirius portal to the Earth. It is also a chamber for communication with the Star Beings from Sirius. In the time of Zep Tepi, when the Earth's vibration was stronger, physical healing was instantaneous. If we were to experience such healing in our times, we would call it miraculous.
- The King's chamber: the place of initiation with the focus being the sarcophagus. When the pyramid is active and we lie inside the sarcophagus, the etheric energy strengthens and extends our crown to the degree we are able. The initiation can act as a path-opener and create circumstances for spiritual growth.

Above the King's chamber are five smaller chambers known as the "relieving chambers." These relieve the weight of the blocks above the King's chamber and prevent the chamber collapsing. The relieving chambers also strengthen and support the crown chakra during initiations. Additionally, the chambers have a vibrational quality and amplify the etheric energy when sound is used in the King's chamber. Toning certain sounds creates amazing etheric energy waves that activate etheric symbols which normally remain in a dormant state.

The Two Hidden Chambers

- The Chamber of the Power of Creation holds the energy of the Central Sun. Beings of Light, known as the first creators, guard this power point. These beings exist as consciousness and hold the key for understanding ascension.
- The Chamber of the Unconditional Love of the Great Mother, the Chamber of Iset.

These two chambers hold the energy that is the basis of creation: power and love. The two powers are the same, two faces of the same coin.

Summary

There is a common belief that the pyramids were built as tombs for certain pharaohs. This is not my understanding. The pyramids were constructed to create energy fields of high vibrational energy in order to maintain a certain way of life in both the physical and spiritual spheres. Today, they still contribute to the etheric energy of the Earth and generate and distribute the Living Light etherically.

During the Golden Times, access to the pyramids was offered to the initiates. At some point in ancient Egyptian history, these practices became secret and were safeguarded within the temple complex of Iunu. Later, at the end of the old Kingdom, the practices ceased for all but high initiates. By this time, the Great Pyramid was completely sealed, and only those who knew the underground passages could access it.

Inside the Great Pyramid, the three known chambers are the Well that links to the galactic center; the Queen's chamber, which is a healing chamber; and the King's chamber, with the five chambers above it, which is the initiation chamber. There are another two hidden chambers which will reveal themselves when humanity reaches a higher level of consciousness: the Chamber of the Power of Creation; and the Chamber of Iset, the Chamber of Unconditional Love.

Spiritual Journey: Walking as the Ancient Initiate inside the Great Pyramid

Preparation

Before you do this practice, meditate and connect with your heart with a pure intention to serve the highest good. Connect to the Great Pyramid and ask permission to enter Mner distantly as it was in the Golden Times. If you receive a positive answer, cleanse your energy field with water (take a shower) and smudge yourself using natural incense.

When you are ready, open your sacred space by asking Iset, the teacher of the Living Light, and Onpu, the path opener, to create a safe and protected space around you.

Journey

Imagine standing in front of the Great Pyramid. See yourself enter Mner through an opening in one of its faces.

The Well/Pit

You find yourself in a corridor. Beautiful Light surrounds you, even though there are no windows. You walk along a corridor and then enter a passage that takes you down into the pyramid. At some point, you find yourself in a chamber. State your intention:

"May I be grounded in my body. May I connect to the Earth and the physical body I occupy."

The Earth chakra below your feet activates, and energy flows into you. Stay in silence for a few minutes as this energy transference anchors you in your body.

The Hidden Chamber of the Light of Creation
Leave this chamber. Walk up and further along the corridor and enter another chamber, made of white limestone. This is the chamber of the central sun of creation. Feel the vibration changing. You are now at the heart of the pyramid.

Say, "May I manifest myself as the Light of All."

Lift your hands, palms upwards, and ask to receive the Light of creation for the highest good. Then bring down your hands. Bathe yourself in this etheric energy for up to 2 minutes.

Three spirit beings, the three Creators, come. They share a message, "The world was created through harmony. The chaos you meet in your daily life is part of eternal harmony. We invite you to consider that everything in the cosmos is connected, and that you are part of this cosmos and harmony. Any disharmony you perceive is part of Divine Order.

The only difference between us is that you are currently unaware of your Divine consciousness. We offer you a blessing of Light."

Stay in silence for a few minutes and receive their blessing. Then thank the beings of Light.

The Hidden Chamber of the Light of Unconditional Love
Come out of the chamber of the Light of Creation and find your way to the Chamber of the Great Mother. Give thanks for being in this sacred place and open yourself to the vibration of unconditional love.

Say the intention, "I am a manifestation of Divine love."

A priestess greets you, dressed as Hat-Hor, the Divine Mother. Hat-Hor nourishes you with the vibration of Divine love and sees you as a being of unconditional love.

Receive the energy of unconditional love for a few minutes.

Hat-Hor asks you to consider the physical manifestation of spirit achieved through the Light energy that creates the physical world and you. This physical manifestation is birthed through unconditional love.

Give thanks to Hat-Hor, the Great Mother, and leave this chamber.

The Chamber of Initiation — The King's Chamber
You walk along a corridor and find yourself in the great gallery. As you walk up the ramp, you leave behind the earthly world and enter the spiritual planes, which become more ethereal the higher you climb. Then step onto the ledge and crawl through the opening into the initiation chamber. Inside is a sarcophagus.

Lie inside the sarcophagus and intend, "May I be re-aligned with my infinite spirit. May I surrender to the infinite that I am. May this initiation be shared with all my lifetimes and existences for I am a multi-dimensional being. May this initiation also be shared with those of my soul group who choose to receive it."

As you lie inside the sarcophagus, affirm, "May my infinite spirit inhabit my body and may I be resurrected as the Living Light of All."

After a little while, come out of the sarcophagus and give thanks for all you have received. Walk out of the chamber and down the ramp, and bring your spirit back to Earth.

Once you are down the ramp, walk to the healing chamber.

The Healing Chamber — The Queen's Chamber
Enter the healing chamber and intend, "May my heart-center open. May I bring all of myself into this moment of now. May I

receive a healing for my current life and body. May any spiritual blockages be purified."

The healing Light from the Sirius Star flows to you. Stay in silence for a few minutes.

Leaving the Pyramid
As you walk out of the healing chamber, you find another corridor that takes you out of the pyramid. As you exit the pyramid, the sun is shining. Imagine yourself as the radiant sun emanating Light in endless space. The more you share the infinite Light of your heart-center, the more it grows.

Radiate the Light of your spirit towards the whole of creation, for the highest good of all, for a little while. The pyramid is an antenna, so you can truly transmit Light around the globe from this point.

Coming Back from the Practice
Give thanks to this sacred space, its guardian spirits, Iset, and all beings of Light who work with you. Your practice is now complete. Ask the spirits to completely protect and seal you and the room and building where you are, before they go.

You may feel tired after this spiritual practice. Take time to integrate these high vibrational energies by resting.

Note: People were asked to meditate and integrate their experience, rather than share their experiences immediately with others. This allowed the process to deepen.

Endnote

8   There is a difference between knowing a spiritual truth and embodying it as wisdom knowledge. I found the best description in a Buddhist mortality prayer, "May true understanding be born within me." This means we know something, not from a book or through a teacher, but because a knowing arose from within.

Chapter 9

Horus of the East

Channeling from Iset:
As the sun rises in the east, you rise out of the darkness. The night of the soul is like the dark soil of the Earth that nurtured the seeds over a long winter. In Divine timing, you find the power to emerge out of the shadow into the Living Light and illuminate the cosmos.

You are the life-giving sun, born into your enlightened state. Your rays touch all beings, bringing life, warmth, and comfort. You cast away the shadows, and your Light shines everywhere.

Wake up Horan of the east. Awaken in your magnificence and rise up in the infinity of the endless horizon.

Traveling on the Boat

In the ancient spirituality of the Living Light, physical existence and the awakening process were compared to a boat journey on the river of life. The soul embarks on the journey by birthing into the physical world. This dual soul journey, through a lifetime and eternity, is a key spiritual teaching from the Golden Times. During the New Kingdom and thereafter, the priests placed a papyrus of this teaching inside coffins to remind the deceased of the eternal journey and infinite nature of the soul.

The journey starts at sunset and lasts twelve eras, or twelve hours: the whole of the night. In the beginning, the moon is full and the stars are bright, and the soul can easily find its way in the river of life. When clouds cover the sky and there is complete darkness, the soul may feel lost sailing into uncharted waters. Sometimes, the boat is stranded on a sandbank, unable to move. Other times, there is a helpful current and the boat glides effortlessly through the water. The soul has to trust the flow of the river.

There are some key characteristics on this journey:

- The journey has a beginning, a predestined course, and an end, as the river is already there. Following the river's course brings the soul to the endless ocean. However, as the sailing takes place at night, the soul can only see what is right in front of it in each moment. If the soul looks too far ahead, it may not see the sandbanks, rocks, cataracts, and waterfalls that suddenly appear. The soul can only move one step at a time.
- The river has its own flow. In narrow places, the water runs fast, and the scenery changes rapidly. In other places, the river widens and the current slows. The boat still moves, but at such a slow pace that the soul may think nothing is happening. Even if the soul is impatient to move on, these are the times of integration. Changes can happen through being present and reliving the same moments.
- There is an absence of light. Before sunset, there was ample light in the sky, and the soul saw everything. This was an all-seeing, all-knowing state. During the night, the soul forgets everything and has to learn to navigate the river of life. Each step of the journey teaches the soul something.
- Practical knowledge of the river has been lost, even though the soul may have undertaken the journey numerous times. The only resource the soul can bring is its inner wisdom and intuition, and the soul supplements this by consciously learning from each situation it meets.
- The soul knows the river leads to the sea, and that after the night, the day will come. This means that the soul

knows that the body will die. In parallel, no matter how long we live unaware, we will become enlightened at some point. However, the soul does not know what it will face on the journey, nor how the journey will unfold. Will there be storms, cloudy skies, and unhelpful winds? Or, will it be plain sailing?

- The soul does not journey alone. There are other beings on the boat, some are helpful and some obstructive. During the journey, the soul discovers who is who, and what each can do to help the boat sail. Some are on board for part of the journey. Others remain for the whole trip. Some are interlopers. They hide under the planks and come out to steal the food, drink the water, create mischief, and steer the boat off course.

A Dual Journey with Two Parallel Cycles

The metaphor of sailing on the river of life towards sunrise describes two parallel cycles: physical life, and the spiritual path of awakening and enlightenment.

The physical cycle starts at birth and ends with death. Sunrise is when a person dies. The soul rises out of the body and returns to the spirit realm. At the time of death, the Light of spirit is so bright it illuminates the sky, like a sun. Free from the earthly body, the soul moves into the higher realms, symbolized by the sun rising in the eastern horizon, after the dark night.

The spiritual cycle starts when the soul experiences a spiritual awakening out of the conditioned illusion. The journey following a spiritual epiphany is similar to sailing a boat in uncharted waters. Our perspective of life shatters. Prior to this moment, we lived according to, or in reaction to, our cultural and family values. Now what we deemed important becomes insignificant. As we begin to think for ourselves, we step onto a path that has few references. Sunrise marks the end of the journey, when the soul awakens fully and rises in the eastern horizon in its enlightened state, as bright as the sun.

This twelve-hour journey, depicted on many pharaonic tombs, has been misinterpreted by some academics. Seeing the pharaoh portrayed as Ausir standing on the boat in a mummified form, they think the drawings describe the soul's journey after death. This is not so. The illustration serves to remind the soul of its journey through eternity, incarnation, and reincarnation. "Life does not end here," the pictures say, "Your journey continues. You are Khnum, the creator. You are Ausir, the primordial essence of the enlightened heart. Remember your journey."

The ancient Egyptians viewed physical life as the death of spirit. Birth was seen as the death of spiritual Light. In the tombs, texts, and temples, when they refer to death, they usually meant physical life. For them, a human being was only alive when they were spiritually awake, when their purpose was enlightenment, for then there was no birth and death.

Unless one is aware of this viewpoint, these esoteric teachings can be confused. For example, the *Book of Coming Forth by Day*, commonly referred to as the *Egyptian Book of the Dead*, is not about death per se but about awakening, which the ancient Egyptians regarded as the only way to overcome death. Death therefore has a double meaning. It can mean a life without spirituality, and the continuous cycle of incarnation and reincarnation.

Accordingly, what we call life, the ancient Egyptians regarded as death, and our death was their life. This is why the journey begins at sunset with birth, and ends at sunrise with death, when we rise into our spirit.

Both cycles bring us an experience of our spiritual essence and luminosity. The first cycle of birth-death-rebirth continually repeats. At each sunset, we return to the boat. We reincarnate and experience the journey under many different circumstances, and meet the challenges of the human predicament. In this cycle, the spiritual experience of our Light at death is temporary. In contrast, the second cycle is permanent. Once we rise into our spiritual essence and ascend as the enlightened spirit, Horan of the eastern horizon, we join the enlightened Neteru and do not return to the boat. We become one with everything, the universal Divine consciousness:

"I go up on the eastern side of the sky and I am born as Horus, as Him of the horizon [...] for Sothis is my sister, the Morning Star my offspring."[9]

Meeting the Challenges of the River of Life

As the boat follows the course of the river, and the river ends at the ocean, the journey of life is predestined to end in a particular way, either through death or ascension. At some point, each of us will die, and at another point, each of us will ascend. The outcome of the journey is certain. It is the journey's duration and how we navigate the river that is unpredictable and determined by our choices.

As we sail down the river, the boat stops every hour in front of a gate. Each gate presents a challenge, an opportunity for learning. This is symbolized by a "monster" who stands in front of the gate holding two knives, which represent the state of duality, the earthly conditioning that can prevent us from moving forward in flow with the river. Challenges may trigger attachments and addictions, and we can lose our way.

The ancient initiates knew sacred power words to help them overcome these addictions and work with the challenges. And although the Neteru and enlightened beings were sailing with them and supported them, it was up to each initiate to overcome their conditioned mind and remain centered. Staying centered meant remaining on the boat, rather than digressing from the spiritual path.

These challenges, or monsters, are the learning experiences the soul meets in life, based on its karma and what it is here to do. As the soul meets a test, two options appear. One, the way of the initiate, is to stay on the boat and overcome the challenges through spiritual practice. It was hoped that the initiate would come to understand the deeper meaning of the test without living through it. When the karmic lesson is learned and the karma purified through spiritual practice, there is, in theory, no need to experience the challenge. If the karma is not purified completely, the boat may be shaken, but in time it regains its course, as the initiate continues to practice.

In the second option, the soul decides to leave the boat and live through the events as they unfold. This does not mean that the soul loses its way. The soul chooses to learn through meeting the situation, instead of spiritual practice. This can be a more difficult and painful path. In both recourses, the result will be increased awareness. Many souls choose both these ways of learning at different times.

Although epitomized as a monster, from the higher perspective the challenges are neither negative or positive. Everything has a purpose and teaching, even distractions. For instance, kindness can be a test. Imagine someone who cannot say no to others and always tries to help. Although kindness is a positive quality, for this person it may be a conditioned response that keeps them separated from themselves, as they focus on others. A soul meeting this challenge can work through it in life or spiritually, or use both options. To illustrate — after constantly helping others, Helen became increasingly tired and unhappy. Eventually, she realized that in taking care of everyone, she neglected herself. Then she understood that her behavior did not serve her. As she reflected on her actions and looked deeper into her past, an understanding arose, and she chose a different approach.

The ancient initiates aimed to stay on the boat all the time. This is similar to the monks and lamas in Tibet who reincarnate in the same lineage and spend lifetimes studying and applying spiritual teachings. However, remaining on the boat is not always possible. Working with the conditioning spiritually may not be enough. Sometimes, life intervenes, and we decide to leave the boat.

Moreover, some people regularly get off the boat and choose to learn through life. In doing so, they may relive similar circumstances in the same or different lives, until they overcome the pattern. If they are stuck, their spirit helpers or higher self may intervene, raise their vibration and offer them an insight during spiritual practice, so they can release the old karma.

Summary

The aim of the spiritual journey is to rediscover ourselves as the Living Light, the sun of creation. This is not something we have to become. We *are* this Light. However, during the night, we cannot see who we are. Our human vision is focused on what happens on the river of life, instead of looking within.

In order to embody the state of enlightenment, called Ra-Horakti, meaning Horan rising like Ra on the horizon, we transform the way we think, act, and speak; and we view the world through the eyes of the sacred heart, instead of the programing. We develop the enlightened vision that is all-seeing, all-knowing, and pervades all aspects of life.

Iset is the path to awakening. Through this path, we open the Eye of the Heart.

Spiritual Practice: At the End of the Journey You Rise Like Ra, the Sun on the Horizon

Start your practice by inviting your helping spirits — including Iset, in her form of the Divine Mother; Horan, the spiritual warrior; and the all-seeing eye, Utchat — to assist you and create around you a safe and protected space.

Imagine you are sitting at the top of a hill, facing east. It is dawn. You have experienced the night, the absence of Light. During the dark times, you searched for the Light, but the darkness covered everything. Sometimes you saw glimpses of it when you gazed at the night sky and saw the stars. Other times, the moon came out, waxing and waning, offering you moments of Light, before hiding again. Now it is dawn, and your journey is almost complete.

What has the journey taught you? Consider all that has happened during your current life. Some experiences were pleasant, and some were difficult. From all these experiences, some were landmarks.

Ask, "What was an important milestone for me?" Stay quiet while your inner voice reveals the information.

As you focus on this landmark, ask the Eye of Ra to open within your sacred heart. Imagine looking at the landmark through the eye of your heart. Ask to see beyond the experience and gain more understanding of this event.

A realization may arise. If it does, make peace with your life and release all suppressed energy around the landmark.

Say, "I have been waiting for the sun to rise in the east, on the endless horizon. May I experience the inner sun, Ra, the sun within me. May I rise as Ra-Horakti, Horan rising like Ra on the horizon."

Visualize: As a result of your intention, your Ka, your etheric self, activates the Divine essence within your Ib, sacred heart. The Light from your heart flows into every cell of your body, and an inner transformation takes place. The inner sun transforms the physical body from its state of Khat, the material form, into its state of Ankh, eternal life. You are the radiant shining spirit Sahu. Your body becomes the body of Light, first changing into the colors of the rainbow, and then into clear energy without form.

The inner self is now whole, and dawn gives way to sunrise. On this new day, the sun rising in the sky is you. You rise effortlessly into the east and out of the "inert" state. Your spirit has awoken and radiates the light of the rising sun that turns night into day and illuminates the cosmos.

Meditate in this space for 21 minutes as you experience the state of luminosity of the sun, the state of Ra-Horakti.

At the end of your practice, slowly come down from the sky and into your crown, third eye, throat, and heart-center. The sun that you are merges completely with your body and illuminates your physical existence. Iset and all the enlightened ones bless you and place protection around you.

Close your sacred space by releasing the enlightened spirits and asking them to completely protect and seal you, your room, and home before they leave.

Note: Some people may do this visualization and deeply experience their Light. Others may find it difficult to connect with or imagine the Light. The mind may start questioning what it is supposed to see and how it should feel. Allow yourself to let go of these thoughts. Even if you do not feel anything, stay in the quiet space. In time, an opening may come. Questioning stops the flow of the practice and creates a barrier. We cannot experience our spiritual Light through the mind. The spiritual path asks us to release the mind's expectations.

Endnote

9   Almond, J. and Sneddon, K. (2002), p. 103.

Chapter 10

Etheric Keys in Sacred Sites

Channeling from Iset:
During the Golden Times, human beings were connected to their star of origin: the place they originated from before incarnation on Earth. Souls from different star systems came to Earth to manifest in physical form, find a way to live together, and learn from each other. Learning, not in the sense of the acquisition of knowledge and skills, but learning about the Self and the magnificence of the Divine Soul. Every star system has a unique understanding of the Self, and expresses a different aspect of the whole in a particular way. Yet within each aspect, the whole also exists.

In Zep Tepi, humans communicated psychically with the higher realms. Communication with star beings of the Light was accepted and encouraged. Star beings from other realms have always observed the Earth and studied the unfolding mystery of human life, and other earthly life forms. They do not interfere directly, as this would contravene the law of karma; rather, they offer support through the transmission of high-energy frequencies.

These energies of Light were harnessed by the ancients through the creation of sacred sites where they undertook spiritual practices and rituals. Even today, a sense of peace surrounds the people who work there as their chakras clear through the healing energy. Gradually, an alignment takes place between the physical being and the Divine, wise Self. The energy download is paramount, as it speeds up the process of awakening. Without the etheric energy and high cosmic vibrations, spiritual practices by themselves take a long time to be effective.

This is why, after hundreds of years, I make these high vibrational energies of Divine frequency available to you, through the Seven Gates of Awareness teachings. You can access these through initiation and a commitment to work for the Light and the highest good. It has always been so. It was only when humanity tried to misuse the energies through the ego and personal gain that the Light was withdrawn, and the world fell into darkness.

The Gift of the Phoenix and the City of the Central Sun

From high in the sky came the Bennu bird, the bird of fire, the Phoenix. Its whole body shone brightly like polished silver, reflecting the rays of the sun. Smoke and fire emanated from its tail. High in the sky it flew, and a loud noise, like thunder, accompanied it, even though the sky was clear and no rain fell. Then its stomach opened, and a large shape fell to the Earth. And despite falling from such a great height, the shape remained intact.

From under the trees and the bushes, the people came and admired the gift of the Phoenix. The gift was elliptical and made of a dark material that had not been seen before. When someone touched it, the dark casing opened like a flower, and revealed a silver egg. The people knew instinctively that this was the egg of the Phoenix, created by the body of the silver bird. They understood it was a gift to the sacred land of Khem from Ra, the Divine sun of creation. They built a tall granite column and placed the egg on top. "May the gift of the Bennu bird stay long on the land," they said, "and our land will be blessed."

Sitting on its high pedestal, the egg sparkled under the sun. It was luminous, like a star in the day. People shielded their eyes to look at it. Iunu, a city and temple complex, was created around the egg after the sun of creation that rises out of the abyss Nu. In time, the city grew and became an important spiritual site. The temple priests took care of the egg, and the egg took care of itself. For unlike earthly silver, the egg never tarnished. It reflected the light of the sun, day after day, for thousands of years.

Beyond the Myth

Many objects of etheric power were taken to Egypt before the end of Atlantis. As the battles raged across the Atlantic and the Mediterranean sea, some Atlanteans were already preparing for the annihilation of their civilization. They wanted to save objects of etheric power that would help humanity in the next step of its evolution, and they used an aircraft to transport these objects to the land of Khem.

The indigenous people of Egypt had no reference for this technology, they saw a gigantic silver bird flying in the sky. Such sightings were rare, as the Atlanteans knew how to make the aircraft invisible in order to safeguard the technology. The Atlantean priests residing at the Giza plateau knew the importance of the silver egg that was given to them by their counterparts in Atlantis. But the local people needed an explanation: was it a good or a bad omen, they wondered. To safeguard the sacred object, the priests created a story, a prudent way to keep it safe. They said that the silver flying bird was called Bennu, and that it was a bird of fire. The three-foot-long silver "egg" that came from the bird was a gift from the Neteru to the people of Egypt. The "egg" was placed on a high column so that no one could touch it or be near it.

The Egg of the Phoenix

Iunu, the city of the sun, is now modern Cairo. In the Ptolemaic era, it was renamed Heliopolis by the Greeks. Apart from a few isolated monuments, nothing remains of the original site.

For thousands of years, the egg remained on the column. When conquerors came, the priesthood hid the egg in the desert and re-installed it when it was safe. What was the egg's purpose? The egg radiated a high vibrational frequency across Egypt and the Earth. It was part of the pyramidal and temple network of the Living Light that sustained the energy field of the Band of Peace. The egg was charged daily by the light of the sun, and its placement on the high column ensured that no shadow fell on it.

This high etheric frequency is presently unknown in our world. Our modern technology cannot reproduce its vibration, which was called the resonance of Divine consciousness. Only when we become aware will we personally be able to channel this energy. Yet, as we grow spiritually and gradually clear ourselves from heavy conditioned energies, we can become a purer channel for increasingly higher vibrations of etheric Light to come through and gradually work towards embodying this Light.

The initiates of the Living Light lived and meditated in the energy of this Divine frequency. The higher aim of these practices was the re-alignment with the Divine self, which the egg facilitated. Sometimes, it was a blissful experience, and people had significant dreams and psychic visions. Other times, it was a difficult process, as the healing of the inner shadow took place.

I have witnessed this same healing process unfolding many times when people visit sacred sites in Egypt. Most of the time, it starts with a physical-energy clearing. A person may experience a healing crisis with flu-like symptoms — including headaches, stomach pains, nausea, and tiredness — as the body tries to expel the heavy energy residing in the tissues. People may have spontaneous moments of awareness of unhealed trauma, from this or other lives. The shadow surfaces to be healed, revealing deep-seated issues, such as unworthiness, anger, and fear. In some instances, we have found a quiet space inside a temple and performed a soul retrieval healing. Such deep healing and transformation is possible through the increased awareness and etheric energy work that these sacred sites still facilitate.

The Fourteen Pieces of Ausir, the Essence of the Enlightened Heart

In another myth, it was said that the good king, Ausir, was dismembered by his twin brother, Set, into fourteen pieces, and the pieces scattered across the land and sacred river. Where Ausir's body parts fell, the Light was born. His soul sister, Iset, retrieved them, except the one eaten by a fish, and carried them to Abydos to be re-assembled. Some of Ausir's essence remained where the pieces had first fallen, and temples were constructed there, safeguarding the essence of the enlightened heart. Since then, Light continues to flow from these sacred sites and touches all who visit them.

After the construction of the pyramids in the Giza plateau, the Atlantean engineers drew up plans to channel the etheric energy from the north of Egypt to the south, following the course of the Nile. The river became a conduit for etheric energy. Its east bank had a positive etheric energy charge, while the west bank held a negative charge. The engineers conveyed this aspect of the Nile by giving it the form of a hermaphrodite, which carries both male and female characteristics.

The transference of the etheric energy from the pyramids to the whole of Egypt was achieved through the construction of temples on etheric power points. These key places, said to carry the essence of Ausir, were selected due to their naturally occurring high frequency. To enhance this frequency, the engineers housed a sacred object at each site.

When these sacred objects are brought together in one place, they can create incredible frequencies of Light energy. However, the myth tells us that one of these pieces, the phallus of Ausir, was lost in the river, eaten by a catfish. As a result, they cannot all come together and create the unique energy field that would fully activate the Divine frequency vibration they carry.

The Atlanteans knew that even if some of the objects came together, they would generate great energy. They also understood that these objects can cause great damage if their energy is misused. So they "lost" the fourteenth object, the one that teaches us about the creation of the Golden Times. In a subsequent part of the myth, Iset recreates the lost object from wood and her words of power. She uses it to create a seed of Light on Earth (the conception of Horan), but is unable to bring the Golden Times fully back. However, the seed of Light can grow and will eventually become a catalyst for a higher dimensional reality to return to Earth. Then, the Golden Times, the reign of Ausir, will follow.

The Temples

The Atlanteans planned temples where the sacred objects carrying the Divine frequency were hidden. Over the years, these holy places have been rebuilt many times, exactly on the same location. After the Golden Times, more temples were built by the pharaohs, who claimed they also housed a part of Ausir in order to attract followers and pilgrims. There is now a plethora of sacred sites, some of which were original and some not.

The Atlantean engineers selected the original sites based on the morphology of the land and the existence of powerful ley line crossings. They opened etheric portals to certain star constellations, celestial bodies, and higher dimensional worlds in the unseen realities. Their aim was to download high vibrational etheric energy into the sites and create an extensive etheric field of the Divine consciousness frequency over the land, known as the Band of Peace.

As in the construction of the pyramids, the first builders created two temples: an etheric temple, made of energy; and its physical counterpart, made of stone. For thousands of years, the priesthood chanted words of power (mantras), channeled energy from the etheric to the physical world, meditated, and facilitated spiritual practices, rituals, and ceremonies onsite. They lived in this high-energy field that communicated with them each time they engaged in the spiritual work of the Living Light. In this way, they maintained their energy vibration.

The ancient temples that are still standing are within these portals of etheric energy. These portals, gateways to higher vibrational realities, are active — albeit to a lesser degree than in the Golden Times. Today, the vibrational energy of the Earth is rising, and these sites are supporting this gradual awakening; evolutionary growth takes place systematically so that it is sustainable.

These portals are also etherically "manned" by beings of Light, wise spirits who bring us knowledge from other worlds. They are not ghosts or lost souls who are stuck. They have purposefully chosen to continue serving the temples and support all who visit them. Today, they communicate with those who are able to connect with them and do sacred work.

Two Main Star Portals — Sirius and Orion

Throughout the ancient Egyptian temple complex, there are two important etheric portals: one to Sirius star, symbolized by Iset; and the other to the Orion constellation, in particular the three stars of the Orion belt, symbolized by Ausir. Through the union of these energies, the overcoming the conditioning, symbolized by Horan, is possible.

The Sirius connection is the first etheric key that unlocks our path to ascension. In order to access the Living Light energy, we first receive an activation from the Sirius star portal through an initiation process. A download of energy flows from the Sirius star, through the crown, into our heart-center, awakening this portal within.

Sometimes people seek initiation and believe there is no need to do anything thereafter; the initiation will provide everything. The ancients knew that although the initiation unlocked the gate to a new path, it was up to the individual to walk it. Similarly, if we do not engage with the etheric energies of the Living Light after the initiation, the mind will draw us back into the dramas of everyday life and the effect of the initiation will be minimal.

This first initiation is the foundation, the key that opens a path towards ascension. Once this initiation is integrated through meditations and spiritual practices, other gates/portals can be opened. These etheric gates, to different star constellations and worlds, are incorporated into everyone's body at birth. They lie dormant, until opened during initiation ceremonies. Through a continual process of initiation and spiritual practice, our vibration heightens, and we can increasingly self-generate the Light of our Divine self — the Light that carries the same Divine consciousness frequency we find in the sacred sites.

Following the initiation that opens the portal to Sirius star, and after some time of spiritual work, the portal to the three stars of the Orion belt can also be opened. The Living Light energy from Orion carries a different frequency that allows us to access the Light of the spirit realms, where souls find themselves after death. This second portal offers us a teaching of "eternity and everlastingness," while we are still alive. Even though physical life is finite, we become aware, through our spiritual practice, of the eternal journey of the soul in the physical and spiritual worlds.

Visiting the Temples Today

Even though the etheric energy field in the ancient Egyptian temples is significantly weaker than in the Golden Times, these places are active. Most of the time, the etheric fields work with people unconsciously. People may visit Egypt as tourists and return home different. The intelligent Light of the portals and spirit beings who work with them etherically may take the opportunity to offer some people a transmission of high vibrational energy. People may experience déjà vu: a spiritual opening they cannot explain.

When spiritual practitioners go to these sacred sites with a pure intention and open heart, and consciously engage with the energy for the highest good, they can receive incredible gifts of Light that boost their spiritual work and align with their path of soul evolution. Practitioners may also spontaneously experience an activation of spiritual gifts they did not know they possessed. The gifts lie dormant until activated by a meditation in a particular sacred site in Egypt. I have seen people who could not see or feel energy having a significant spiritual opening inside the pyramids and temples and subsequently being able to feel the Light. Some saw psychic colors and heard the Light beings for the first time. Others received an activation in their throat chakra that opened their voice center, and now Light is transmitted every time they sing mantras. We all carry different gifts and, at different times in our soul's journey, we will access them.

Sometimes, if people carry a lot of trauma and issues from difficult life situations, the energy can reveal their shadow. This may cause people to discharge their own fears and pain onto the site and criticize the temple for carrying heavy energy. There is a conditioned tendency to project our human predicament to others or the sacred.

These spiritual openings, in whatever form they take, cannot be based on expectation. We cannot say to a temple site, "I want the gift of clairvoyance"; this is the egoic mind making demands. I advise you to humbly acknowledge you are in a sacred place of Light and open to the experience that is right for you in the moment. Trust that whatever you receive will be exactly what you need for your soul evolution.

Summary

There are so many temples and sites one can visit, principal and minor. Throughout the great history of ancient Egypt, the Golden Times and the Pharaonic Times that followed, a plethora of temples were built across the land. There are two foremost portals that radiate through the main sites: one is the Sirius/Iset portal, the other is the Orion/Ausir portal.

Spiritual Practice: Connecting with the Portal of Sirius Star

Welcome Iset in her form as Mut, the Mother of unconditional love that creates the physical world out of her body; the initiates of the Living Light that worked in her temple for the highest good; and any spiritual guides you work with. Ask them to create a safe and protected space around you.

In the practice, you connect with the Great Mother in Dendara. Imagine yourself as a kite, the bird of Iset. See yourself flying beyond space and time and arriving at the temple in Dendara. Visualize the palm trees, smell the perfume of the beautiful lotus flowers, and feel the energy of unconditional love emanating from this holy place. Then, take the form of a human being: it may be your current body, or if you had incarnated in the Golden Times, you could see yourself in that body.

Notice the magnificent stone buildings, and hear the chants of women and men. The men's voices anchor you to the Earth. The women's voices respond to the men's, chanting in Light language codes of power that open your third eye. As a result, the symbol of the eye of Horan, the eye of awareness, appears in the middle of your forehead.

A priestess and priest come to greet you. They take you to a building at the rear of the temple. This is a small chamber where the energy of Iset, the portal of the Sirius star, has been downloaded and radiates the Light of Sirius-Iset. On the back wall is a statue of the Mother giving birth. The priest and priestess invite you to enter the chamber alone. This is your time in this sacred space.

Say to Iset, "Divine Mother, sacred womb of creation, I am the cosmic traveler. I have been wandering this universe and parallel worlds for thousands of years. Now I have arrived at this moment. Please take me back into your sacred womb. Let me feel that I am part of creation. Let me feel your support around me. I am the Divine Child."

Imagine yourself inside the womb of the Great Mother. You are supported and nurtured by her body. Immerse yourself in the Divine love that is holding you.

The Great Mother says to you: "I have created this world so that you can experience physical form. The whole world is my body, and I nurture and feed you. You are my precious child born out of my body; you are the Divine child. Trust that you have all that you need and all that makes you happy. I walk beside you in your life. The sacred bond between us can never be severed. Go and experience the beauty that I create, the beauty in you, and the beauty that exists around you."

Take some time to feel the love of the Mother.

When you are ready, consciously decide to be reborn into the wonder of physical life. Say, "May I be born out of the womb of the Great Mother as in the first time I ever came into being. May I be born whole and complete."

Feel the Great Mother birthing you into the world. She holds you over her heart. Feel her heartbeat. The Mother looks at your heart-center and sees the portal of awareness. She blesses you with infinite blessings. Receive her blessing and listen to what she may say to you, as you meditate for 15 minutes, or as long as you wish.

When you feel the meditation is complete, Iset appears and offers you the Ankh on your third eye, to help you become aware of the eternity that you are. She places your hands on top of your heart-center, breathes her sacred breath all around you, and places etheric protection over you.

It is time to return to the present. You exit the chamber, and the priest and priestess greet you and offer you a cup of sacred water. Thank them. Then, see yourself once again as the kite and fly back into your current body and your time.

Slowly come back. Imagine you have etheric cords that extend from your root chakra and feet into the Earth, grounding you. Give thanks for this ceremony of rebirth, to Iset, and to the ancient initiates of the Living Light in Dendara Temple. Say that your practice is complete. Ask them to close and seal you, your room, and home before they go.

Chapter 11

The Divine Mother Speaks

Channeling from Iset:

The Voice of the Divine speaks through the one who has followed it in many lifetimes. The Voice speaks, and the Voice guides, and some walk the path that the Voice shows. Many hear the Voice but do not follow it. The Voice asks much of you, because this path will consume your life. It is the path where your intention becomes one of personal fulfillment through the awakening process, instead of achievement in the world. The mind does not wish to walk a path guided by the Divine's Voice because it does not know what will happen and has no reference for the Voice. It becomes confused and frightened. The mind does not understand how someone can forfeit "security" for something as abstract as spiritual awakening. The mind cannot comprehend the deeper calling of the soul and the joy of the heart opening. The mind does not know, yet it seeks.

And those who seek, shall find. But what then? What you do when you hear the calling is as important as its discovery. The spiritual path does not end with the discovery of the grail; this is only the beginning. Once you find the treasure of the sacred teachings, you are then called to embody it. Then you will have followed the Voice of the Divine instead of the chattering of the conditioning. Each time you connect with these sacred teachings, you follow the infinite spirit, and release part of the conditioning. So I speak these words to your sacred heart. I speak with the Divine Voice. Hear me, and do not let me go. Be with me on this journey. Travel with me and answer my invitation to become the Living Light.

The Energy of the Living Light

In Zep Tepi, humanity lived in a temperate climate supported by the high vibrations of the Living Light, which are self-generated. The technology, machines, homes, and temples were powered by a type of etheric Light energy that generated powerful spiritual energy fields. In these fields, people had access to advanced psychic abilities. Etheric communication with beings of Light beyond space and time, psychic awareness, and inner knowing were commonplace. Concurrently, people connected with the cosmos, their Star ancestors, and Star of origin. The Star ancestors visited the planet, offering humanity etheric gifts of power and Light.

The technology available during Zep Tepi is unimaginable to us today, in the same way that a medieval man would be confused by us switching on lights. While we currently rely on physical elements to generate electricity, the ancient Egyptians could create it out of the etheric field, called the Ether, the spirit. Spiritual energy is much more powerful than the energy we have now. It nurtured and sustained life, instead of compromising and polluting it. The predicament is that spiritual energy cannot be made, nor can it be manipulated. It exists everywhere, within each one of us and within the cosmos. The only way to access it is through spiritual evolution.

In the future, people may try to create energy and control machines mentally, using the power of their intention and consciousness. They may realize that if they focus their minds, especially collectively, they can create movement, thus energy. This is only a first step. It is nowhere near the spiritual energy of the Living Light.

In order to work with the spiritual, etheric energy of the cosmos, we need to have the key, the awareness that we are Ankh, eternal life. We have to consciously decide to let go of the conditioning and engage our spiritual Light. And this we cannot do if we are attached to the ego-mind. There are no shortcuts in this process. The mind may say, "You only need to believe you can do this, and it can happen," but this is not so. The energy of the Living Light is protected by the fact that its high vibrational frequency is aligned with our sacred heart-center. It is only through the awareness of the heart that humanity can return to the First Time of Zep Tepi. Accessing the Living Light frequency and working with it to support our lives constitutes a huge leap in our evolution, individually and collectively. And we can only do this if we follow the rule of Ma'at.

Physical Life Is a Teaching About Ma'at

Ma'at was seen as a path of Truth. This meant that the ancient Egyptians differentiated between the ego's voice and that of their sacred heart. They understood that the mind's voice can be distorted by desires: it may want something so badly that it persuades us to follow its biased rationalizations. In my therapy work I have had clients, women and men, who were in controlling relationships. All said that they somehow knew, before entering the relationship, that their partner was not right for them. This was a moment of truth, a moment of Ma'at. Yet, they silenced that voice. The ego-mind desperately wanting a relationship, said: maybe your partner will change through your love; maybe things will be better once you get married etc.

In Zep Tepi, people were educated to follow Ma'at. They observed their mind and learned from life every day, for life is an important teacher for what Ma'at represents. We are tested continually, and lessons repeat until we learn them.

The same principles apply when engaging with Ma'at in the collective. We can easily accept what we are told because we are taught to follow the voice of authority. From a young age, our ability to think critically is diminished, and our personal power compromised, usurped by parents and the education system. So when we hear the voice of the media, politicians, doctors, and spiritual leaders, we may automatically believe them and continue to give away our power. Even if our inner voice questions what we are told, the fear of not conforming, also instilled in us, silences the doubts. Ma'at is absolute truth. Life invites us to break through the conditioned limitations and find freedom of thought, and then freedom of action will follow.

A friend studied for many years with a spiritual master who had never travelled outside his country. His students routinely flew to visit him. My friend wanted to go to a workshop and she thought she needed a visa. The master told her there was no need. Inside, she felt she should apply (the voice of Ma'at), but her conditioning said, "Obey the master." When she shared the story, she said she never thought the master could be wrong, even though he had never been on a plane.

Life is designed as a training ground for discovering Ma'at. This means we will meet situations and people who challenge us to make decisions that are true for us in each moment. In the bigger picture, these people and situations are our teachers; without them, we may never learn about Ma'at.

Most people wish to follow Ma'at, but when faced with a challenge, they usually adhere to their programing. Each time we break the rule of Ma'at, our etheric Light dims and our vibration lowers. In the rule of Ma'at there are no exceptions, no matter how much the egoic mind justifies our actions.

Awareness of Ma'at and the transformation of the egoic mind is possible through spiritual work. The high vibrational energies of the Living Light clear our Divine connection from the cloud of the conditioning. We start to open the pathway of the sacred heart and share the spiritual gifts we carry within. We find the path of manifestation through Light, instead of mental energy.

Mental Manifestation and Spiritual Manifestation of a Higher Reality

Everything is energy, including our physical body; in the body the energy is denser and only appears solidified. The physical world is a manifestation of the Light energy that is born through the intention of the Divine Consciousness we all are.

In this earthly theatre of life, we forgo our memory of being the Divine Consciousness in order to experience various physical forms and circumstances. The key is to be aware and present in the experience. This is what our Ka and Ba do. These higher aspects of ourselves observe and record all the events we experience and our actions and reactions. Gradually, through our spiritual practice, we become more like our spirit, aware of what we are thinking, feeling, and doing. In doing so, we are sometimes granted leeway, the power to manifest part of our experience on Earth. This is a first stage of manifestation, which uses mental energy.

A few times in my life, I have been granted the ability to do this. These times occurred in places of high etheric energy. One was on a pilgrimage in Nepal. After arriving in Kathmandu, I received an email from my workplace in Scotland: a crisis had arisen.

Instinctively, I knew I could remove the problem. This was not an emotional decision. I felt no fear or stress. I was completely detached from the situation and connected to something bigger. I consciously decided that I did not wish to live through this experience. I received an email from work the next day saying a solution was agreed. There was nothing for me to do.

There have been only a few times in my life when I felt this clarity that I could manifest my reality and change events. It is not something that usually happens. It is a gift of perception that is generated through increased awareness.

Apart from this type of mental manifestation, I have experienced spiritual manifestation numerous times. The latter has the quality of a miracle and has filled me with gratitude and a sense of grace each time. Until the age of twelve, I could feel and see Mother Mary. I would pray to her, and she would grant me what I asked. I asked for simple things that were important to me in the moment. And every request was given. This type of manifestation was created through the open heart of a child. I was very innocent and did not dream about money, status, etc. I had no fear, and manifestation from this state of purity was a natural process.

In spiritual manifestation, there is a conscious choice to join with the Divine element to create our reality. My Divine element was Mother Mary. I had such trust in life because I knew I was not alone and surrounded by love. This sense of absolute love, goodness, and grace came from this Divine source. It was not something in my mind. When I started high school and my mind took over, I lost the innocence that had given me the perfect Divine connection. The power of spiritual manifestation diminished.

Conscious Manifestation: Conscious Thinking and Conscious Surrendering

In these instances of mental and spiritual manifestation, I never felt a lack, threat, or fear. My manifestation was a conscious choice born from a strong intention. It was also accompanied by an expansive feeling of gratitude. If I could describe a formula of manifestation, I would put the following ingredients in the magic cauldron: awareness, gratitude, acceptance, and surrendering to the Divine will.

In February 2022, when writing an article for the monthly newsletter for the ISIS School of Holistic Health, Iset offered the following teaching on manifestation through conscious thinking and conscious surrendering to the Divine. I include her words below:

***

To manifest a higher vibrational reality, you do not need Divine intervention. You are already the Divine. What you need to do is discover and embody your Divine nature. We, the enlightened ones, offer you the path of ascension into the Divine being that you are. We invite you to do the personal and spiritual work with the high vibrational Light that is flowing to your planet at this time, and walk this path. Do not look to us to change your world reality.

You were born in these times to experience the power of Light that you are. In previous centuries, you petitioned the Divine to change things for you. And in the process you believed yourself to be unworthy, and relinquished your power. These ways do not serve you. These times ask you to become conscious manifestors through the Light of the sacred heart within you.

The key to conscious manifestation is twofold:

- *Conscious Thinking:* Be aware of the power of your thoughts and harness this power by staying in silence and engaging consciously with the process of thinking when you need it. Say to your mind, "Stop talking. Only speak when there is something I need to do." For example, if you need to clean your house, say to your mind, "I wish to clean my house. Please guide me through all I need to do to accomplish this. Do not speak of other things." And when you think about a situation, do not go into anything negative. Say to your mind, "This is the situation I am dealing with, help me resolve this. This is the outcome I envision." Think of your thoughts as energy. Every time you think in this conscious way, you create an energy seed that you plant in the heart of creation. Your thoughts are

filled with power. They are no longer feeding the cloud of the conditioning. They become powerful intentions.
- *Conscious Surrendering: The conditioning pines for what it does not have. It lives in a world of lack. It is incapable of gratitude and seeing the beauty of life. It focuses on the negative and tries to create a reality based on what it thinks it needs. To become a conscious manifestor, surrender your desires, needs, and wishes for the future to the Divine heart. For instance, if you dream of a high vibrational Earth, feel it as if it is here now, then surrender the dream to the heart of creation. To be a conscious manifestor, you surrender everything to the Divine Light and trust the Divine wisdom to bring you exactly what is right for you at each moment. And when the Divine Light brings things, accept and respond.*

In order to engage in the process of conscious manifestation and develop conscious thinking and conscious surrendering, we suggest that you do the inner work that enables the healing and transformation of the shadow, and the experience of high states of consciousness through Light work. These two ways of shadow integration and Light work are essential for you to discover and embody your Divine Self.

Summary

Hat-Hor creates the physical world, the body, so that the spirit can experience physical life. Her name in hieroglyph is a square symbolizing a house, the physical, within which is the falcon Horan, symbolizing the spirit. Thus, her name literally means the House of Spirit.

When the spirit within activates, it experiences its Light and opens up the eye within the heart-center. It fully accepts the body and can then manifest the awakened state. The union, the marriage between the Creation (body and physical world) and the Creator (Spirit, Divine Consciousness) takes place. *The gift of the Mother is the physical state, and our gift to the world is the awakening and luminosity of our spirit whilst living.*

In ancient Egypt, the mysteries of the embodiment of spirit were celebrated through the sacred marriage of Hat-Hor and Horan. The statue of Hat-Hor was taken from Dendara on a sacred boat down the Nile, first to bless all the different temples along the way and finally to arrive in the south, at the temple of Horan in Edfu. There, the two statues of Hat-Hor and Horan were placed together, symbolizing a sacred marriage ceremony. Following the marriage, the statue of Hat-Hor was returned to Dendara, and 9 months later, Ihy, a male Neter representing happiness, was born in the world.

In the tradition of the Living Light, the sacred marriage is the marriage between body and spirit. This marriage takes place at soul level and is achieved through self-realization — the embodiment of one's spirit, the actualization of the enlightened state.

Part 2

Initiation as a Channel of HEKA

Initiation is a spiritual process that involves the transmission of exponential amounts of etheric energy via the teacher to the initiate. The teacher merges with a Neter in a sacred place, and the Neter, the enlightened being channeled by the teacher, conducts the initiation. The purpose of the initiation is to raise the etheric frequency of the student-initiate so that they can channel the Living Light frequency.

"The Living Light" energy that I and my guides refer to was known as HEKA, translated as "The Divine invisible power that rules all." Another translation is "The mystical Divine power that creates the manifested world." During the initiation, Iset works through me to bestow HEKA, and the ability to channel HEKA, to the initiate, to the degree that they are able.

An initiation is the beginning of the journey, the crossing of a threshold where initiates dedicate themselves to the sacred path of Light. After this, the initiate is encouraged to practice the teachings and harness their ability to be a pure channel of Light. HEKA can then flow through them for the highest good, creating harmony and supporting healing.

HEKA works in conjunction with the rule of Ma'at. If someone tries to misuse the energy and the teachings, the ability to channel HEKA is withdrawn, and the person will generate heavy karma. It was the misuse of HEKA by the ego that created the circumstances for the fall of the ancient Egyptian civilization. Problems began when the pharaohs and high government officials bypassed the initiation process and appointed priests, priestesses, and high priests (sometimes referred to as prophets) in an ad-hoc manner. This broke the link between HEKA and Ma'at. This ancient karma is still affecting our world.

Initiation and the Three Main Paths of HEKA

Three spiritual paths were open to the initiates of HEKA in ancient Egypt.

The first path consists of the Seven Gates of Awareness and Five Ascension Circles. This path was taught in the temples throughout Egypt and was governed by the Hat-Hor priesthood. It unites the teachings of Iset–Sirius–Life, and Ausir–Orion belt–Death. This is one of the most beautiful, loving, and sacred paths of this work.

The second path is the embodiment of the nine primordial Neteru. This initiation involves building the etheric temple of Light inside the heart chakra and in the initiate's sacred space in their home. The temple is held by the nine Divine principles that govern creation and ascension. This path, taught throughout Egypt, was governed by the Priesthood of Atum, in the temple of Iunu (Heliopolis), which also had jurisdiction over the pyramids of Giza. Initiations were undertaken inside the temple complex and Great Pyramid.

The third path was for those who wished to delve further into the philosophy of ascension. Initiates worked with the eight Neteru who oversee abstract principles that can only be understood through experience, fasting, retreat from the world, and long spiritual practices over many years. This path was governed by the temple of Djehuti in Khemenu. This was a difficult path with no guarantees. It was only open to initiates who had mastered the first two paths, which also included some of the teachings of the third path.

In these three paths, the Initiator is Iset. Iset governs and bestows HEKA as it flows to the Earth through the Sirius portal.

The Ancient Initiates

Inside the temples, sanctuaries, and desert hermitages, the ancient priesthood, through initiations, activations, and a life dedicated to spiritual practice, were gradually able to shed the human conditioned programing and emerge as a being of Light who is the embodiment of HEKA.

After initiation, initiates were taught the teachings of the Living Light. These teachings explain how our infinite spirit incarnates in the physical realm, loses its luminosity through interaction with the earthly realm, and then returns to spirit by embodying the Divine consciousness of its essential nature. As initiates continuously brought HEKA into their body, they gradually awoke from the Earth's base consciousness into the luminosity of their spirit.

Becoming an Initiate of HEKA in the Modern World

Since 2006, Iset has offered me spiritual teachings that have reintroduced the path of the ancient initiates of HEKA. The aim is for new initiates to embody their essential nature of the Living Light and shine like spiritual suns who "dispel the darkness of the long night of the soul," meaning the Earth's social conditioning. Through these teachings, Iset invites people to step onto their path as Light workers and support the huge shifts that are taking place on the Earth towards awakening and ascension.

In ancient Egypt, these initiations lasted many hours, and sometimes days and weeks. In our present way of life, this is not practical. Consequently, Iset has restructured the teachings to account for our current lifestyle, whilst maintaining the integrity and depth of the spiritual work. The teachings contain references to ancient Egypt, as this was the last time the HEKA teachings were practiced.

I explain the process of initiation and offer practices for you to work with HEKA. However, no one can be initiated by reading a book. Although you will access the Light and feel the energy, and may recall hidden memories of ancient Egypt, I would strongly recommend that you consider receiving initiation into HEKA and practicing the teachings of the Living Light for the highest good.

Chapter 12

The Goddess Iset and the Seven Gates of Awareness Initiation

Channeling from Iset:
 From the ancient times, the calling comes.
 Listen to the sound of the sistrum, the ringing of the bells,
 and bring your voice to the temple of Light.
 Sing the sacred words of power that help you see beyond the veil,
 and open to the Living Light that you are.
 May the Winged Goddess bestow upon you HEKA,
 the power of transformation and rebirth.

Iset — The Guardian, Governor, and Bestower of HEKA

Iset is identified as the wisdom keeper of HEKA as it flows from the multi-dimensional portal on the Sirius Star to the Earth. The last time this path was available was in Zep Tepi. In those times, evidenced by the pyramids of Giza, the Sphinx, and the Osirion temple in Abydos, human beings lived in a higher vibrational frequency and channeled and worked with HEKA in the physical and spiritual dimensions. These teachings were also practiced in Lemuria and Atlantis. Now Iset has made them and the etheric energy available again to spiritual practitioners.

Iset bestows:

- The gift of healing and connection to the higher realms by activating the crown chakra. On the crown is an energy point called the throne, which enables connection to the multidimensional Divine self, the Ka, and Ba.
- Access to spiritual teachings, by opening a path towards ascension, spanning many lifetimes.

- Resurrection from the inert state. As with Ausir, Iset finds the dead/dissociated parts and re-assembles us after the many dismemberments we experience during this and other lives. Iset brings us back to life.
- Protection from chaos. As with Horan, who was hunted by Set-chaos, Iset extends her wings of Light around us protecting us from harm.
- Access to our spiritual gifts. When we accept Iset's invitation to work with her, she transfers wisdom teachings and knowledge to us. Iset offers us spiritual gifts so we can heal ourselves and others, serve the Light, and fulfil our soul's purpose.
- The experience of unconditional love of the Great Mother — we receive the nourishment from her breast and reconnect with the love that we are.
- Access to the Light of the world so we become that Light.

I have worked with Iset in many lifetimes. She has asked me to again be her teacher for the Living Light-HEKA, and share these teachings.

The Seven Gates of Awareness and the Five Ascension Circles

This is the main path of HEKA that was taught throughout ancient Egypt. It was governed by the Priesthood of the Goddess Hat-Hor, whose main temple still stands in Dendara. The priesthood were known as "the Hat-Hors." Their aim was to support initiates' rebirth into the Living Light and Divine love that lies within.

The seven gates are energy portals that exist within our body and within the heart of creation — as above so below. The seven gates is a circular path. It begins with access to the Living Light vibration and moves full circle to reincarnation. Each time we walk the path, we begin a cycle within a previous one, spiraling ever deeper into the center of our being.

The five circles of Ausir focus on death, rebirth, life, awakening, and ascension. These teachings center on the human experience of life as viewed from "the upper regions of the sky": the spiritual world we access after death. As we integrate the journey of life and lives, and the journey of dismemberment and death, we build a strong inner foundation.

These teachings are vast. Each gate and circle must be understood and assimilated mentally, physically, and spiritually.

The Wings of Iset

Iset opens our crown to the high dimensional realities, helping us increase our understanding and channel higher vibrational frequencies of HEKA. And she offers us a healing gift through the "Opening of the Wings."

The ancient priesthood merged with Iset and discovered that, like her, they also had wings of Light extending from their backs, down their arms. Many eons ago, beings of Light who inhabited the Earth had wings. These beings are now referred to as the bird people. As we lost access to the higher frequencies, our bodies became heavier, and our wings disappeared. Some of the bird people who remained in the etheric realms now serve the Earth as angels.

The wings are still attached to us, but no longer visible. Through energy work, we may feel our wings. Iset herself is portrayed with wings.

Iset has given me a sacred chant called the Opening of the Wings, which I teach in the Spiritual Path of Iset. This is a fundamental chant for the whole of the teachings. The chant is in a Light language that Iset calls the universal language of the cosmos, and is accompanied by hand positions. By chanting these words and performing the hand positions, HEKA streams into us, raising our frequency and increasing our awareness. Many times I have managed to resolve issues by going to my meditation/temple room and opening my wings. As I chant the invocation, I feel the love of Iset surrounding me, and often an answer arises in my mind as if from nowhere.[10]

The Opening of the Wings chant is part of the teachings of HEKA and part of the initiation ceremony of becoming a channel of HEKA. However, our life circumstances may not allow us to begin a spiritual path and take initiation; it may not be the right time in our life. Taking initiation is a significant decision. Accordingly, Iset has given me another powerful chant and practice to connect with the wings of Light that is available to everyone.

Summary

Iset is the guardian and wisdom keeper of HEKA, the Living Light of Creation, and the associated teachings of the path of ascension. One of her emanations is Hat-Hor. In ancient Egypt, the priesthood of Hat-Hor, based in Dendara, were responsible for the teachings of the Living Light and the spiritual and healing Path of Iset. These teachings begin with an initiation and are based on the Seven Gates of Awareness — seven portals and associated energy fields — and the Five Ascension Circles. This is a vast teaching that is circular: each ending births a new circle within the previous one, taking us deeper into the core of our being. Iset's Wings of Light chant helps us activate our etheric wings, increase our vibration, and elevate our awareness.

Spiritual Practice — The Wings of Light of Iset

Creating an Altar for the Practice (optional)
You can create an altar that will become a focus point for the energy during your practice. This will raise the vibration of your

room. The altar can be temporary or permanent. A permanent altar is like a lightbulb that is always on and any objects placed on it will be cleansed and etherically charged. The power of the altar depends on how much Light you bring in. The more focused and regular your spiritual practice, the brighter the altar may become. The opposite is also true, so be discerning of the energies you bring into your sacred space.

Build your altar on a little table covered with a cloth, do not place it on the ground. The altar on a table represents the in-between plane; it accesses spiritual energies and brings them to the Earth.

On the altar, place a picture or statue of Iset, or a feather standing upright. In front of this, place a red candle, the preferred color for Iset; light incense, such a myrrh, to purify your energy bodies and open your energy channels; have a glass of water, which you drink at the end of the practice; add crystals — carnelian is associated with Iset, black crystals with Iset's emanation as Hat-Hor; add any other power objects you have; place flowers to represent beauty, especially red or red and white flowers; and have a little plate with offerings of fruit and sweets that will be charged by the power of your spiritual practice. Afterwards, eat the offerings, share them with friends, and leave some outside in nature, giving thanks to the land and raising its vibration.

After you create your altar, light the incense and smudge the room.[11] Walk around your space three times anti-clockwise with the lit incense, asking that any energies that do not work wholly and fully for the Light leave or be transmuted. State that the room now belongs to the Earth Mother and will be a temple of the Living Light. Then place the incense on the altar.

The Practice
Ask the Divine Mother Iset to be with you. Invite any helping spirits of the Light that you work with to support you. Ask them

to create a sacred space around you and your room. Light the candle.

Speak the invocation to Iset, "I invoke the Great Mystery of creation. Iset, Divine Mother of all, you are the Gate of Awareness that leads me back to my sacred self. You are the keeper of the portal in Sirius. You are the Living Light that disperses the darkness of ignorance and reveals my sacred self, hidden within. Through your intercession I walk the Earth as an awakened spirit in a human body. I invoke you Mut-Iset, Mother Iset."

Chant: Iset-Sothis, three times.

(This means Isis-Sirius. Sothis is the mystical name of Sirius. Do not use Sepdet, the everyday name of Sirius.) As you chant Iset-Sothis, connect with the multi-dimensional portal of the Living Light that exists on Sirius.

Ask to be a channel of the Living Light. Say, "May I be a pure channel. I invoke the power of the Divine Mother Iset's sacred wings of Light that surround all beings. May they surround and heal me so I feel the love and peace of the Great Mother, for I am the Divine child. I invoke the power, Light, and healing of the sacred wings of Iset for all beings, including myself."

Chant the Mantra 108 times: CHA-NE, Iset, HET-HET, AN

(Meaning: From the center of the luminous Iset, the energy flows to me and the Divine Wings of Light activate within me.)

Then chant three times: MA AN SA

(Meaning: Great Mother, Divine Source, Light of Creation.)

Visualization

Imagine that Iset is in front of you. As her wings open and surround you, your wings open. You are now Iset, the Great Mother of unconditional love, and you radiate the infinite Light of the Sirius portal. You are the star in the night sky, illuminating the darkness. Stay in this state meditating and radiating the Light of awareness for at least 21 minutes.

Afterwards, blow three times into the glass of water. Drink a little of the sacred water and sprinkle some over yourself. Say, "May the sacred essence of Mother Iset, Mut-Iset, protect and guard me, forever and ever."

To close, offer gratitude to Iset and all the Neteru, the enlightened spirits you work with, and to yourself for practicing the teachings. Say to the spirit beings that your spiritual work is now complete. Ask that, before they leave, they protect and seal you, your room, and home.

Endnotes

10 When I narrate this to a class, some people think that from now on all they have to do is open their wings and their problems will be sorted. It does not work like that. Sometimes you may go with a problem to your meditation space and realize that what you are worrying about is unimportant. Or that what you are facing is part of life, and you are being asked to surrender and accept what is occurring. Many possibilities may appear when we open our wings, channel HEKA, and find a deeper connection with our wise self.

11 People may not be able to smudge due to fire alarms. In that case, go around the room with the incense unlit.

Chapter 13

The Light of Atum Initiation

Channeling from Iset:
Nine Words of Power
Nine Keys to Nine Doors
Nine Beings of Light
The Nine Primordial Neteru form a circle around you;
each with their own story,
opens a portal within you.
As you chant, so you become
Atum, Shu, Tef-Nut, Nut, Geb, Iset, Ausir, Horan, Nebt-Het, Atum.
Rise, ancient initiate of the Living Light.

The Energy of the Living Light

In Part 1, we worked with the myth of creation and the nine primordial Neteru that govern all life. In our enlightened state, we are the Neteru, as we are a manifestation of the Living Light. Through our spiritual work, we consciously and gradually ascend into our Light bodies.

Atum and the other eight Neteru are keys that unlock our potential towards ascension; each is a stage we pass through in our soul's journey. We start as Atum and finish as Atum, becoming all the primordial Neteru in the process. Each of these divine consciousnesses offer teachings and is an energy field that we can open in our body through an initiation that builds the etheric temple of the Living Light inside our heart chakra. Then we create an altar/temple in our home that mirrors the inner temple. The inner and outer temple work in conjunction and help us access the Living Light within, and in the world.

The Nine Primordial Neteru

Below is a brief description of the nine primordial Neteru and their attributes.

- Atum: the Living Light, the power of creation, the etheric energy of Divine Consciousness that creates the physical and spiritual universes and beings therein, through the power of unconditional love. Iset says to you: "Seek no path that is only a path of knowledge; if you wish to awaken, find the way of unconditional love." The Primordial Lotus name is Nefer-Tem, meaning the beginning and the end. In birth and death, in creation and destruction, in the physical reality and ascension into the divine consciousness of the infinite spirit, we access the lotus and become the power and state of unconditional love.
- Shu: the cosmic wind of manifestation. The Living Light streams forth from the abyss, and the wind Shu, representing constant movement and change, brings Atum into manifestation. Shu is action based on the universal laws of Ma'at, Divine Order, that govern everything. Shu is the application of Ma'at in the creation of the different realities.
- Tef-Nut[12]: the celestial waters, has two attributes. The first is the enlightened state. These waters carry the state of wisdom and symbolize the ocean of stillness and inner knowing. In this state, the soul experiences infinity. The second aspect is Tef-Nut's contribution to the process of creation. When the celestial waters flow into the world, they become individual drops — a multitude of souls that inhabit the manifested reality.
- Nut: the sky realm. Nut is the vastness of the sky that covers the Earth. This realm includes worlds of different dimensions, inhabited by beings of higher consciousness.

- Geb: the Earth realm, the physical world, and the Earth's life-force etheric energy. The Earth reality is a place of experience that contributes to the evolution of all creation. Geb, the male Earth, fertilizes Nut, the female sky. Power and Light is birthed within us through this union.

The next four Neteru govern the awakening process that human beings experience:

- Iset: the Divine Mother, the guiding Light into spiritual ascension.
- Ausir: the Divine Father who is in his heart. Having been dismembered by the conditioning, Ausir was re-membered by Iset through her knowledge of HEKA and returned to life. He opens the path of death and resurrection.
- Horan[13]: the Divine child that rises against Set, the forces of chaos, to obtain the enlightened vision and become the sun in the eastern horizon. Horan reclaims his ability to rule himself.
- Nebt-Het: is portrayed on the outside of sarcophagi with her sister Iset, as she helps resurrect and re-member Ausir. In this teaching, Nebt-Het is last, indicating it takes years of practice before the initiate meets her. Nebt-Het says, "I am the voice of the night, the power of silence that brings the soul back to its primordial state of being. I am the sacred one inside the shrine of the holy of holies. I have full access to the conscious and unconscious self and see all worlds beyond the veil, yet I remain humble and speak few words."

At the end of the teaching, we become again Atum, the Living Light, no longer the individual drop but the awakened consciousness of the ocean of eternity.

Summary

This second path of HEKA is the path of transformation into the nine primordial Neteru, the nine enlightened beings that govern creation and un-creation, the transcendence of the physical reality. This path was governed by the temple complex of Iunu, the city of Atum, the place of the Living Sun. Each Neter unlocks a field of etheric energy and esoteric knowledge that lies dormant within us. It is also a stage on our journey of soul evolution. The initiates walked a circular path from Atum back to Atum. When one circle finished, a new circle began inside the previous one, and initiates met the teachings again, until they found themselves inside a tiny circle through which the Living Light flowed. From this circle, they returned to the state of Nu, the Abyss, the emptiness of enlightenment. Nu was the focus of the third path, governed by Djehuti.

Working with the Nine Neteru — Spiritual Practice

In this practice you will need a notebook and pen.

Each Neter is a sacred teaching that helps us unlock our enlightened state. In the ancient Egyptian temples, the initiates connected with each Neter through different mantras and practices. Each Neter had to be known, accessed, activated, and integrated.

In the spiritual practice, you meet and receive a description of each Neter. Working with the Primordial Neteru is a very powerful experience. The fields of Light that open within you are strong. It is best to prepare. Remove all distractions from your space, such as electronic appliances. Take time to sit peacefully and calm your mind.

After the practice, you will need time to integrate and may feel tired. It is best not to go to work, or into busy public places, as your senses will be heightened and you may find yourself overwhelmed. Savor and digest the spiritual practice in peace.

You can build an altar as described in the previous chapter. If you kept any sacred water from that practice, sprinkle some of it on yourself and then smudge yourself, altar, and room with incense; go around the room three times anti-clockwise as before. Create your sacred space by connecting with Atum, the Divine Light of Creation. Also, invite any helping spirits of the Light that you work with. Ask them to create a safe and protected space around you and the room you are in.

Speak the invocation, "May I be aware. May I be aware of myself as the primordial Neteru — the nine powers that govern creation and un-creation. As the manifestation of the Living Light, I am all these powers."

First, invite the presence of Atum. Ask Atum for a word that represents him, an aspect that you are ready to manifest. Write down the word you receive. Say to Atum that you wish to manifest this aspect, and ask for an activation. Wait for approximately 2 minutes.

Then call in Shu. Repeat the process with Shu and the rest of the Neteru. Write down the word you are given by each Neter and receive the activations.

At the end, return to Atum and say, "I am all these aspects. I am the Living Light. I am the Light of Creation, and I radiate Light everywhere."

Meditate in this state for at least 21 minutes. Then gently come back. If you have a glass of water near you, blow nine times into the water, once for each of the Neteru. Drink a little of the water and sprinkle a little over yourself. Keep some for future practices.

To close, offer gratitude to Atum and release and thank all the Neteru as below. Start with Nebt-Het and finish with Atum:

"Sacred one, you are a manifestation of my sacred being. I thank you and release you. I see myself as Nebt-Het, the holy of holies.

Sacred one, you are a manifestation of my sacred being. I thank you and release you. I see myself as Horan, the spiritual warrior who has overcome Set and is in his sovereignty.

Sacred one, you are a manifestation of my sacred being. I thank you and release you. I see myself as Ausir, the Divine Father who is in his heart.

Sacred one, you are a manifestation of my sacred being. I thank you and release you. I see myself as Iset, the Divine Mother, the bringer of enlightenment and the path of awakening.

Sacred one, you are a manifestation of my sacred being. I thank you and release you. I see myself as Geb, the life-force energy of the Earth and the physical world.

Sacred one, you are a manifestation of my sacred being. I thank you and release you. I see myself as Nut, the sky realm that is vast and encircles the world with her arms.

Sacred one, you are a manifestation of my sacred being. I thank you and release you. I see myself as Tef-Nut, the celestial waters of the enlightened state.

Sacred one, you are a manifestation of my sacred being. I thank you and release you. I see myself as Shu, the wind of manifestation.

Sacred one, you are a manifestation of my sacred being. I thank you and release you. I see myself as Atum, the Living Light.

I thank all the Neteru who work with me. I thank myself for practicing sacred teachings. Enlightened ones, my spiritual work is complete. I offer gratitude and release you. May you protect and seal me, my room, and the building before you leave."

You can either keep your altar in place or take it down. In the latter case, smudge everything and put the items away. Ideally, the items should only be used for your spiritual practices.

Endnotes

12   Egyptologists translate this being as moisture or rain. The esoteric translation is celestial waters.

13   Initially in the place of Horan was Set, the hidden, conditioned shadow. Horan defeated Set and takes his place in the invocation. If you wish to invoke Set instead of Horan, be aware that this is a very difficult energy to work with, and you may not be able to release it easily.

Chapter 14

The Wisdom of Thoth Initiation

Channeling from Iset:
The Mysteries of Djehuti are the mysteries of the Divine, which can only be revealed by becoming the mystery, becoming the Divine. This is one of the most sacred paths, for it requires immense trust, acceptance, and surrender to the unknown. Let go of all you thought you knew. Open yourself to learn like a child who discovers things for the first time. Your ego that was your friend and enemy must leave you completely, even though you have no idea how to exist without it. An empty mind arises that is also full of knowledge. This is the wisdom-mind that is limitless, and you will discover that it is the same with your being. The physical world does not exist, but you do. And who are you? The infinite mind, the infinite consciousness.

The Way of Djehuti: Accessing the Inner Well of Wisdom

This was a teaching that was reserved for initiates who had mastered the other paths. Even then, it was a teaching that people were invited to attend; one could not apply. The path was arduous for the body and spirit. The body needed to be flexible and adapt to the intense, high vibrational Light that the path opens. To receive this fire energy, one needed to be the fire: unlike the previous paths, where the initiate's vibration was raised through the initiation process, the student of Djehuti needed to have reached this high vibration already.

How did it work? The initiate practiced for many years with the Living Light and healed deeply. Consequently, their frequency was sufficiently raised for them to access a wisdom with the same frequency. Then they entered an unlit underground chamber to meditate and have an awareness of the spiritual Light they were. These chambers can still be found in some ancient Egyptian temples, such as Dendara, where the walls are adorned with sophisticated hieroglyphs of the finest quality. The Egyptologists, unfamiliar with this sacred tradition, describe these chambers as crypts or storage rooms.

The initiate entered the chamber alone, with no one to guide them. In the dark, they invoked Djehuti, and visions were given to them. The visions were an initial guide; they had to go past them into the deeper truth. Initiates needed a strong, healthy body and mind. They had to have solidity, inner strength, and be grounded. If the person was unprepared, they could go insane, as their issues, fears, and unresolved traumas resurfaced and plagued them.

The initiates also had to sustain their body through life-force energy. There was no food and only a little water.

Visions in the Dark — My Experience

I remained inside the dark chamber for days with no way to assess time. All aspects of life, such as meal times and going to bed when the sun set, were gone. In the beginning, my body's clock remembered its routine, and I would feel hungry when it was dinnertime. After approximately 2 days, this sensation diminished and then left. This is an important aspect to overcome. Since birth, we have learned to eat and drink. It is the first time the conditioning enters the form, for it is part of life's instinct: without food and water, we would not exist. When my body's clock stopped, and I no longer felt hunger, I did not know if it was day or night.

Then I found myself in an unknown place, and I began to see in the dark. I saw the energy and the hieroglyphs on the walls. Was I dreaming? Were they real? They appeared very real to me. I began to see the multilayers of the story the hieroglyphs depicted. However, an inner awareness cautioned me to pull back and not lose myself in the story. I needed to stay grounded in my body. The transformation had to happen from within and include the body. When the stories became lucid dreams, I detached from them and sent them away.

Encountering this phenomenon, I knew I had to connect with my inner essence and allow it to expand so that my frequency matched that of the hieroglyphs. And, as the Light flowed from me, the vibration emanating from the walls paled into insignificance, for my frequency became greater than the glyphs. I could now see beyond the walls and into every room of the temple, as if there were no walls. All this time I did not move, astrally or physically. I remained present in my body and saw with my all-seeing eye.

And then the experience ended. I was in the dark again. Was that it? Am I ready to come out? Should I try and see it again? Instinctively, I knew the experience was complete. Although I felt the temptation to stay, I knew it was unhealthy. If I succumbed to the temptation, I may go too far and lose my mind. The visions may trap me and I may not be able to return. I remembered that safety was the best policy, and came out.

Afterwards, there was a 3-day integration. I was so luminous and needed to rest, sleep, and remain quiet with few people and distractions. I ate simple food, starting with a starchy fruit and some clear liquid. Slowly, I reintegrated. I walked around the temple, looked at the stars at night, and the sunrise in the morning. Then the teachers asked, "What happened?" As I described what I remembered, the experience solidified within me. I realized I knew more than I thought. And speaking about it helped me comprehend the immensity of what I learned.

There was a book in the temple, the Book of Djehuti.[14] It was a long papyrus that initiates who went into the dark to find the Light added to. Some wrote long paragraphs, others a sentence. Written is the pearl of wisdom each initiate received. Once I had written in the book, I could study the whole papyrus. Before, I would not have been able to understand what the others had recorded. Djehuti, the wisdom keeper, opens this gate for us.

The Path You Walk Alone

I was tempted to return to the dark chamber and see if I could re-experience the profundity of the inner Light. This was not usually allowed. My channel had been opened by the experience, and now I needed to work with it myself rather than force it to open further through another extreme practice.

At first, working with it myself could be frustrating. I experienced luminosity and wished it back. "Where is it now?" I wondered. Life was full of distractions, and I could not find the luminosity in the material plane. I met with other initiates, discussed the papyrus, and shared the teachings. I had to choose what to focus on. What did I wish to know?

There are two paths for the soul to incarnate through: the male aspect and the female aspect. Two opposites. Yet these opposites come together and create anew. So the initiates had to choose, "Do I work to understand the female aspect of the Abyss?" If Nanuet interested me, what did it mean? My mind gave me information, but the information came from other sources and the teachings, not from direct experience. And how can Nanuet take me to Nun, its male counterpart? And what about Nu, the primordial state of both, or is it their union?

Every day my mind was overwhelmed with these abstract aspects, and in the daily sharing with other initiates I explained my reasonings, and they gave their input. The teacher listened to the conversations and usually remained silent. Another day passed and the quest continued. After a while, I thought I had an insight. In truth I did not; my mind had grasped something and made it a fact when it was not the real experience. I became tired and impatient, and a little desperate.

When I reached this state, it was time to seek the truth outside the temple walls. I went into the desert to the power places, where Set roams the land, the dead walk at night, and the jackals howl. Despite this, I felt safe. The voice of the desert touched me, and the emptiness of the place filled me. Here, there were no debates, no distractions, only the quiet space. The desire to write in the book of Djehuti left, and I laughed about any desires and goals I had. "Why did I try so hard. What was the point?"

Everything in the desert was alive and communicating with me. The desert has a sound, and I listened to its music. Then I heard a voice. My mind thought it was the wind, then I began to perceive more clearly, and insights I had about Nanuet fell into place. The immense beauty of this truth slowly revealed itself and made complete sense. I did not have the words to explain it, but I knew it. I always did. I knew it in the temple, but only as separate fragments. In the emptiness of the desert, the wind Shu brought it into one absolute truth, and I was awed by the revelation.

This moment also passed, but the understanding of Nanuet was born within me, and remained. I was tempted to stay in the quietness of the desert and savor the gift again, but I knew it was time to leave. The desert can take as much as she can give, and she could claim my mind if I overstayed. I returned to the temple, and after another period of integration, I related my story and shared the teaching. Again, I was invited to write in the book of Djehuti. Once I had recorded my realization, I read the pearls from others, and understood them at a deeper level.

Awakening That Never Leaves You

For many days, months, and years you walk this path. You seek, you understand, you integrate, you grow. You become a pillar of wisdom and truth. Life flows, and you master many aspects of yourself. You are centered in your axis, and Iset's ladder upon your crown connects you to the enlightened wisdom-mind. Your mind is quiet most of the time. You live withdrawn from the world in a sacred space, a temple of the Living Light.

And then it is time to see if you can retain your awareness in the world of Set. Are you truly immune to its snares? You leave the temple and venture into the world. You live an everyday life. You have a job, perhaps a relationship, and a family. Can you retain your vibration and calmness when your child wakes in the middle of the night? Can you be in the beauty and harmony of Djehuti's teachings in the human world? Can you serve this world and support the transformation of those who seek wisdom?

At this point, you learn one of the most beautiful and powerful lessons, compassion. Compassion for yourself, compassion for others. Compassion for the human predicament. And you learn detachment, the detachment that the Divine state inspires. What is the highest good in each situation? Are your heart strings pulled in ways that do not serve you, and therefore do not serve others? You live your teaching. You live your wisdom. You are no longer the wise pillar of the temple; you are the wise pillar of Life.

As you continue to walk the path of Ma'at, gradually everything clears in the most unexpected ways. You see the conditioning for what it is, a cloud of no substance that cannot touch you. You stare at the clear sky that can never cloud over, because your Light is so bright that any clouds evaporate. This is it. What you sought emerges by itself, and again you realize it was always there, so obviously there. The conditioning is insignificant, for you embody the immensity of the enlightened spirit.

This state will stay with you always. Even if you lose it in another life, part of you will remember it and rediscover it. It is who you are. It is who we all are.

Summary

There are not many words to describe the Path of Thoth, Hermes Trismegistus, or Djehuti — the many names of the scribe who records the journey of the soul and brings forth enlightened wisdom. This is a path that can only be experienced when our vibration reaches a certain level. In our modern times, we no longer have temples with dark rooms and caves in the desert for our spiritual quest. Through initiations and wisdom teachings, Iset has given us a way to work with this path in our modern lives. I hope that as more of us bring into being the Living Light and raise our consciousness, these ancient practices will be re-established and the book of Djehuti will be re-opened.

Introduction to Spiritual Practice

As above, so below. The Nile, as the river of life, becomes the Milky Way. How can one travel along this river? The ancient *Egyptian Book of the Dead* contains cryptic messages that show a way. It is said the path was opened by the shining spirits so that human beings can travel this road. The journey starts from the River Nile, where the day bark and night bark ferry the traveler into the higher realms of consciousness.

Understanding the spiritual significance of the Nile is an important first step. In the material plane, we see the river as the creator of life; without the Nile, Egypt could not exist. This green strip of land is a physical reminder of the contrast between life and death. Life is full of sounds, colors, food, and possibilities to create in the world. And death is silence, nothingness. The desert is where nothing grows, and the dead rest with their face turned to the north wind. In this place, you may lose your path, for the landmarks quickly change. You may run out of water and die. It is hot during the day and bitterly cold at night. Yet this is also a place of possibilities of a different kind, of spiritual awakening. Egypt carries the threshold of awakening that exists between life and death.

And, as with everything, the physical and spiritual, the green land and desert, each exists within the other. The Nile strip is where you find the temples of the Living Light located on the east bank, guiding the spiritual seeker to become Ra-Horakti: Horan who rises in the east like the sun and becomes enlightened. And in the desert, there are places where the water gathers and creates an oasis, a pool of life amidst the desert of death. In the material sense, the desert is emptiness; the Nile strip is fullness. And in the spiritual sense, it is the opposite: the desert is fullness, and the Nile strip is emptiness; it literally strips you away from your spiritual power and focus.

These two states of being exist next to each other in Egypt. This is why the ancient Egyptians practiced the mysteries of life and death equally, knowing the importance of death in the soul's journey.

In 2014, I stayed on the west bank of Luxor (ancient Thebes) with another initiate. Our local Egyptologist suggested we visit the temple of Djehuti, which exists in a part of the desert west of Luxor. This is not a temple that tourists visit.

After walking into the desert for three hours and climbing two hills, the most incredible terrain could be seen: crescent moon canyons, chasms, valleys, and more hills. We then climbed another small hillock, and on top were the ruins of a small temple of Djehuti, built with mud bricks, many of which remained.

We took turns to sit in the sun and the little shade the ruins offered. It was too cold in the shade and too hot in the sun. This was an incredible pilgrimage, to come to a sacred place where the seekers of truth gathered. We sat by ourselves, gazing at the empty horizon and meditating.

Now it is your turn to visit this place of wonder.

Spiritual Practice: The Temple of Djehuti in the Desert

Start by calling your guides, teachers of the Light, and Djehuti, and ask them to create a sacred space around you. State your intention to retrieve a pearl of wisdom from your infinite inner well of unconscious knowledge.

"To walk on the road of the Neter Djehuti is to be filled with Light; great are the advantages gained by those who discipline themselves to follow it."

(Extract from the hymn to Djehuti, tomb of Pet-Osiris, High Priest of Djehuti, in Khemenu.)

Visualization

It is time to leave behind all that you are familiar with, including your responsibilities to others. This is a time for you. Make a commitment to walk into the emptiness of the desert to the temple of Djehuti and meet the ancient scribe.

See yourself walking on a path that takes you deep into the desert. A jackal appears and you follow it. The jackal can be a guide or a trickster. If it is a guide, you will reach your destination; if it is a trickster, you may become lost. Make an offering to Onpu, the Opener of the Ways, to guide you safely to your destination. What should you offer? Onpu asks for a necklace or ring you have been wearing for years. You remove it and offer it to the desert, and follow the jackal.

The jackal takes you deep into the desert, up hills, and through valleys to a place of wisdom. Without realizing, you have been releasing many of the burdens you carry from your life. The desert has the capacity to draw moisture and remove old energies from the body. Offer the desert all that you wish to leave behind.

After the purification, the jackal takes you up another hill towards the temple of Djehuti. As you climb, ask yourself: "Why am I here? Why have I left the comfort of my home to come to this arid place?" Reflect on these important questions as you continue up the hill. The walk is difficult. It is a steep hill and the sun is burning you with its relentless fire.

Once you have found your answers, you realize you are at the top of the hill. The temple gates are open and you and the jackal enter. You meet Djehuti, either in his form of an ibis-headed man or a friendly baboon. He asks you to follow him and guides you further into the temple.

As you enter, Iset appears in the form of a woman. She is the teacher and offers you a sacred papyrus. You unfold the scroll and see a word or a phrase for you to meditate upon and discover its true meaning. You think you already know it, but she asks you to remain silent. She takes you to a place that has been prepared specifically for you, and asks you to remain here and contemplate what she has given you, as she spreads her wings around you. Meditate for as long as you wish.

When you feel the practice is complete for now, slowly bring yourself back. Thank Djehuti and Iset, as well as your guide, Onpu, the jackal. Ask them to close, seal and protect you, the space, and building you are in before they leave.

Note: You can continue with this practice over days, weeks, months, or even years by calling these beings and asking to return to the place they have created for you inside the temple. Once there, meditate on the word or phrase that was given to you by Iset. When a pearl of wisdom arises from within, your time in the temple of Djehuti will be complete, and your path will take you to a different spiritual landscape.

Endnote

14   This book has never been found.

Part 3

Mystical Esoteric Practices of Ancient Egyptian Spirituality

We embark on a journey of spiritual resurrection and rebirth. We follow Iset inside the Great Pyramid and meet our Divine spirit. We astro-travel to the world of the dead and walk a journey of self-renewal. This spiritual work parallels what happens when we die, enter the spirit realms, and reincarnate. Like Ausir, we reincarnate as Horan, the one who becomes aware of being the spirit in the body.

We participate in a mystery play of resurrection and rebirth. Our soul is familiar with this play, for we have lived many lives.

We start our narrative with one of the oldest myths about death, resurrection, and reincarnation.

The Myth

In Zep Tepi, Ausir, the embodiment of the heart, reigned. He was kind and generous and taught people how to live with compassion. He saw the beauty of the Divine soul in everyone, and under his reign, the land and people prospered.

Ausir's twin brother Set, representing the mind, wanted to be in charge, to be king. Set contrived a trap for Ausir. On Ausir's birthday, Set brought a beautiful sarcophagus made of precious wood, proclaiming that it belonged to whomsoever fitted it exactly. Everyone tried the sarcophagus, but Set had made it to fit his brother. When Ausir lay therein, Set closed the lid and had the coffin thrown into the Nile. He returned to the palace and sat on his brother's throne.

Iset, wife of Ausir, sought Ausir and eventually found him and took him back to the palace. Set pretended the incident was a joke that had gone wrong, and persuaded Ausir that no harm was intended. Ausir immediately forgave Set.

Set was livid. The mind was determined to rule. Next time, Set cut Ausir into fourteen pieces to ensure he could not return. The mind killed the heart.

Iset and her sister Nebt-Het found all the pieces of Ausir, apart from one, the phallus, which Iset refashioned out of wood. As Iset reassembled Ausir, she joined with him in sacred union and became pregnant with Horan. Ausir then left for the domain of the dead. "I cannot stay in this world, for it cannot sustain me," he said. "I will move to the spiritual realms of the Light." The time of the heart was over. The mind now reigned, and the people grew unhappy but did not know why. They tried to work things out logically, not realizing they missed their sacred heart.

Iset kept young Horan alive. Horan represents the spirit who has to overcome the conditioned mind. He battles the mind, for the mind does not relinquish its position easily. In the struggle, Horan gains the enlightened vision and begins a new reign, where the awakened spirit is in charge. People have awakened into their divinity. They experienced the loss of the heart and supremacy of the mind, and then found the spiritual path back to their infinite spirit.

Activation of the Golden Times

When we were conceived, we were all like Ausir, the awakened heart. Then, as in the myth, the mind locked the heart in a box and put itself in control. Living life through the mind is a process that dismembers the wise self and renders life arduous. We grow unhappy, afraid, and dissatisfied, until we become aware of our spiritual self. Horan, the spirit, awakens within, fights for his space, and transmutes the conditioning. We gradually reclaim ourselves and our life. We re-member.

Dis-memberment and re-memberment is a continuous cycle, personally and collectively. The Golden Times were the age of Ausir, innocence. Then the cycle ended with the emergence of Set. For thousands of years the egoic mind has controlled us, individually and collectively. It is the age of separation from the sacred heart. Still, the seed of Ausir is present. During the era of Set, Ausir reincarnates as Horan, the spiritual warrior, who reawakens his Divine connection and overcomes the social programing by facing many challenges. The spiritual awakening that many are now experiencing signals the birth of a new era, the reign of Horan.

After the time of Horan, another era will emerge — the next Golden Times and the re-emergence of Ausir.

After Zep Tepi, the priesthood worked to re-activate the Golden Times within themselves and the world. In the temple of Abdju (Abydos), the mysteries of resurrection continued. The fourteen pieces of Ausir were brought together in a sarcophagus, and through ceremony and theo-drama (sacred theatre), a re-enactment of Ausir's resurrection occurred annually. Even during the pharaonic times, when Set reigned, it was believed that the resurrection rituals contributed to the upholding of Ma'at. These rituals, described in the *Pyramid texts* and the *Book of Coming Forth by Day*, invite us to work with them so that we re-member and gradually bring the Golden Times back to ourselves and the planet.

This third part takes readers into a process of re-membering, resurrection, and re-activation of the Golden Times.

Chapter 15

Activation through Iset

Channeling from Iset:
I call you to walk the path of resurrection of your spirit and retrieve your innocence, lost in the world of Set. The magical life of the sacred initiate is one where you recover your essence, the sacred heart. The shadow, pain, and hurt you carry must first be healed through the power of love. No evil can exist when you are in your sovereignty as a being of unconditional love. To heal the evil of the world — the hidden serpent Apep — become like me, the Great Mother, who subdues, overcomes, and transforms all separation.

***

As we journey back to the Golden Times, we encounter two Divine principles who help us remember that we are the Divine essence incarnated: wisdom and love, Djehuti and Hat-Hor.

Djehuti: Mystical and Applied Knowledge

Djehuti encompasses the aspects of knowledge which are essential to the spiritual seeker who aspires to wholeness.

The First Aspect of Djehuti — Mystical Knowledge
This includes knowledge of the Divine self, ourselves as multi-dimensional beings, the cosmic principles that govern life on Earth, the universal laws, and the etheric energies of Light. This is the knowledge of the path of the mystic. On this path, mentally understood knowledge, does not serve us, and may hinder us. We can lose ourselves in definitions and theories, believing we know what we are talking about. This is a tragedy.

Sacred knowledge is awareness. First the initiate reads the texts, learns the theory, and listens to lectures — symbolized by the Papyrus plant. And slowly, a birthing of the knowledge arises from within. Only then can someone claim to know something — symbolized by the ibis bird. Thus, sacred knowledge consists of two parts: theoretical learning and inner realization. Paradoxically, awareness also emerges independently of theoretical learning through spiritual practice or by living a sacred life.

Each cognizance is an experience of awakening. It is rediscovered wisdom. When we die, our soul retains some awareness of this knowledge, and it becomes more accessible in subsequent lives. The knowledge is the jewel we always possessed that was hidden in a drawer. One day, we open the drawer and, astounded, find the jewel, sparkling and shining. To access higher states of awareness and sacred realizations, we also do spiritual work with high vibrational etheric energy and learn the art of detachment.

The Second Aspect of Djehuti — Applied Knowledge
This aspect of knowledge is utilized to serve physical life — help humanity evolve. Examples of applied knowledge are architecture, writing, technology, astronomy, medicine. With applied knowledge, initiates must be cautious. In the etheric, knowledge-Djehuti is a Divine principle and exists in pure form. When it is brought into the third dimensional reality, this knowledge enters the realm of duality, and can be used positively or negatively. For example, someone with herbal knowledge may work positively with plants to heal people, or negatively to poison someone.

In the same way, etheric Light has been misused throughout human history via black magic and cursing. Access to the etheric Light energy is key to the soul's evolution. When a misuse of the Living Light is attempted for whatever reason, even if the person thinks their actions are justified, the use of the highly evolved frequency is withdrawn. In the previous example with the jewel, when we misuse the energy, we still know the jewel is in the drawer, but it no longer shines. It is energetically dead. This is because our vibration has lowered, and it takes a huge amount of spiritual and personal work to clear the karmic seeds that the misuse of energy creates. It is not just a matter of regretting the action.

The Story of the Priestess
A priestess lived in a temple with her son whom she adored. She tried to teach him the way of the initiate, because she wished to keep him near. But when her son became a man, he had no wish to be a priest. He found the liturgies boring and was tired of the restrictions of temple life. He wanted to become a soldier and seek adventure.

The priestess was devastated. "What will happen to me if he is killed?" She approached a priest and begged him to speak to her son and lie to him, if necessary. Her colleague said her son refused to come to the lectures, or left half-way, and had no aptitude for the priesthood, and they must respect this. The priestess was unhappy but pretended to agree with her colleague. Her mind told her that, as a mother, she had every right to protect her son. And so she used the etheric energy to create a spell and stop her son from leaving. The next day, she felt as if she was no longer in the flow of life. Few people now came to her for healing, whereas before she saw fifteen people daily. She had expected promotion, but nothing happened. Each time she tried to do something, obstacles appeared.

Eventually she realized that what she had done was wrong. She took back the spell and apologized to the Goddess. "I did not realize what I was doing," The Goddess Iset said that no one has the right to interfere with someone's free will. Her actions had broken the law of Ma'at, and consequently, her frequency fell. Obstacles that her vibration blocked now appeared. Iset surrounded the woman with her wings and filled her with unconditional love. But even Iset could not restore the woman's vibrational frequency. We all have to purify the karma that our thoughts and actions create.

Hat-Hor — The Vibration of Divine Love

The path towards enlightenment and ascension is through the opening of the sacred heart. In generating higher states of awareness, we are touched by the love of the infinite, a love that brings tears to our eyes, for it is incredibly beautiful. This love asks nothing of us and accepts us unconditionally. This state is symbolized by the white lotus flower.

It is important to realize that we have to overcome the ego through the opening of the heart. No matter how much knowledge we acquire and how many spiritual gifts are activated, it is the open heart that fuels soul evolution. When I asked Iset why she invited me to be her teacher, she simply said, "Because of your heart." Knowledge and spiritual gifts may lead us astray. We can lose everything by falling prey to the ego, because we have not fully opened the most important center: the sacred heart-center.

Our earthly self has no idea what Divine love is. In the story about the priestess, she appeared to act out of love for her son. However, her actions were based on her needs and fear of losing her son. Her ego-mind said she had every right to manipulate her son's future. This is conditioned pride. It is not Divine love.

In our world, we may equate Divine love with our earthly experience of love, the love from our relatives, friends, parents, or partners. Yet, in most cases, this love, beautiful as it is, is still conditional. Could we love these people even if they did not love us? This is how the Divine loves us. No matter who we are, what we do, or if we reciprocate the love, Divine love is unconditional and fully accepting.

To generate such love, we need to experience it. Sacred work leads us to moments where Divine love flows to us. This love has the potential to activate our heart-center, the place where our enlightened consciousness lives in the body. Through the activation, we become more aware of the love that we are. But it takes time. In our everyday life, we may feel that we access Divine love and then it leaves us. This is not true. Once the heart-center is activated, it continues to generate these states, at the right time. Each experience is a precious pearl that builds on the previous one. Have patience and allow the process of awakening to unfold organically within you. Be careful not to attach to this goal. *Desire stops the flow.* Allow yourself to surrender to the continuous opening of your heart-center without conditions.

One way to learn about Divine love is to experience it through contact with the enlightened helping spirits. They offer this gift to assist our soul evolution. Our task is to receive it. The biggest obstacle in accepting Divine love is that the mind does not value it. It thinks it should receive something more important: a special gift, knowledge of the future, or the fixing of our problems. By coming into contact with unconditional love, and learning how to self-generate this state, we pave the way towards the embodiment of the enlightened consciousness that we are.

As we start to generate states of Divine love, we become detached from drama. We find inner strength and remain centered in our heart and body, rather than being hooked by external events. In this way, Divine love becomes Divine wisdom. Knowledge and Love, Djehuti and Hat-Hor, come together. We know when and how to act for our highest good, instead of being influenced by the collective consciousness. We generate compassion and, paradoxically, are not affected by the world's problems.

Overcoming the Empath Within
Problems arise when we develop Divine love but lack sufficient grounding in deeper wisdom and develop the "empathic archetype." Empaths feel the pain, emotional and physical, of others, and take on that pain. Gradually, they are unable to function in everyday life, as the suffering becomes unbearable.

Being an empath is challenging. Sensitive souls, with an open heart, may have learnt that being a good person entails feeling the pain of others, if not, they are selfish. If they are healers, they often manifest the illnesses of their clients and eventually burn out: feel emotionally, mentally, and physically exhausted, and give up their caring or healing career.

Another misconception is that an empath epitomizes compassion, and that giving up this identity means wearing armor over your heart. This is not true. If you continue working spiritually, your compassion will grow infinitely. You will also be in your strength and Light, and this will encourage your clients to find their strength and Light. Here are some key principles towards overcoming the empathic trait:

- *Set good boundaries.* Empaths commonly attract people who are looking for sympathy and an opportunity to offload their problems. Many empaths also draw narcissistic partners, or clients, and people who are energy vampires. If you are a healer or working in a caring profession, state the intention before a session, "May I take nothing from my client and may my client take nothing from me."
- Empaths feel the issues their clients carry as psychic information, which helps them identify what needs addressing. For example, if a client has knee pain, the empath will feel pain in their knee. Problems arise when the empath carries the pain after the session. Make another strong intention, "I will know instinctively what

my client's issue is, as information, without having to feel the pain. If I feel anything, once I acknowledge it, the feeling will completely cease. I will be the observer only."
- Moreover, there are people whose wounding will resonate with your wounding. In a similar way to open sores, it is easy for infections and foreign matter to settle in. An empath is essentially a deeply wounded healer. This is a signal to work on yourself, release any self-blame and criticism, and extend self-love and self-forgiveness to your past.
- Empaths may be understanding towards others but very self-critical. While they offer love to their clients, they deprive themselves of love. To heal the traumas of the past, reverse this trait. Forgive yourself and offer the understanding and compassion you share with others to yourself. You have to come first.
- When someone gives so much to others, a part of them is looking for friends, loved ones, and clients to acknowledge, respect, and love them. This trait is part of the empathetic shadow that you are called to heal. In doing the deeper work, know that you have to give yourself the self-love. Do not look for it from others. It is your love that you crave.

Overcoming the empathic trait is deep work, and an enormous gift to offer yourself. You will be much happier and your life will transform when you are fully in your body, free of the pain and suffering of others, and the collective.

I-Set: I Exist Outside Set

In the name Iset, we find the word Set. Set means the conditioning that expresses itself as inferior, superior, jealous, proud, angry, attached, and ignorant. Set silences the voice of love and integrity, and believes that no matter how unfair and harmful he is, it is his right. He always finds a way to justify himself. Set thinks he can get away with everything and suffer no consequences. This is not true. Eventually, through the law of karma, or the rule of Ma'at, Set will experience the effect of his actions.

The headdress of Iset, the throne on the crown with the three steps, exists in all of us. This heavenly ladder activates and enables a raising of our etheric vibration, and offers us the potential for a deeper spiritual connection with the upper realms.

The First Step — The Seeker
Initially, we experience an opening, an awakening, a shift in perspective, a dream of initiation, or a spiritual being suddenly manifests in front of us. Or perhaps nothing tangible happens, but something ignites a desire to seek spiritual knowledge and follow a spiritual path. Circumstances steer us towards the study of the mysteries and the experience of the etheric. We answer the calling, immerse ourselves in the Light energies, and slowly become aware of the conditioning that we carry.

Our conditioning does not understand this new endeavor. Our mind tries to stop us. It tells us it is dangerous to meddle with such things, and that we are wasting our time and precious resources. Friends and family, who become the voice of the conditioning, may express their doubts about our newly found passion.

This first step can last for a while. It is a pleasant time. We explore different aspects of spirituality and are supported by the Light energies. Some may spend their entire lifetime in this first step, moving from one spiritual discipline to another, and remaining on the surface instead of going deeper. The duration of this first step is different for each person.

The Second Step — The Adept
At some point, we come across a spiritual path of Light that has the capacity to take us into higher states of consciousness. Accordingly, Djehuti and Hat-Hor start to generate within us. Our seeking becomes focused. We practice teachings that enable the birthing of deeper realizations. We find ourselves in states of Light, joy, and connection. We open to our Divine wisdom and Divine love. However, this path is steep. On one hand, we immerse ourselves in experiences of Light. On the other, our shadow surfaces and asks for our attention and healing.

The spiritual path of Light is not straightforward. We can climb high, but each step takes effort. We have to see what we carry, surrender to the path, and trust in the Light, instead of actioning the wishes of our ego. We heal and release the trauma held in our cells, instead of projecting it. We learn to let go of the conditioned desires and judgments, which stem from our upbringing, and any expectations we hold about what our spiritual path should do and provide for us.

Sometimes the ego hooks us, and we fall off this second step, and then give up. What keeps us steady on the ladder is continuous spiritual practice and personal work — the constant immersion in higher states of consciousness, the constant seeking of truth.

As we climb this second step, we have help from the etheric realms, even if we do not always appreciate it. No matter the difficulties we face, we can surrender into the peace of the Living Light and find assistance. From the higher perspective, we may see a bigger picture. This is the gift of awareness that comes by channeling HEKA.

The Third Step — Embodiment of the Shining Spirit Sahu
In this final step, the path of the Living Light becomes our way of life. Our life is a ceremony, a spiritual practice. The Light transforms our body at cellular level. Every part of us emanates

HEKA. Issues, even physical illnesses, fall away. We experience spiritual and physical transformation. Our body becomes the body of Light, Sahu.

Summary

The initiates practiced the self-generation of two Divine principles: Divine wisdom that arises from within and Divine love that takes place through the activation of our sacred heart. The aim was to align with and gradually embody the Divine self by walking a spiritual path of Light. The Neter Iset opens this path towards enlightenment and spiritual ascension. On her crown, Iset carries a throne with three steps, which define the way the path unfolds. The activation of the crown chakra enables access to the etheric energy of the Living Light, to the degree we are able, so that we can find our way home to the Neter that we are.

Spiritual Practice

The ancient initiates worked with the headdress on top of Iset's crown, the heavenly ladder. They brought themselves into meditative states where they became aware of the structure of the "throne" on their crown chakra. They visualized climbing the steps, to experience higher levels of consciousness, and then brought these vibrations back into the body.

Apart from fueling their spiritual development during their life, they practiced these ways to learn how to exit their body at death. The throne is aligned with the central channel of our meridian system. When we die, our consciousness may have the opportunity to exit our body through the crown, move up the etheric ladder, and reunite with the infinite self.

The ancient initiates spoke the invocation below, calling the path of Iset, during their life and at death. The reference to being just and true means they are in their authentic self, which is always true.

***

"O grant to me a path so that I may pass in peace, for I am just and true."[15]

***

Start your practice by inviting Iset and any helping spirits you work with to support you and create a sacred space around you.

Imagine lifting the veil of time and entering the time of Zep Tepi. Visualize yourself standing in front of the Great Pyramid, which is covered with white stone and capped with a golden pyramidion.

As you approach the pyramid, Hat-Hor greets you. She appears as a woman dressed in white, wearing a headdress consisting of a circular disc attached to two rods shaped like cow horns. The circle symbolizes the brilliance of her spirit. The cow horns denote unconditional love. Her eyes radiate love towards you, and she welcomes you into this sacred space.

She invites you to climb the steps and stand at the entrance of the pyramid. She lights incense from the lotus flower that symbolizes awakening and inner knowing through the opening of the heart. Hat-Hor smudges you with the incense and asks you to state the intention, "May anything that masks my true nature and authenticity be taken away by the smoke of the incense. May I enter the pyramid and receive the empowerment of my true self, as much as I can, at this moment."

Hat-Hor takes you into the chamber of the Great Mother. Iset manifests in front of you, in a female form. Her wings are outstretched towards you, emanating waves of Light. Say to Iset, "Lady of Light, I thank you for your presence. I offer you all the conditioning that I have outgrown and am ready to release. Although these conditioned ways served me, they are now no longer appropriate."

Activation through Iset

Iset takes the conditioning that you offer with no judgment, and asks you to release all self-judgment. Take a moment to listen to Iset as she shares with you the value the conditioning had in your life.

Iset now comes close to you, carrying a model of the "throne," made from the purest white alabaster. She asks permission to place it on your crown. If you accept, she places the throne on your head. A download of etheric energy flows from your infinite spirit into your central channel and spreads throughout your meridian system. Receive this activation for a while (15 minutes).

At the end, Iset removes the crystal throne. She offers you an amulet of protection, called the "Knot of Iset." If you wish to receive it, Iset will place it around your neck.

Iset now asks you to focus your awareness on your central channel, the central axis of your body. Lift your dominant hand to eye level right in front of you, palm facing you. Your hand chakra opens, and Light flows from your hand into you. (Hold this position for at least 1 minute). Your "throne" on your crown is now active. Bring your hand down.

Iset offers you the Ankh, eternal life, and places protection around you. Give thanks to Iset for this activation of the throne in your crown chakra.

It is now time to leave the room. Hat-Hor, guides you outside the pyramid. As you step outside, there is so much Light. Everything sparkles because you sparkle. Look at the sun in the sky and see yourself as the Living Sun, the radiant being.

Now see the veil of time descending, go through it and return to the here and now. Connect with the Earth where you live and take a few minutes to radiate the Light of your practice to the land. The energy that you radiate becomes a circular river of Light that flows around the Earth, and then back to you. This is the Light that connects all.

Offer gratitude to Iset, Hat-Hor, and all the enlightened spirits who work with you. Say that your practice is complete and release them. Ask that they protect and seal you, the room, and the building before they go.

Endnote
15   Almond, J. & Seddon, K. (2002). p. 126.

Chapter 16

May I Pass in Peace: Death and Eternal Life

Channeling from Iset:
I open the Gate of Death, the death of the conditioning that has served you for a while and now you have overcome. I reveal the Gate of Awareness, which leads to your Divine self. With your last breath, a path may open for you; when you experience physical death, may you soar into the Light of your spirit. There is no death, only a shift in consciousness, an awakening from the dream that is physical life. You can also pass through the Gate of Death while living: consciously embodying your spirit while in the body.

Eternal Peace Is a State of Mind

The invocation from the ancient *Egyptian Book of the Dead*: "O grant to me a path so that I may pass in peace, for I am just and true," spoken before an initiation, was recalled at death, when the initiate's spirit left the body. Death is another door towards awakening. At the time of passing, if the consciousness is centered inside the central channel, it can move upwards through the crown and onto the "throne," Iset's ladder. The etheric energy then intensifies as the higher frequencies of the Living Light, transmitted through star portals, help the human consciousness experience a profound state of peace. This enables us to fully detach from the earthly realm. Free from the body and supported by the energy, the consciousness awakens and may even become enlightened.

At death, the initiates were supported by the Neteru and spiritual allies they worked with during life. They were further aided by their spiritual community. When the door of death opens, the state of luminosity generated by the person dying lifts the people who are supporting them through prayer and spiritual practice, in person or distantly, into a higher state of being. People may experience a deep state of grace for days afterwards. This only happens if they are in a state of acceptance, peace, and meditative stillness.

The initiates had no fear of death. They understood it was a natural process that everyone experienced. In making peace with death, they treasured each moment of life. Death rituals were doors that generated a shift in consciousness to a higher awakened state.

The Creation of Peace on Earth

In the necropolises, the ancient Egyptians created places where people could experience the peace and Light that is potentially available during death. To achieve this, they used sacred architecture and high vibrational etheric energy, and opened portals of Light that may still be active today.

Im-Hot-Tep was the job title given to the chief architect and engineer of these sites. These high initiates of Djehuti were master builders and adepts of spiritual knowledge; in order to create places of silence and peace, they had to be able to self-generate these states.

In many of the older pyramids there are empty sarcophagi. These pyramids are not tombs, as Egyptologists suggest; they are chambers of initiation and spiritual connection. The sarcophagi are placed inside etheric portals, each of which has a different purpose. The initiate would lie inside for a while, with the lid slightly closed, in order to expand their awareness, travel to alternate realities, and enter higher states of consciousness. One of these sarcophagi lies in the Necropolis of Sakkara, inside a pyramid built by the pharaoh Unas, who lived during the fifth dynasty.

A soul is able to experience the awakened consciousness when it exits the body during the death process, and the sarcophagus in the pyramid of Unas facilitates this experience for the living. Like the ancient initiates, by lying down and meditating inside it, even distantly, we can open to the higher states of consciousness we normally experience at physical death.

Sakkara was a place for the living to practice the spiritual arts and overcome the conditioning. It was a healing sanctuary where people stayed when they experienced illness. All types of physical, emotional, and mental illnesses were successfully treated there, through the holistic medicine of the healers, priesthood, and physicians. Most of the time, the energy was so high that people could not stay awake and fell into a deep sleep or trance. No hallucinogenic substances were used; the main medicine was the etheric energy.

Sakkara was also a cemetery. People wanted to be buried in this area of high vibrational Light to access the spirit realms more easily, and capitalize on the potential that the death process offered them to awaken. Unlike the foreboding atmosphere of some of our current cemeteries, the ancient Egyptian necropolis in Sakkara still emanates the energy of peace it was designed to convey.

Imprisoned by the Conditioning: Etheric Thoughtforms

The conditioning is collectively created and maintained by all our thoughts, beliefs, and ways of life. We make agreements about what to believe and how to behave. Most of the time we automatically believe what the conditioning says and do not challenge it, either individually or as a society. We then pass these agreements to our descendants, through our family values, education systems, and organizations. These conditioned ways are strengthened by our collective attachment to them. In continuously abiding by these beliefs, we have energized them and kept them alive for generations.

These beliefs become thoughtforms: they have an energy of their own that takes the shape of an etheric being. Thoughtforms have no Ka, no soul, and yet they exist. To keep themselves "alive" they attach to the aura of human beings and hold them captive through their endless negative chattering. Thoughtforms create a cloud over the crown chakra which stops us engaging with our wise self. Their intention is to shift the etheric energy emitted by the crown chakra sideways so that the vertical etheric connection from the crown chakra upwards is skewed.

Thoughtforms have no respect for human beings. Their survival depends on us living in negative states: fear, violence, unhappiness, anger, hopelessness. They try to generate fear of death; for when we exit the body, it is much harder for them to affect us. Some souls, however, can become trapped by thoughtforms, even at death, and resist moving to the spirit reality.[16]

In the pharaonic tombs and in the ancient *Egyptian Book of the Dead*, the conditioning is portrayed as a being holding two knives, which represent duality. Sometimes, this being is shown as a monster that holds the soul back. Other times, it is shown as a person, symbolizing the earthly self under the influence of the conditioning. The two knives demonstrate the polarity of the world: one thing and its opposite. For example, the conditioning may say, "You are the best. You should be on top." Then it might say, "You are insignificant, no one respects you." These are the two knives at work, lifting us up and putting us down. The knives prevent us from resting in the middle ground where we find peace and balance through self-acceptance and self-respect.

Over time, the effects of the conditioning and thoughtforms can manifest physically as dis-ease, and unresolved emotional pain adds to the physical issue. In ancient Egypt, healing was holistic. It identified the connection between mental, emotional, and physical illness and the conditioning. It re-established the spiritual connection with the person's Divine self that could instigate a deeper level of healing and open a door towards awakening.

The emphasis was on creating a harmonious relationship with life: for life to flow, instead of being a struggle. The aim is to be at peace with ourselves and with life. And when our time comes, to be at peace with death.

Awakening — Two Key Activations

The ancient sites of Egypt create the potential for two key activations, which are an essential part of the awakening process.

- The consciousness centers inside the central channel at heart chakra level and an alignment takes place with the higher chakras. Effect: access to higher realms and their pool of knowledge opens to us. We channel and understand spiritual and cosmic truths we did not know before.
- Activation of our inner Light, the awakening of the Ba inside our Ib. Effect: we feel an incredible sense of peace and love emanating from our heart-center. Power in the form of etheric energy flows from us in waves of Light, working for the highest good. This power may create miracles in our life and the lives of people who come into contact with us.

Everyone possesses such an inner Light, for everyone has a Ba inside their Ib, but unless it is activated, we remain unaware of it. We only know this Light through experience. Start by setting an intention. Repeatedly ask yourself during meditation, "What is my inner Light?"

With power and knowledge comes responsibility. Following the direct experience of our Light, it is important we stay in our heart. Others will sense this Light, and may be attracted to us. Unfortunately, people can fall prey to their ego, be seduced by the power and admiration that others bestow, and lose their heart connection. This phenomenon happens in our world in the same way it occurred in ancient Egypt. Many priests and priestesses reached high levels of awareness, only to be trapped by unhealthy pride. They fell off Iset's ladder and could not self-generate the etheric Light that once flowed from them. They also became vulnerable to the thoughtforms that their inner Light had kept away.

Summary

The ancient Egyptians practiced sacred teachings that prepared them for death. Their architect-initiates built necropolises where high-frequency energies subdued the human conditioning. They capitalized on the presence of ley lines and erected pyramidal structures, in which they placed etheric portals that re-created the feeling of peace a person may experience at death. Initiates lay in the sarcophagi inside these structures and received attunements and activations. These portals and sacred temples are still available to us today, when we enter them with a pure intention to meditate for the highest good.

Spiritual Practice: Inside the Sarcophagus of Death and Eternal Life

Invite Iset, Im-Hot-Tep, and any other helping spirits of Light you work with to support you and create a safe, protected space around you.

Imagine lifting the veil of time and space and finding yourself in ancient Egypt. Walk through fields of emmer wheat and grass towards a river. As you approach the water, the initiates of the Living Light of past, present, and future, who work totally and wholly for the Light, greet you with palm leaves, an offering of peace. Im-Hot-Tep, the chief architect of the sacred sites, is your guide. Follow him as he takes you onto a barge, and cross the sacred river from the east to the west bank, arriving at Sakkara, the city of the dead, the place of silence and peace.

First Activation
Meditate in this energy field, asking for the alignment with your higher self to be strengthened. Im-Hot-Tep sits in front of you radiating his inner Light. Sacred geometrical symbols flow from his third eye to you. He says:

***

"*I see you. I see your Light. Everyone has the spiritual Light of Divine Consciousness. Etherically, your Light has been restricted, covered by the circumstances of your life and the heavier energy of the Earth reality. You have lost access to Ra, the state of the shining spirit. Access your inner Light and break through this dark cover. Your inner sun, Ra is within you. Shine your Light.*"

***

As you shine your Light, you may become aware that inside your Light is a sacred geometrical structure. Meditate now in this space of silence for 15 minutes. As you meditate, this sacred structure is strengthened.

Second Activation: The Door of Death and Life
Im-Hot-Tep takes you into a pyramidal structure that is accessed via an underground ramp. You enter a hallway and then turn right into a chamber. Inside there are two pictures: a depiction of Horan, the human being who has overcome the conditioning; and a human being in their luminous state after death.

At the end of the room is a sacred sarcophagus, placed inside the portal of death. Imagine lying in the sarcophagus. Intend, "May I become aware of my Light and express it in my life for my highest good." As the lid closes, imagine you are lying under the night sky, and above you is the whole of the cosmos.

Im-Hot-Tep says:

***

"Imagine that you are at the point of death, where you become aware of you Light. Your higher self begins to merge with you. Your earthly body, which was like a drop of water, now flows into and becomes the whole ocean. You become the whole of creation. All the universes and galaxies are inside you. You are one with everything.

To do this practice when you are alive is to become aligned."

***

Meditate in this space for 15–30 minutes.

See yourself coming out of the sarcophagus. Im-Hot-Tep blows the sacred breath of Iset into your third eye. Your third eye opens. He offers you the Ankh-eternal life, and places protection all around you.

Im-Hot-Tep thanks you for practicing these ancient truths. Exit the chamber and leave the pyramid. Above is the sun, Ra. Intend to embody the state of Ra for a few minutes and radiate Light in all directions. The more you radiate as Ra, the more your Light grows and burns away the conditioned clouds.

The veil of time and space descends. Walk through it and back to your own time.

Offer gratitude to Iset, Im-Hot-Tep, all the enlightened spirits who work with you, the initiates of the Living Light, and to yourself. Say that your spiritual work is now complete and ask that before the spirits leave, they completely protect and seal you, the room, and building.

Endnote

16 There are three reasons that lead a soul to remain around the Earth instead of moving to spirit, and multiple remedies. I refer you to my first book: Chapter Four — Surrendering to Death, before, during, and forever after. *The Golden Book of Wisdom: ancient spirituality and shamanism for modern times.* (Adrimi, 2018)

Chapter 17

The Universal Law of Ma'at: Divine Truth and Justice

Channeling from Iset:
In the world of duality, you were taught right from wrong. Yet what you call right action changes according to the times you live in, your culture, and beliefs. Your view of right and wrong is conditioned. There is a higher truth that you only know through opening your sacred heart. Your entire life is a teaching about this higher truth, about Ma'at. Everyone learns about Ma'at, even if they do not know that this is what they are doing. When you die, your whole life passes in front of you, and tears of gratitude and joy flow for the miracle you experienced, and the wisdom of your soul that created this incarnation to know Ma'at.

Ma'at as Truth — The Gift of the Times of Set versus the Gift of the First Time

We have lived many lives in different times of the Earth's history. Each incarnation offers a unique experience that our soul wishes to savor. The soul does not see life from the human perspective. Earthly challenges are regarded as opportunities for inner growth and personal expansion. And each era of human history, from Zep Tepi, the time of Ausir, to the modern times of Set, offer our soul a gift, a unique perspective of itself. Akin to the principle of yin and yang, there is never one aspect without the presence of the other, for this is a world of dualism. In the Golden Times, the seed of Set, conditioning and corruption, was there, but it rarely manifested. In our times of Set, where the chaos of the conditioning is visible, living life in an awakened way is not the norm. Still, the seeds of a harmonious reality are here, within everyone. During this time of transition from one era to another, these seeds start to sprout.

Ausir and Set are linked; in the myth they are twins. They create different cycles and life circumstances for us to reach the enlightened state. Generally, we say that the time of Ausir provides humanity with the opportunity to awaken through happiness. Whilst the time of Set teaches through lack and suffering. This is a period of hard, fast growth where the soul's evolution can accelerate. After Set is the age of Horan, where we acknowledge, transform, and heal from the influence of Set, and consciously choose to live in joy.

For the past few thousand years, humanity has adopted the law of survival of the fittest. We may think that this is the law of nature: that the stronger animal kills the weaker one. This only applies to some species. A younger stag may kill the older one, but the natural world has many examples of harmonious living. Elephants take care of their young and elderly, and live in community.

In the Golden Times, people lived in community, and everyone was valued. No one was more important than another. Society's collective wish was for each person to thrive and develop their inherent gifts. Knowing and developing our inherent gifts was part of creating Ma'at in our life. By being true to our calling, we honored the rule of Ma'at.

In contrast, the times of Set are a battleground between Set and Horan, within ourselves and in the world. The conditioning, ours and the collective's, discourages us from engaging with alternative spirituality, while the inner spirit yearns to manifest itself. The merits of this era are growing into our power, reclaiming our Divine self, and honoring and sharing the gifts we bring to this life, despite inner and outer obstacles.

In the world of Set, the individual rarely matters. As long as the whole continues to function and people conform, society is not interested in what happens to individuals. Hence, from a young age we learn to compromise our needs. This way of living is outside Ma'at. Ma'at always begins with ourselves. And when we disregard our needs, life is seldom harmonious, joyous, or satisfying.

Living in Accord with Divine Justice

In the Golden Times, people had compassion for everyone and endeavored to stay in their Divine connection of unconditional love. They understood that order is created when Divine love reigns. Without this soul connection, they knew that chaos would predominate and destroy their harmonious way of life. Hat-Hor, who had the title "She Who Creates Order," was seen as the manifested Ma'at, the order that makes corruption impossible.

To stay in their sacred heart and honor Ma'at, people lived a life of awareness. They examined their life, finding the places where Set crept in through the back door. They identified unskillful actions motivated by the conditioning, and looked for the deeper causes. What triggered them to do what they did? With compassion for themselves, they looked within for answers.

If someone created chaos, they were not judged or blamed. Help was offered rather than recrimination. They saw everyone in their Divine Light. They understood the state of Set as an illness or outside force that had deprived the individual of the ability to act skillfully. Divine justice has no condemnation for anyone. Blaming creates negative energy that is directed towards someone, or even ourselves. When we live in Ma'at, no matter what we or others do, we accept and forgive. Every life circumstance, and our response to it, is seen as an opportunity for learning. Then we apply the learning and act differently next time.

In this context, how could society hold the space of Hat-Hor for those manifesting the chaotic state of Set? In Zep Tepi, people saw the person who acted inappropriately as a valued member of their community who was projecting their inner suffering. This was something the community needed to address and apply the deeper principle of inner connectivity and oneness. As an analogy, if one part of the body ails, the whole organism suffers. For instance, your legs may be fine, but you have a migraine and cannot run the marathon today. Therefore the community looked beyond the person's actions for the deeper reason that motivated the soul's behavior. "Perhaps the person is unable to self-examine," they thought. "Maybe we can support them to see more clearly."

The rule of Ma'at works with the law of karma: everyone experiences the effect of their actions, thoughts, and words, positive and negative. When someone knows this law in their heart, they recognize that acting unskillfully towards others is an act of self-harm.

Set can only be abated through the development of the Hat-Hor state. Hat-Hor brings order where Set creates chaos. If a society wishes to thrive and grow, it must overcome Set by developing the higher awareness state of Hat-Hor.

People acknowledged that the virus of Set could spread in many ways. Maybe the person acting unskillfully experienced deep trauma, soul loss, which the ancient Egyptians referred to as "the wandering Ka."[17] Or, it could have been due to environmental psychic causes. An outside force, such as a lost soul may have attached to the person, influencing their thinking. Perhaps the spirits of the land where this person lived were upset. Maybe the ceremonies of gratitude to the Earth were neglected, or construction took place without first asking consent. External factors were examined and the relevant ceremonies and healing rituals were carried out to restore balance in the person and the community.

Sometimes it was recognized that some people carried an issue from a past incarnation. This karmic baggage could cloud their judgment and make them susceptible to the wiles of Set. However, the person incarnated in this community for a reason. No one is born by accident. There is order in everything, and the community looked deeper at the situation to discover the gift the person was bringing them.

In some rare cases, despite all the ceremonies, healing rituals, help, counseling, listening, and good advice, the person either refused to take responsibility for their actions or the deeper community work had no effect. The community then petitioned the star ancestors. It was believed that everyone who incarnated came initially from various star constellations. Each soul on Earth is a star seed. This may be why it is difficult for some people to feel at home here: the soul yearns for the place it originated from.

The star ancestors are the distant ancestors of the soul who resides in another cosmic place. The soul on Earth is not cut off from them, although it may have no idea of this connection. When we incarnated, we came as a representative of that star system, and our star ancestors observe and learn from our experiences of earthly life. When we are in difficulty, they may intercede and offer assistance.

In invoking the star ancestors, the community petitioned them, saying, "You are the star ancestors of our brother. We call on you to take care of him. He is stuck. We have tried to help him, as you have seen, but he is unable to live by the law of Ma'at and is harming himself and the community. We love him, but we can do no more. Please help your relative."

This invocation to the star ancestors was very effective. Many times, the person caught by Set had an epiphany that showed them the futility of their unskillful actions. The members of the community welcomed them back. The door was always open.

Then the person had to "balance the books," restore Ma'at, as much as possible. With the help of their elders and spiritual teachers, they decided how to compensate those they hurt in a fair way. For example, if someone stole from their neighbor, they may decide to work for them until the debt was repaid.

Changing Cycles: From Set to Horan

In Zep Tepi, everyone aspired to live in Ma'at. They knew that to live outside Ma'at would jeopardize their civilization, and the Golden Times would be lost, as they indeed were. They were aware that they lived in a precious time, and that this time of the heart would eventually cease and the time of Set, the corrupted mind, would come. They understood that in the beginning humanity would welcome Set, for Set knows how to cajole, influence, and manipulate. However, after thousands of years in this cycle, people would long for a harmonious way and would rise up and overcome Set.

We are currently living at the cusp between cycles, when our spirit calls us back to Ma'at while we still have full experience of Set. As more of us feel this calling and engage in personal development work, we see with growing awareness the damage the conditioning creates in ourselves and the world. As we unveil the Light of our inner essence that is always in Ma'at, we find the world of Set incompatible with this Light and are motivated to change our way of thinking, living, and being.

The world of Set creates difficult circumstances. It is full of drama, pain, destruction, and a lack of joy. Set is like a hungry monster that is never happy.

Set is neither good nor bad. Seen outside duality, Set acts as a mirror. It manifests the various circumstances where we see the issues we carry. Set knows our buttons and pushes them. Set shows us the hurts and unhealed trauma. Set is strong and does not release its hold on us easily. We may find ourselves reliving similar circumstances, even when we know they are not good for us, and our inner voice asks us to make better choices. Overcoming Set is not straightforward.

The Egyptian prophecies speak about this time of transition. They say that the era of Set will come to an end when three things happen:

- First, the papyrus plant will appear. The papyrus represents learning about esoteric and mystical ways. People will be drawn to the study of spiritual arts and discover their inner abilities.
- Second, the ibis bird will arrive. Ibis is Djehuti, Divine wisdom. We will detach from the conditioning and access our inner wisdom. We will apply this wisdom in our life.
- Third, the lotus flower will emerge. The lotus has two meanings: awareness (blue lotus) and unconditional love (white lotus). We will open our all-seeing eye and see clearly. We develop unconditional love so that we can reach the enlightened state.

Invoking the Star Ancestors for Help to Be in Ma'at

We can work with our star ancestors and ask for support for ourselves and for the world community.

Invocation to the Star Ancestors:
"My star ancestors, in the Golden Times we came to you and asked for help with members of our community. At that time we knew our Divine connection and the way of Ma'at. Now our world is governed by Set, and we are on the brink of destroying the Earth and ourselves. There is much pain, and sadness, and goodness too. Underneath the hurt and pain, we are always Ma'at, for this is our inherent state. However, fear and trauma have taken us out of Ma'at. I ask you to help me and my human tribe understand the ways of Ma'at. I ask for your help to live in balance and release Set."

After such an invocation, I received a channeling from the star ancestors for all of us on the spiritual journey:

The Star Ancestors Speak About Our Times:
We come with so much compassion for you. We have heard your words. You may believe sometimes that you are lost, that you have not done enough, and do not have enough time. And collectively you may think, "I look at this world and see injustice and corruption, and nothing changes." Set is truly with you and in your world. The purpose of these times is to find and grow into your power that says, "I will overcome Set and reclaim my power. I will keep saying no to Set."

This is the shift that is happening in these times because you can see Set now, even if it is only a glimpse at a time. When you see Set in yourself, say, "I have suffered enough by giving away my power to what Set tells me to do. I find the way to my Divine connection, through my Divine heart." This is the road you must take. There is so much support for you and everyone who has the intention, "I truly wish to awaken. I truly wish to find a way back to my Divine self." Even if you think the road is difficult, and you should be further along in your development, know that this road is perfect for you.

Thank you for walking this road. You are not lost. We have such respect for you and are in awe of what each of you is doing. It is a high mountain to climb, but you are strong. Thank you.

Summary

In Zep Tepi, people lived in Ma'at, in supportive community. The rule of Ma'at spoke about Divine truth. One of the invocations the initiates worked with was "I have not spoken lies wittingly, nor have I done aught with deceit. I am in Ma'at."

Ma'at means Divine justice, the universal law of cause and effect, known also as karma. Our life experience is based on this law, as we learn about ourselves through our responses to different events. Divine justice is based on the principle of awareness rather than punishment and recrimination. In our world of Set, it can be difficult to live in accord with the principles of Ma'at. At such times, we develop compassion for ourselves and connect to our star ancestors who support us in our earthly journey.

Spiritual Practice: Restoring Ma'at — Truth and Justice

Open a sacred space by inviting Iset, Ma'at, and any spirits of the Light you work with. Ask them to create a sacred space around you.

Imagine being inside the Great Pyramid, in the healing chamber connected to Sirius, as it was in the Golden Times. Ma'at comes to you as a woman with wings wearing a long white feather on her head. She holds the scales of justice. On one scale, she places the white feather, and on the other, your heart. She says that through life circumstances Set has come over your heart. "Now I invite you to release all that you hold in your heart that is heavy: regrets, pain, doubts, let go of anything that stops you being in Ma'at. Allow your heart to be light and free."

Energy flows around and through you, helping you release. Say, "May my heart be as light as the feather. May the scales of Ma'at be balanced."

Ask that your heart be as light as the day you were born. All the heaviness, regrets, trauma, and suffering are not who you are.

Meditate in this space for 10 minutes. If any doubts or difficult thoughts arise, say, "I release you; this is not who I am. I am Divine essence. I am Light."

After a while, imagine that the scales are completely balanced. The inner you is Ma'at — Divine truth and Divine justice. Ma'at comes to you again, holds her feather, and touches your third eye. She says, "May you have awareness of Ma'at in your life." She takes the feather and places it inside your heart-center. Merged with the feather, you become Ma'at.

In front of you, imagine the Earth as it is currently. Radiate unconditionally the Light of Ma'at to the planet for 5 minutes.

Ma'at thanks you for offering Ma'at to the world. She places protection around you.

Your spiritual work is complete. It is time to leave the chamber. Slowly bring yourself back.

Close your sacred space by thanking Iset and Ma'at, and other enlightened beings you invoked. Ask that, before they go, they seal and protect you, the room you are in, and your home.

Endnote

16   Soul loss: when we experience trauma or shock, part of our soul may leave the body as life becomes too challenging. We may feel numb inside, as if our spark is missing. (Adrimi, 2018)

Chapter 18

The Universal Law of Ma'at: Divine Order and Manifestation

Channeling from Iset:
The law of Divine order is the law that keeps everything in the universe in place. The law speaks about creation and manifestation and governs change and destruction. Creation — birth, life, and death are all under the law of Divine order, for nothing can exist unless it is in Divine order. If anyone tries to manifest something that is not in Divine order, for example through the corrupted powers of Set, it will fall. The rule of Ma'at is absolute. Even the chaos of Set is in perfect Divine order.

Ma'at as Truth, Justice, and Divine Order

The ancient initiates worked consciously with three aspects of Ma'at:

- *Ma'at as Truth.* They practiced honesty and aspired to always speak the truth. In our everyday life, we may lie, even to ourselves. Our inner voice tells us something and we ignore or placate it and choose to believe an untruth that is more comfortable. For instance, Mary knew instinctively that her husband was unfaithful, but in her conditioned mind she held the image of a happy marriage. Even when her husband's boss confronted her, she called him a liar. When we fib, we lose part of our life-force energy. Even if we lie so as not to offend, or to keep the peace, we still lose power; our soul and life hear us denying the truth.

- *Ma'at as Divine justice.* In the Golden Times, all strived to live a just life, respecting themselves and each other. And people took responsibility for their actions. In the concept of oneness, each person is part of us, and being unjust to another is an act of self-harm.
- *Ma'at as Divine order.* This is a fundamental principle that creates flow in our life and inner freedom when understood and applied.

The Universal Law of Divine Order

This law permeates all aspects of life, all dimensions and realities. It declares that everything that exists in the manifested world is in perfect Divine order. Everything is balanced. Even the chaotic states and destruction we experience on Earth are in perfect order.

To begin to comprehend the workings of this law, we regard life from the soul's perspective prior to incarnation. Imagine your soul is in the spirit realms of the Light, what the ancient Egyptians called "the upper regions of the sky." Your soul looks at the theatre of life on Earth and all the possible opportunities for expansion. The soul wants a diverse and enriching journey so that it can evolve through various experiences, clear any karma, and open up to its Light and authenticity. Conversely, when we incarnate and adopt the ego state, our conditioned mind aims to protect us from experiences and live a life with few ups and downs. Thus the soul plans a journey incorporating many landmarks and different places to visit, and the egoic mind finds a road that avoids as many of these places as possible. The ups and downs of life have been designed by our soul in absolute Divine order to wake us up from the Lethe of the conditioned reality so that deeper understanding arises from within.

All that we experience individually in any given moment, even the difficulties, are in Divine order. There are no accidents and no coincidences. Things are as they are meant to be. Every circumstance carries within it a pearl of wisdom. When we live life immersed in the conditioned mind, we are oblivious to this. With hindsight, we may realize why things happened in a certain way, and that even the most onerous situations contributed to who we are today, even though we would not wish to relive them.

Life challenges can be met more easily when we accept what is happening. Then we observe the situation from a detached perspective, perceive its purpose, and gather the pearls. The ancient initiates viewed life as a teacher. They had great awareness, developed through years of dedicated spiritual practice with HEKA. Spiritual truths and gifts of knowledge arose from within, and life brought experiences that they worked through. Facing a challenge, they adopted an objective view and asked, "What is the gift of this situation? What is the karma? What is this experience teaching me?" They asked these questions in meditation, creating an intention for deep realization. At some point, an answer emerged and offered greater clarity. When such a cognizance happens, it is like a "eureka" moment. In Tibetan Buddhism these moments are compared to being struck by a lightning bolt.

Often, by knowing what is behind a problem, we see another path or find a solution we may not have envisaged. Sometimes, the understanding is sufficient and nothing needs to be done. Other times, the issue diminishes. For example, Frank had a debilitating pain in his back and could not sit down. Through his spiritual work, he resolved the issue energetically: he saw the emotional trauma that triggered the pain and then worked to release the stuck energy. (Dr. Sarno, a late Professor of Rehabilitation Medicine at New York University Medical Centre helped thousands of patients by encouraging them to find the emotional cause of their chronic physical pain, instead of pursuing mainstream medical treatment. (Ozanich, 2016))

Once the gift of awareness comes, we often do not need to live through the experience again, either fully or partly.

We can apply the same principles when affected by world events. We are part of the collective, and our souls chose to incarnate during these times. In difficult global situations, instead of going into fear, anger, and despair, we can look deeper and find the gift in the situation. And when we find the gift, through surrender, acceptance, and awareness, we ride the waves and improve our life experience. Even when a fire consumes the forest, a tree may be unscathed. The tree accepted the fire and death and surrendered, so the fire said to it, "You no longer need me." We can all be that tree.

Manifesting a New Reality through the Rule of Ma'at

The law of Divine Order is determined by our vibration as etheric beings. We all have a particular band of etheric energy frequencies we work with. At different times throughout the day, our vibration rises and falls within this band. For example, when we meditate, we access a high frequency within our band. When we become angry, frustrated etc., our vibration lowers. When we open our heart, we expand into higher frequencies again.

This band of frequencies creates a resonance that attracts specific situations to us. Think of the scales of Ma'at. We are on one of the scales with our distinct band of frequencies. On the other scale are all the life circumstances that resonate with this band. In order to alter our life circumstances and manifest a higher reality for ourselves that is in Divine order, we will have to raise our vibration, to initiate and experience a leap in frequency to a higher band.

Frequency is linked to awareness. As we grow in spiritual wisdom, we can clear our vibration and shift our frequency to a higher band. Creating such an energy shift takes time. It is not instant. And when we engage in such shifts, life becomes more stable and quieter. We are protected and almost secluded from the world so that we can focus on our spiritual work. Our needs are met, and nothing much changes in our external circumstances. How long does this quiet period last? This energy shift and increased awakening has its own unique timescale. It cannot be hurried, even if our mind is impatient. Once the energy shift is complete, life changes by itself. Miracles, synchronicities, and events manifest a different reality for us. This new resonance with the outside world will then attract different circumstances to us.

Working with Divine order for the purposes of manifestation requires considerable surrendering, spiritual practice, and awakening to our inner wisdom. Maybe there is a deep wish within us to create a new reality. Does this wish come from our heart or our ego? If it is ego based, even if we manifest it, the new reality will not bring us the joy and expansion we anticipated. And eventually it will fail, sometimes in a challenging way that shows us this was not a wise choice. This is why our wish for a new reality needs to come from our sacred heart.

Our heart may show us an incredible dream and potential, this may even be our life's purpose, that will take time to materialize. Creating a new reality for our highest good requires a huge leap of faith as well as a leap in frequency and patience. The challenge is to continue nurturing our dream whilst staying true to ourselves and the wishes of our soul. As time passes, our ego-mind may get disgruntled and disheartened. We may get angry with ourselves and jealous of people who have manifested what we wish for. In ancient Egypt this energy of the disappointed ego was portrayed as a monster or as a hungry animal that is never satisfied, called Ammit. This animal nature can consume our heart, erode our confidence, dampen our Light, and cause us to give up.

Manifesting through Divine order is the most perfect manifestation. Through our continual spiritual and personal work we grow into the person, situation, and way of life we wish to create. Our soul finds its deep calling. We embody more of our Divine spirit and gradually awaken into the being of grace we are. We are filled with gratitude and awe for the gift of life. What an incredible life this is, we think.

In the Halls of Ma'at — The Weighing of the Heart

In many pharaonic tombs and papyruses, we find the depiction of a fundamental ritual used in many initiation practices. This ritual, currently referred to as "The Weighing of the Heart," was widespread and demonstrates the teaching of Ma'at as Divine order.

In the ritual, the key Neteru were present in their role as the Lords of Karma to ensure that everything was done in accordance with the universal laws. Their presence created a sacred space for the ritual to take place. In the center, the priest of Onpu, representing the guardian of the keeper of the ancient knowledge that leads to awareness, held the scales of Ma'at. Onpu is also a guide who enables the Ka to access the higher realities, for this ritual was done in the in-between space between physical life and the spiritual realm of Light.

The scales of Ma'at were significant. At the top of the scales was a statuette of a baboon, symbolizing Djehuti, the wisdom of the enlightened state that comes through contact with the spiritual Light. Djehuti, in his form as the ibis bird, was the scribe who records the wisdom that the scales share. In this role he is the keeper of the Akashic records that document each soul's journey of awakening through incarnation and reincarnation. Another key presence stood next to the scales. This was the infinite spirit, the Ba, of the person for whom the ritual was conducted, portrayed as a bird with a human face. The Ba was the observer of its earthly counterpart. At one end of the room were the enlightened spirits of the ancestors living in the harmonious state of spirit, and at the other end was Ammit, representing the physical duality and the ego-mind.

The feather of Ma'at was placed on one scale, while a papyrus with the name of the person in hieroglyphs, symbolizing the heart, was placed on the other. The person then connected with what they wished to manifest. If this was in Divine order, the scales would balance. Otherwise the request came from the ego-mind and the ritual was deemed unsuccessful.

Initiation into the Priesthood

During the Golden Times, part of the temple complexes were accessible to everyone. All could enter, experience the Living Light, and receive teachings. Some people wished to deepen their spiritual journey and become initiates, the living channels of the etheric energies. The priests and priestesses were called "the Servants of Ma'at," translated as "the Servants of Truth."

Those who wished to join the priesthood would live in the temple for a while. They would receive an initial initiation and then go through a preparatory stage where they studied foundation teachings, practiced meditation, undertook energy work, and served in the temple in some way. When they felt ready, they could ask to receive the main initiation into the priesthood and become an initiate of the path of Iset, the living channel of HEKA.

Their entrance into the priesthood was determined through the ritual of the weighing of the heart described above. They would meet Ma'at, and if their frequency resonated with that of the priesthood, if there was Divine order and the scales balanced, they were admitted.

On the day of the initiation, the person was blindfolded and led through different gates of the temple so that they would become disorientated, unaware of where they were. Each part of the temple carried different etheric portals, seven different gates, known as the Seven Gates of Awareness. As the potential initiate passed through each of the Seven Gates and was immersed in the different energies, their ego subsided, as did their need to know what was happening.

After this walk, the person arrived at the initiation chamber, the Halls of Ma'at, and the blindfold was removed. Priests and priestesses dressed as the Neteru, wore the relevant headdress, carried their respective staffs, and merged spiritually with these beings. A priestess of Ma'at asked the potential initiate standard questions. These questions had fixed responses which the candidate had memorized. This helped them feel relaxed and confident about the process. Then, the priestess asked questions channeled directly from Ma'at. The aim was to help the candidate and temple staff decide whether this was the right path for the person. Was the person drawn to the mysteries because they had an open heart and wanted to serve the community, or did they seek power and recognition? Was spiritual study a part-time interest, or was the person willing to make spirituality a way of life?

After the questions and answers, the priestess of Ma'at removed an ostrich feather from her headdress and, with her eyes closed, placed it on one of the scales of justice, held by the priest of Onpu. On the other scale was the papyrus with a drawing of the heart and the name of the candidate written in the sacred language of hieroglyphs. Depending on how the feather was placed, the scales would be balanced or lopsided.

If the scales were balanced, the candidate was admitted into the priesthood. They would then be prepared through meditation, fasting, and silence, to receive the initiation into the First Gate of Awareness. If the scales were unbalanced, the priestess of Ma'at channeled guidance for the candidate, which the priest of Djehuti wrote down and gave to the person. For example, they may be invited to take part in a purification ritual, go on a pilgrimage to a holy shrine, or meditate in a particular temple and discover more about themselves. Suggestions were given to help the candidate open their heart and establish a stronger spiritual connection.

Most people were rejected the first time. This was deliberate: to test the candidate's commitment to walk a spiritual path. Many candidates were saddened or angered by the "rejection." Elder priests waited outside the chamber to encourage the candidates, but some wanted guarantees. They asked, "If I go on this long pilgrimage, which is a big sacrifice, will I be accepted next time?" Of course no human person could tell them what Ma'at would say, or what the feather of truth would do the next time. It was said that only the feather knew what was right for each person, as it could see into their heart.

The Story of My Spirit Guide: Every High Priest Starts from Somewhere
One of my spirit guides experienced an incarnation as a High Priest during the Golden Times. He appears to me as a humble, respectful man with a witty smile. He is originally a star being from Sirius. In his quest to enter the temple, he was turned away six times. His seventh attempt was so joyous he gave thanks for all the other "failures." He shares his story.

"I arrived at the temple when I was sixteen. From an early age, I wanted to become a priest, but I had to wait until my brothers grew up and could help in the fields. As soon as my family released me, I left our village to go to the magnificent temple that we had visited many times. As I child, I somehow knew I belonged there. I had dreams telling me this was my path, to become a priest, a Servant of Ma'at.

When I arrived, I was initially accepted and welcomed by the temple community. My teachers were kind and encouraging. With their guidance, I could see auras, even the Neteru appeared to me. I could truly channel, feel, and see the energy. I could do this without the main initiation into the Gates of Awareness. My teachers were surprised and happy for me. They recognized me as an old soul. My classmates admired how quickly I was progressing. When the time for the initiation came, I was almost sure I would get in first time. I had a big expectation about the outcome.

I was blindfolded and taken round and round the temple and finally arrived in the Halls of Ma'at. The teachers and priests were all dressed as the Neteru and looked very serious. A priestess of Ma'at asked me why I was there, and I had to speak aloud my intention of wishing to be a Servant of Truth. The priest who was merged with Djehuti wrote down my intention and my name in hieroglyphs and placed it on one of the scales. Ma'at approached the scales holding the feather. The feather did not even touch the scales. It dropped straight to the floor. The priestess looked at me and said my heart was not ready. She advised me to focus on the meditation practices for a while and then, if I wished, I could try again.

I was devastated. I took the papyrus from Djehuti and went outside. The old priests were waiting for me. They were sympathetic, telling me that almost no one was accepted first time. I was disappointed but did as I was asked. I focused on meditation for a few months and tried again. The same thing happened. Ma'at told me my heart was not ready, and this time she said I should go on a pilgrimage to the turquoise temple of Hat-Hor, in the desert. This was a big undertaking that required a lot of preparation, resources, food, and I had to find a caravan that would take me there. It seemed so difficult. Yet when I came out of the room, the priests encouraged me to find a way, and somehow I made it happen. I came back from the pilgrimage and tried again. And again. All together I tried six times. I saw other classmates being accepted, and my mind was so angry, as I was much more psychic. I wanted to tell myself that Ma'at was wrong; she was a stupid priestess who just did not like me. Many times, I almost walked away. But something kept bringing me back.

Finally, I tried for the seventh time. It was a magical day. I woke up with such joy that I found everything beautiful, even the voices of the donkeys that used to annoy me. I realized that everything on Earth had been created with such care and love, even myself; I was a

Divine child of love. I fell to my knees and cried because my heart was breaking open with gratitude. I tried not to think about the ritual, as I did not want to lose this feeling of joy. After the tears, I was elated. I loved the temple so much, and knew this was where I belonged.

At first, I so wanted to be a priest that I thought it was my right. In my mind I had already planned on becoming the High Priest, such was my inflated opinion of myself. But that morning, I knew it did not matter how I served the temple. I would sweep the floors or wash the dishes just to be there. The realization brought me peace and happiness, and the dread of looking again at what the feather would do subsided.

This time in my initiation, Ma'at looked straight at me. She never closed her eyes. She put the feather on the scales without breaking eye contact with me. And I saw her for what she is: Divine order, everything connected to everything, the celestial bodies, the cosmos, every single life form being part of Divine order and having a place. Mesmerized by the vision of Ma'at, I never looked at the feather. Then, in the distance I heard people cheering and ululating. I had been accepted. Divine order had been restored within me, and I had a place. No matter how far I went into the priesthood, even becoming the High Priest towards the end of my human life, I never forgot the teaching of that day.

This is my story of initiation by Ma'at: truth, justice, and order. In your world, there are no such rituals. Ma'at speaks through your life, even if you do not think so. The feather always knows. Trust the process of your life. Trust in Divine order to guide you and open you up to serve your highest purpose, to serve the truth that you are."

Summary

Ma'at has three different aspects. In the beginning, Ma'at is seen as truth, then she transforms into justice, and finally, we meet Ma'at as Divine order. Everything is created in perfect Divine order, even the challenges and chaos in our life have an important role to play as they have been designed by our spirit to lead us on a path towards enlightenment. As we develop our awareness through spiritual work, we realize that our frequency and vibration have a resonance with the experiences we meet in life. Ma'at is cosmic order, and we are part of that order. As we evolve and become conscious manifestors of our reality, our etheric frequency rises to match the vibration of what we wish to manifest. Spiritual expansion gradually shifts us to the next stage of our life.

Chapter 19

Death, Resurrection, Reincarnation

Channeling from Iset:
Imagine you are inside a small room and can only see outside through two tiny windows. You only hear certain sounds that come from two little openings in a wall. You only smell what is in front of you. In this space, you are restricted to the limited view of what exists around you. This room is your body. The tiny windows are your eyes. The openings in the wall are your ears. Your body limits your ability to perceive. As you step onto your spiritual path and practice the ways of Light, you start to see with your spirit eyes and hear with your spirit ears. You start to sense there is another world to discover, yet you are still limited. At some point, you find the door into a world of Light you only glimpsed before. It looks familiar and welcoming. Death is the door that takes you into this place of wider perception. However, this room you have been in may feel so dear to you that you are loath to let it go, even as it crumbles and disintegrates around you. Walk into the Light, child of the Divine consciousness, and open your spirit eyes, your spirit ears, and your spirit mouth. When it is time to go through the spirit door, do not turn back; a new life awaits you. Walk into the Light free, with no regrets.

The Death Door to the Enlightened Self: The Way of the Initiate

The ancient initiates prepared for their physical death. They saw death as a gateway to a new life in spirit. During their life, they enacted the process of death. When actual death happened, they hoped to automatically go into their practice and peacefully leave the earthly world. There was also a secondary benefit.

By enacting their death whilst living, they connected to the Ka and Ba, the multidimensional self and the infinite spirit respectively, and brought this essence of spiritual Light into their body, increased their vibration, and progressed on their spiritual path.

For the ancient initiates, life and death were just different states of consciousness. In the former, they experienced the physical world through the conditioned reality and the five senses, and observed the shaping of the personality and its transformation into the spiritual self through their mystical practices. In the latter, the personality was a redundant vehicle. As the spiritual self emerged, they reclaimed the aspect that is eternity and everlastingness.

For the initiate, the intention behind life and death was the same: soul evolution, enlightenment, and ascension.

The Death Meditation of Merging with the Spiritual Self

Below, I have included the spiritual practice that the ancient initiates worked with during their lifetime, in order to prepare for death and also transform the earthly self through the Light of their spirit.

***

"A path opens for you; a path calls you. A path opens for you on the horizon, a path of clear Light. As you walk this path, you enter the sphere of Light that exists in your eighth chakra. The path takes you into states of higher awareness. As you ascend this path, you leave behind material life; you become the infinite spirit." (Channeling from Iset).

***

The Death Practice

Open your sacred space by welcoming Iset and any enlightened spirits you work with. Ask them to create a protected space around you. Then follow the practice below.

In a peaceful state, take your awareness into your body, as if you could see inside your body. Focus on your central channel, the central meridian. Imagine that inside this channel exists a sphere of brilliant Light. Connect with this sphere and merge with its shining Light.

Imagine a bright, luminous path opening in front of you. The path leads upwards through your chakras. Allow yourself to float upwards inside this path. The path ends at the top of your crown chakra where everything becomes clear and you are embraced by peace. Above your crown is the eighth chakra: a large ball of brilliant Light. Take your awareness into this ball of Light and merge with it. This Light is peace, harmony, and infinity. Stay in this space for 10 minutes being the Light.

Afterwards, it is time to return to your body. As this immense Light, see yourself floating back down into your body through your crown, third-eye, and throat chakras into your heart-center. Stay in your heart chakra and allow your spiritual Light to expand and radiate into your whole body, every cell. You have done this before. When you incarnated, you brought the infinite self into the physical body. Welcome yourself back into the body: your home for now. Allow the Light that you are to fully embody your physical self.

Meditate in this space for 21 minutes, bringing the infinite peace and spirit that you are into your body and life.

At the end of the meditation, close your sacred space by thanking Iset and your helping spirits. Ask that, before they go, they completely seal and protect you, the room, and place you are in.

Note: This is a very powerful practice. When you come back into your body as the infinite self, the Light that you bring may dislodge parts of the conditioning in your body. The conditioning is of a lower vibration compared to your spiritual Light. As it is released, you may feel nauseous, or have visions of the situations that created it, which may be from other lives. In the Golden Times, people had support from their peers and they received healing, counseling, and therapy work so that they could transform the heavy energy. When things arise, you may wish to find a therapist who will help you release the conditioning and heal the trauma you unknowingly carry.

How the Practice Works

Inside our body lies our consciousness. While living, we are not aware of this Light consciousness; there is no distinction between the body and the consciousness. We identify with our body. At the time of death, the consciousness tries to exit the body. At this point, if we relax, a path of Light opens, and our consciousness rises inside the central channel to the top of the head, where there is a direct link with the spirit realms through "the throne of Iset." This link takes us into the eighth chakra, above the crown, where the Ka, the multi-dimensional self resides. We then merge with the Ka and leave the physical realm. We enter the spirit worlds in our Ka with an increased level of awareness that has the potential to instigate full enlightenment: a permanent state of oneness where the soul may choose not to reincarnate.

When you do this practice, you may enjoy the Light of the infinite self but also discover how heavy the body is. Some people find it difficult to make peace with their physical life and wish to escape. They may have had suicidal thoughts in the past and wonder why they should stay in the world, when the Light consciousness is so beautiful. Escape is not the aim of the practice. It is important to accept the physical reality and what it is showing you. Instead of running from it, work to transform it. If you die prematurely, you will have to come back and revisit the issues you sought to avoid. The aim is always to embody the Living Light consciousness while in a body: to become enlightened while living. As you prepare for death, it is vital to honor your life in the best way you can.

Meeting the Neteru at Death — Another Way Home

The initiates practiced these meditations and rituals throughout their life so that they could embrace death, merge with their Light, float upwards, and enter the spirit state. However, no matter how much we practice, no one can know in advance how they will respond at the time of their passing. What if we experience a sudden or traumatic death? What happens if we panic and cannot relax? What if we go into shock and completely forget our training? There is another door, another possibility towards spiritual expansion at death.

When an initiate felt they were dying, the community came together to help them remember the spiritual teachings. They created sacred space and repeated this intention to them:

***

"May I become like Ra, a Shining One amongst the Shining Ones. May I become like the untiring stars, the stars that are never tired of shining their light, illuminating the darkness."

***

Then, as a precautionary measure, the community invoked the Divine principle the deceased worked with most during their life. If they were, for example, a priestess of Iset, the community would primarily chant specific hymns that invoked Iset. Then the deceased would merge with the Neter. If the community was unsure of who to invoke, they invoked Ausir, the enlightened heart in the spirit world. The more the initiate allowed themselves to enter the spirit state and detach from the physical world, the greater the possibility for the door of death to become a door of spiritual expansion. If they followed their spiritual teachings, they bypassed what we call the first death (see the following section) and moved immediately to the state of the Infinite Spirit (second death state).

To recap, these are the possibilities open to initiates at death:

- The consciousness merges with the Ka in the eighth chakra: possibility for full enlightenment.
- The consciousness merges with the Neter: a lesser possibility for full enlightenment and most probably experiences the second death.
- The consciousness is unable to see the Neter and follows the deceased ancestors: experiences the first death and then the second death, similar to everyone who is not an initiate.
- The consciousness refuses to move into the Light and is stuck in the physical realm as a ghost (or Khat).

Another Door That Leads Back Home: The Way of the Everyday Person

The practices above were the ways of those who dedicated all or part of their life to the spiritual teachings of the Light. However, in the ancient times everyone received help. Below, I offer an account of how death was approached during Zep Tepi.

Everyone understood that death was a natural process in which the physical body died and the soul survived. All were taught that at the time of death the spiritual self emerged out of the body and became ever-present. What died with the body was the Khaibit, the ego-self, the conditioned personality. The ego is afraid of death and panics, because once the spiritual self emerges, the ego dissolves. The fear people experience when they think of their death is the ego's fear.

When the body dies, the soul must leave. Even if the soul resists moving out of the body, at some point the body will disintegrate. As a person approaches death, their spirit helpers, deceased ancestors, and friends come to offer comfort and support and show them the way to the spirit realms of the Light.

Sometimes people's fear of death keeps them attached to this reality and they ignore the path of Light that opens. Or, they may feel the love and emotional pull of their living relatives who do not wish to let them go. Either way, these people do not enter the higher awareness of the spirit state. They may become ghosts or stay trapped in lower realms (known as the lower astral plane). To avoid such a fate, the ancient Egyptians had complex rituals that offered help to the person who died.

Prior to the body being placed in a tomb, a priest would perform a ritual called "The Opening of the Mouth for the Dead." The aim was to remind the soul that they were alive and that they needed to move on to the spirit realms in the company of the Neteru. The priest recited a sacred text and touched different parts of the person's mummy with an instrument made of meteorite iron that had three prongs. For example, the priest touched the person's mouth and said, "Your spirit mouth is now split open; you can speak." He touched the nose and said, "Your spirit nose is now open; you are alive; you can breathe," and he touched their eyes and said, "Your spirit eyes are now open; you can see."

The priest encouraged the person to let go of the "inert state." Inert because the body was dead and also because the spirit was also energetically stuck and not moving to the other side. The meteorite instrument was a sacred object. When the priest channeled Light through it, it acted as an energy flint that lit a spark and activated the person's etheric body.

After the rituals, the body was taken into the tomb, which was then sealed, physically and etherically. This meant that the tomb was now in the in-between place, between the physical world and the world of the dead, the door to the spirit realms. The inside of the tomb had painted or carved doorways, which archeologists refer to as "false doors." These doors were portals that opened etherically to the spirit realms of the Light. The soul of the deceased could stay for as long as it wished inside their tomb and move to the spirit realms through the portal when it was ready. The physical and etheric seals ensured the soul could not leave the tomb and harass the community. If someone could not afford a tomb, a miniature terracotta house was constructed, and they would seal the soul there until it was ready to move on.

Every day, till the soul went to the spirit realms, a priest or family member would visit the tomb or miniature home. They would greet the person and make offerings of food, saying to them that they were alive, remembered, and encouraging them to move on. Inside the tombs, there may have been images of the spiritual realms of the first death, showing the deceased that they could still enjoy everything they loved during their life. For instance, they might see themselves dining with their family, walking in the fields, and hunting. By looking at the familiar pictures, it was hoped that the deceased would feel comfortable about passing to the other side. The message was: "You have not missed out by dying; everything you want or need will be provided for you."

A soul cannot be forced to move into the spiritual realms; it needs to be the soul's choice. Everyone has free will, and each soul decides when to move on. At the same time, some souls are not in a peaceful state of mind when they die. So the community would wish to help them but also protect itself from ghosts by placing etheric boundaries around the tombs.

Most of the tombs people visit nowadays in Egypt are empty; souls either moved on when they died or shortly afterwards. However, there are a few cases where souls remained in their tomb for thousands of years. Time is only an aspect of the physical reality. In the spirit reality, time does not exist, and people may have no notion that they have been inside their tombs for millennia. When the tombs are opened, the etheric boundary disappears. This may be distressing for the soul, as their world is disturbed. The soul may attach to a living person in an effort to find help, and inadvertently cause this person mental or physical illness.

The First Death

Those who do not follow the mystical ways of death experience a double death. Immediately after physical death, the soul's awareness multiplies, as the etheric portal from Orion radiates Light frequencies towards them. The soul begins to release their earthly self and move on with a greater understanding, following deceased relatives. If they manage to pass to the other side, they have a life review, and they find themselves in a world of Light, illuminated by the Light of their own spirit. The first place the soul moves to is the realm of the first death. They meet their loved ones, and everything is made to look familiar. For instance, they may find themselves in a lovely home specially prepared for them, where they can do the things they enjoyed in their earthly life. They experience instant manifestation: if, for example, they wish for a sports car, it appears magically in front of them.

Gradually the soul's awareness grows as they heal from the earthly existence through love and release all that happened to them in life. They realize the deeper purpose behind the various circumstances they experienced. They heal their etheric body, and all traces of disease and trauma are alleviated. At this time, they may look towards their living relatives and try to help them, or go through a medium and offer messages of support and comfort. This state of the first death may last a long time. Some people stay in this place until their loved ones, their partner, or children die, so as to reunite with them.

At the same time, the soul may wish to expand. In the spirit realms, there are many opportunities to increase our spiritual awareness. One of the most coveted "jobs" is to become a spirit guide to the living. Souls may seek out people who do spiritual work such as healing, therapy, or mediumship to become a helping spirit and develop further. Unfortunately, with so many people living a material life, jobs for spirit guides are at a premium. If you wish to work in holistic healing and help others, do not wait until you are dead. Take the opportunity to do this work in your life, right now.

A Dream for the Healer

As I was facilitating a 21-day retreat, I had a significant dream. When I shared this with the participants, who were all initiates, many found a deep resonance. Perhaps it has relevance for you.

"In the dream, Mark had trained as a healer, but lacked confidence. He wanted to do healing work, but his mind held him back. Mark was not psychic, and he felt that if people came for an energy healing, they would expect him to be a medium. Many times he thought of offering sessions, but his mind always discouraged him. Unbeknownst to him, Mark had a spirit guide from his neighborhood who had died young in a motorbike accident. This person, called John, had experienced the first death and was looking to train as a spirit healer. He saw that Mark had completed energy healing courses and was hoping Mark would

work with people. John had so much to teach Mark. Unfortunately Mark never did anything. Two years later, Mark died from a sudden heart attack.

When Mark passed, he realized that part of his life journey was to do healing work. This would have helped other people as well as himself. Now it was too late. Mark thought his only option was to work with a person as a helping spirit guide, and he was keen to do this. As he experienced his first death, Mark met up with John, who told him of his own difficulties in trying to find a living person to work with. He told Mark that he had waited for a long time for him to do healing work. But that day never came.

The Second Death

Soul evolution does not stop with death, and it may accelerate after we pass. In the spirit realms, the soul can continue to expand and will, at some point, experience what is called the second death. This is when the soul experiences a shift in awareness and sees itself as the pure consciousness of the Divine spirit. There is no attachment to earthly life and no wish to support relatives or involve itself with earthly affairs. This is the ultimate healing for a soul. All experiences from all incarnations become wisdom. The soul can then share this wisdom with all, because it is aware that it is all. The soul experiences oneness.

In the ancient *Egyptian Book of the Dead*, they describe how the initiate of the Living Light, who has spent his life in spiritual practice, finds himself in the pure state of the Divine essence.

***

"Here comes the Initiate Hunefer, who is united with Ausir victoriously. You possess the essence of the essence of Horan. You possess the essence of the essence of Djehuti..."[17]

***

Initiates who followed the path to the Ka or merged with their Neter could potentially bypass the first death and go straight to the second death and merge with the Divine Consciousness. However, this path opens for everyone eventually. Prior to reincarnation, we all have the option to merge with the Divine Consciousness momentarily and experience our spiritual essence of infinity and everlastingness.

Reincarnation
Reincarnation takes place when the soul, from the state of the infinite spirit, decides to resume its journey in the earthly realm. As a result, its perception changes. From being oneness in spirit, the soul re-enters the physical world and begins to identify once more with the body until it gradually forgets its bigger perspective. This cycle of reincarnation — physical birth, life, and death, first spirit death, second spirit death, rebirth — continues until the soul experiences full enlightenment and ascends permanently into the state of the infinite spirit.

Summary
The ancient initiates prepared for the door of death throughout their life. They saw death as a change in consciousness and an opportunity for full enlightenment into the infinite self that we all are. The spiritual practices they undertook were an enactment of what the consciousness may experience at the time of death. This was a time when people were supported to die well. The ancient Egyptians were aware of a double death. In the first death, the consciousness experiences a comfortable lifestyle in the spirit realms akin to their earthly life. Gradually, the consciousness increases its awareness until it merges fully with the infinite spirit, the Divine, during the second death. At

reincarnation, the infinite spirit descends once again into the physical body and develops the personality and the ego-mind that is a feature of earthly life.

Endnote

17 Extract from the ancient *Egyptian Book of the Dead*, The Papyrus of Hunefer, Seleem, R. (2001), p. 79.

Chapter 20

Releasing the Dead and Healing the Living

Channeling from Iset:
You have lived in many dimensions and experienced diverse existences. All these offered you something: a gift of awareness, a gift of knowledge. As you step onto the spiritual path of Light, you have the opportunity to bring all the gifts from these incarnations together, heal deeply, and gradually transform into the Living Light that you are. The Hall of Records opens its doors, and the eternal scribe awaits to show you the endless papyruses of your lives. None of these lives are real; they are all dreams, dreamt by the Divine consciousness and created in Divine order. Now you can look at your dreams and bring your consciousness into the dream, becoming conscious in a world of illusion. Consciousness is the only reality that exists; everything else, including the physical and spiritual worlds, are projections. When you awake from the dreams, all you are is Divine Light and love.

Souls Stuck in the Earth Realm over Lifetimes

The ancient initiates lived a life of awareness, where death rituals were an integral part of their path. This is the path of transformation of the individual into the Light, the Living Sun, that we already are in our Ba state (Saleem, 2001), which also enables a smooth transition at death. The initiates practiced by resonating with the sun and working with their own luminosity and radiance.

***

"I advance in eternity like the rays of the sun. What does that mean? It is light itself."[18]

***

At death, some may not be able to find the Light. Instead they become stuck in the Earth reality, in their Ka, their double. The double is an exact image of the physical body, and it carries the karmic seeds, memories, and energy of all that the body experienced. For example, if someone had an illness that was not cured during their life, the double holds the memory or seed of that illness. And although the person is dead, the earthbound soul still experiences pain until the double heals through transitioning to the spirit realms. In that realm, an instant healing of the Ka can take place. When the consciousness remembers that it is perfection, all traces of illness and trauma are healed.

The perfection state only exists in spirit. In the material plane where everything is ephemeral and duality reigns, we cannot achieve perfection.

In the realm of the first death, a healing of our mental state also occurs. In life, many of our thoughts are unconscious, and we often speak harshly about ourselves, others, and the world, often without realizing it. This directs negative energy towards ourselves and others. Fortunately, these unconscious thoughts do not manifest instantly, and life offers us many opportunities to become aware of what we think and say and change our mindset. For example, one of my clients used to tell herself, "I hate you. Go to hell." In physical life, the cumulative effect of this self-judgment created difficult circumstances, as she attracted people who hated her or made her life hell. Life is always listening and trying to teach us a better way, sometimes through challenges. Generally, the more our vibration has heightened through spiritual work, the quicker our thoughts will manifest.

When the consciousness moves to the realm of the first death, its awareness increases. Our thinking becomes clear and focused. Spiritual growth takes place that enables the consciousness to detach from the egoic self and seek a higher purpose, working only for the highest good. For instance, a dead father may wish to offer comfort and healing to a living child who is ill. The spirit father will only do so if it is for the child's highest good. If the illness is acting as a teacher for the soul, the dead parent will not intervene. It will respect the wishes of the child's soul.

In the first death realm, following the life review, the double heals completely. And so a question arises, "Why do people carry illnesses, patterns, and issues from a past life, if a state of healing is reached?" There are two possibilities:

- *The person has unfinished business from a past life.* The soul lesson has not been learned, and there are unresolved issues with other souls that still need to be addressed. To illustrate, during life a father was unkind to his son, and at death his son still carried unresolved resentment towards him. In another life, these souls meet again and may exchange roles in order to bring closure. Souls manifest similar issues until awareness occurs.
- *A soul leaves part of itself behind through soul loss,* what the ancient Egyptians called "the wandering Ka." Parts of a soul may freeze in time and detach from the main Ka. Although there is an opportunity for a soul to reunite with all its lost soul parts at death, this does not always happen, and only the main part of the soul moves to the Light. In the next life, the soul looks for wholeness. It may develop the same issues, illnesses, and behavior patterns

to attract similar situations in order to gain awareness, heal, and reunite with the lost parts.

A key aspect of another of the death rituals conducted by the initiates included the invocation of the two sisters Iset and Nebt-Het. The initiates read out a sacred text, where the newly deceased was seen as Ausir, who, in the myth, had been dismembered by Set into fourteen pieces. Iset and Nebt-Het reassemble the fourteen soul parts lost through trauma, heal the soul and etheric body, and restore it energetically.

Iset and Nebt-Het govern incarnation and reincarnation. In this role, Iset represents the spiritual path of awareness through the infinite Light, and Nebt-Het the awakening of the unconscious self and its hidden unmanifested potential. Iset and Nebt-Het were called the hidden eyes of the Divine. They are spiritual powers that instigate healing, transformation, and awakening in life and death.

***

"The truth manifests itself through reincarnations. Iset and Nebt-Het cause these reincarnations to take place [...] Iset and Nebt-Het are the two hidden eyes of God, in the realm of the soul."[19]

***

Transforming Ammit in Life and Death
In the halls of Ma'at, we met Ammit, the hungry monster who is never satiated. Ammit carries the characteristics of three animals: the head of a crocodile, the body of a lion, and the hindquarters of a hippopotamus. These symbolize, respectively, manipulation, viciousness, and ignorance.

Ammit is a negative force in the world of duality that holds back the consciousness from awakening during life, and moving on after death. Until full enlightenment, Ammit plagues all beings on Earth to a greater or lesser degree. The vicious animal aspect creates addictions in the mind and body, and demands constant attention. Although we try to starve it, it can hook us back into unhealthy behaviors.

Sometimes this force prevents the soul from moving to the spiritual realms by generating difficult mind states at the time of death. The deceased is not at peace. They wander the physical world in their double, but cannot sustain themselves. The double is linked to the body and is sustained by the life-force the physical body generates. Now there is no body and no life-force to sustain it. Therefore the double of the distressed soul needs to find the body of a living person to attach to and feed off their life-force energy. The living person may experience tiredness and illness, and manifest the unhealthy emotional states of the attached spirit person. The living person's personality may also change, and they may hear voices that nudge them towards addictions or suicide. The spirit person does not want the living person to awaken and does all it can to keep them captive in negative thinking, whilst feeding energetically from their unhappiness.

These souls are like Ammit, for they too are never satisfied. They are unconcerned about the chaos they cause in peoples' lives and have no awareness of the distress they engender. These lost souls operate through fear and manipulation and feed off shame, guilt, pain, and anger.

Healers and Light workers may be able to perceive these attached souls and remove them from the living. Many times I have performed such healings. The spirit person usually tries to threaten and frighten me, adopting grotesque forms and becoming hostile. In one case, an aggressive spirit that had taken over a client's body tried to strike me. However, I am always safe and protected. Spirits are only shadows — they have no power of their own — and I stay in my power and Light surrounded by my enlightened guides. If it does not get its way through fear, the spirit may play victim. They say they have nowhere to go and try and manipulate the person's good nature. This is not true. They can move on to the Light if they wish, and the Neteru can be invoked to help them. Unfortunately many lost souls do not wish to move on, so I try and persuade them that this is their only healthy option.

There is a lack of understanding of what happens after death. People who die suddenly or traumatically may be angry and unable to step into the Light. Those killed in war, for example, may remain stuck in our world for hundreds of years. We do not know how to care for these trapped souls, and they can impact the ancestral line. Collectively, these wandering spirits lower the vibration of the Earth and create disharmony globally.

We cannot destroy or banish these spirits. The Light's way is to offer help. These spirits are lost and desperate and have forgotten their humanity. Yet, inside, a Neter still exists. Even Ammit cannot remove the god-form state from them, only stop them from accessing it. In helping these souls, we invoke the spiritual warrior Horan, who, in fighting Set, learned what chaos can do. Set is the human being who is acting out Ammit, and in the myth Horan has lost both his father and his inheritance to him. To overcome and subdue Set, Horan had to regain his power and find his Light. Set and Ammit are powerless before the awakened Horan. With his all-seeing vision, Horan defeats Set and castrates him, which is a metaphor: Set is rendered impotent and powerless. The initiates would say to Horan:

***

"Strengthen me in the same way as you have strengthened yourself and show yourself upon the Earth. For you have returned and withdrawn yourself and let your Divine Will be done."[20]

***

And Horan would say to them and the lost souls, "You have called me, but I am not the one to help you. You are hungry like Ammit, but this is not who you are. You have been slaves to Ammit, slaves because you cannot be satisfied. The more you eat, the hungrier you become. Even when you take from others, there is no relief. Remember, you are a Neter, a Divine one. You do not need others' power, for you are the Divine incarnated. I am not here to give you Light, for you have it already. Find the eternal Light, the sun Ra, within you. You are eternity and everlastingness."

The initiates practiced radiating their Light like Ra to transform themselves and Ammit. This Ra state can also support lost souls to remember their own spiritual nature and be free. We overcome Ammit by transforming into the Divine nature we are.

Summary

At the time of death, people can sometimes become stuck in their double, instead of moving forward into the spirit realms of the Light. Our state of mind at death determines how we approach this gateway. In ancient Egypt, they compared the conditioned mind and unhealthy emotional states to a hungry monster that can never be satisfied. This force, which affects everyone living and can prevent souls from moving on in death, was called Ammit. We can help lost souls by reminding them of their Divine essence.

Spiritual Practice: Transformation of Ammit in the Halls of Records

This is an advanced practice. It is best to allow 2 hours for the practice and have quiet time afterwards.

Open a sacred space by inviting Iset, Horan, Ma'at, Onpu, Djehuti, and the other Neteru and helping spirits of the Light you work with. Ask that they create a safe, protected space around you. Your intention is to heal yourself and past incarnations from the state of Ammit, and heal the planet by assisting the transition of souls who are stuck in the physical reality.

Firstly, connect with the enlightened consciousness that exists within your heart chakra. Intend to engage your inner voice. Ask your enlightened consciousness, Ib, to activate and become more present in your spiritual work and everyday life. Chant Ib three times to activate it and then stay quiet for 5 minutes, while the activation takes place.

Imagine that before you is the veil of time and space. Lift the veil and see yourself in the Halls of Ma'at. The sacred Neteru are already present and welcome you. They say you are now in the spirit realms at the time of the first death. Your infinite spirit, your Ba, welcomes you with love.

Self-cleansing and Self-healing Practice for This and Other Lives
Djehuti comes to you as the record keeper. He offers you a papyrus containing all the wisdom you have gathered from your existences. You have numerous gifts, and many have actualized in your lives. Hold the papyrus next to your heart-center and feel its energy. Ask to release any difficulties you are carrying from your incarnations.

Intend, "May I release the aspects of Ammit, which I have been carrying from life to life. May I release any shame, guilt, pain, illness, suffering, and anything in my records that is heavy."

As you focus on the intention, Ammit appears. Surrender all of this energy to Ammit and release it without judgment or attachment. The fear and pain belong to Ammit, not you. Ammit opens his mouth and swallows it.

Feel the papyrus again. Does it feel lighter? Perhaps the work is not finished. Ask the papyrus, "What is the main obstacle that prevents me from embodying my Light?" Stay quiet and acknowledge what your inner voice tells you. Ammit comes close to you, smelling the energy that belongs to him. Ask this energy to leave your body. Feel it and release it to Ammit, who devours it. Let all the energy of Ammit leave your cells. You may feel it moving out of your body — keep releasing it.

Now, call any soul parts that are ready to return and ask them to come back in their Divine essence. They come to you as a Neter, in total perfection. Fully accept and welcome these parts. Allow them to merge with your current self and fully incorporate.

At the end, hold the papyrus and feel it radiating the essence of your sacred heart Ib. Intend, "May the Light of my sacred heart transform me into my essence of the infinite spirit."

Helping Souls Pass to the Spirit Realms: A Healing Practice for the Collective
As you hold the state of Ra and radiate Light from your heart chakra, lost souls enter the Halls of Ma'at, attracted by the Light. They are tied to Ammit by chains of addiction, suffering, and negative thinking, and chains of resistance to move on. These chains prevent them from seeing the beauty of spirit. They need help but do not know another way to be.

To help them, welcome Horan, the spiritual warrior. Horan comes in his spirit form as the falcon and stretches his wings of Light and illuminates the whole place. He wears the double crown of the two lands — the physical and spiritual worlds —

symbolizing he has complete sovereignty everywhere and within himself.

He stands in front of these souls and says, "You are in a vicious cycle. You can never satisfy the conditioning. Wake up in your Light. This is what will heal you."

As you hold the state of Ra, imagine that, like Horan, you also have wings. Open your wings and radiate Light everywhere. You are the awakened Neter.

The lost souls see your Light and remember their luminous state. Onpu and Djehuti appear and open the gate to the spirit realms of the Light, where these souls can go, if they wish. As the lost souls manifest their Light, the chains around them loosen and they walk free. More souls come and move on, from battlefields, cemeteries, and all over the Earth. Ammit consumes all that the souls release as they go through the gate. Then Onpu and Djehuti close the door.

Activation of Horan

Horan comes in front of you as the falcon. He offers you an activation that will increase your awareness and access to the physical and spiritual worlds.

Horan takes the double crown from his head and places it on your head. Receive now the activation from Horan for 21 minutes.

At the end, return the double crown to Horan. Your crown chakra has been activated and holds the etheric essence of the double crown. You are Horan, the spiritual being living in a physical body.

Djehuti comes and offers you another papyrus, the record of all your lives. Open the papyrus and observe new lines appearing in a cryptic form that you cannot read. New possibilities for spiritual expansion will open in your life. Offer the papyrus back to Djehuti. Onpu joins you and opens the door for you to return to your life. Lift the veil of time and space, leave the Halls of Ma'at, and return to the physical reality.

As you come back, bring your awareness into your heart-center. Allow your Light to radiate inside your body, into every cell. Your physical and spiritual self become one. Take some time to integrate by staying in meditation for a few minutes.

Thank all the Neteru and your Ba for all you have received and the healing of the lost souls. They offer you the Ankh, eternal life, and protection for your inner vision, your third eye. They place protection all around you, and completely seal you, your space, and home before they go.

Endnotes

18 Extract from the ancient *Egyptian Book of the Dead*, The Papyrus of Hunefer, Seleem, R. (2001), p. 99.
19 Extract from the ancient *Egyptian Book of the Dead*, The Papyrus of Hunefer, Seleem, R. (2001), p. 84.
20 Almond, J. & Seddon, K. (2002), p. 139.

Chapter 21

Initiation into HEKA: Walking the Path of the Living Light

Channeling from Iset:
I fly swiftly as the kite, opening my wings of Light around you. The Great Mother's presence awakens your soul, opening a path for you to walk towards your radiant self and know yourself as the Light Eternal. I have gathered all the pieces that detached from you due to the conditioning. I reassembled your members and breathed the Sacred Breath of Life into you. Behold, I say, here stands the initiate of the Living Light.

Resurrection of Ausir as the Tree of Life

In the resurrection myth, Iset and Nebt-Het find the pieces of their soul brother, Ausir. They take these parts to the temple of the Living Light and the dismembered Ausir is re-membered. The myth is symbolic of our human journey. After the dismemberment of the heart by the ego state, we find the spiritual path that returns us to wholeness. We work with the Light energy (Iset) and the unconscious self (Nebt-Het), and gradually embody who we are.

As part of our resurrection from the "inert" state, we become fully present and connect Earth–body and sky–spirit. Our etheric channels, especially our central channel, is strengthened.

Each year, in the Osirion temple in Abydos, or Abdju, the priesthood re-enacted the Ausir mysteries through theo-drama. Two priestesses, channeling Iset and Nebt-Het, raised a pillar that was lying on the ground. The pillar represented Ausir and was called Djed. As they lifted the pillar, the priestesses said,

***

"We restore our brother Ausir from the inert state. We lift the tree."

***

The tree symbolized three things, all representing Ausir: the tree of life, the central meridian channel, and the backbone.

The resurrected tree is Ausir standing fully in his power and bringing awareness, stability, strength, and the flow of life-force energy to the Earth. When our backbone is straight and in good condition, it supports our body. In the same way, when the Djed pillar was raised, it supported the land, the people, and the spiritual work of the initiates. A spiritual practitioner was seen as a tree of life, with strong roots that connect to the Earth so that they can reach the sky, the infinite spirit. They also needed to develop awareness, stability, strength, and life-force energy, and become the Djed pillar.

The tree of life, either as a tree, or the Djed pillar, features in many temples and tombs in Egypt, particularly temples dedicated to Ausir built on the west bank of the Nile, the place of the dead and the spiritual realms. These places include pathways for walking meditation that symbolized the journey from the physical to the spirit realm and back. The path ended in the temple's holy of holies (representing the spirit realm), where the initiates would merge with their infinite self and experience rebirth. Then they would walk back to the physical reality. The first chamber after rebirth had a representation of the tree of life, Ausir, restored and resurrected, like the initiate.

These resurrection mysteries were re-enacted throughout Zep Tepi and the subsequent pharaonic times. Even when the world fell into the chaos of Set, the priesthood continued to raise the pillar and bring awareness, stability, strength, and life-force to their community. This is the way of the Light; it continues its work no matter what the world does. This is the path we sometimes walk alone, when the majority of the collective is mired in the conditioned reality. Sometimes we can become discouraged when our spiritual work appears to have no tangible effect. For example, people may take part in peace meditations and then be disheartened by the continued wars and violence. The initiate finds the way of peace within the storm and continues the work no matter the external circumstances.

A Myth of Resurrection of Our Innocence

Iset found the sacred sarcophagus containing the body of Ausir on an island in the River Nile, by an acacia tree.[21] *The tree had a strong trunk and bloomed in all seasons, and its flowers exuded a beautiful perfume. Everyone felt peaceful standing beside the acacia tree — their hearts opened, and they accessed the state of the innocent child.*

Iset opened the coffin and looked into the face of her soul brother, who was smiling even in death, and her heart was moved. Reuniting the power of Earth and sky within her, Iset chanted the words of power that heal all ills, even death. She knew that life and death are not separate, but states through which the enlightened soul Ra travels. The resurrected Ausir and Iset thanked the acacia tree, which was made sacred through the power of the two Neteru. Iset took a branch from the tree and gave it to Djehuti to plant in the temple of Iunu, in Heliopolis, the city of the central sun.

The acacia tree became the tree of life, and was cared for in the temple. It was said that Djehuti wrote the names of all the initiates of HEKA on its leaves in gold ink. Under the sun, the leaves shimmered. Perhaps, your name is written on the leaves of the tree of eternal life. Djehuti and Iset look after all who walk the path of the Living Light, ensuring they are protected and strengthened by the tree.

Since that time, Iset was known as Iset Shontet, the Lady of the Acacia Tree, the lady who safeguards innocence in the physical world.

Initiation

An initiation is a process of rebirth and a gateway that places us on a path of knowledge and higher awareness that comes from dedicated spiritual work. In the initiation of the Living Light, our vibrational frequency changes as we go through a door of etheric power. Our central channel, our Djed pillar, is stabilized and strengthened, so we can channel HEKA. This energy had specific names in ancient Egypt that were shared amongst the initiated, as these were words of power. The energy was regarded as the infinite spirit and wisdom, in its form of Light.

The initiation into these mysteries is a gate, not a destination. It is a new beginning. The path opens and we have to walk it. If we focus solely on receiving the initiations and do not work with the teachings and spiritual practices afterwards, the effect is minimal. If you wish to take initiation because your heart calls you to this path of Light, do not open the door and stay at the threshold. Allow the mystery to unfold within you by engaging with the Light in your daily life. Like a tree, our spiritual practice needs to be nourished by the Earth and watered by the sky. May our channel be in alignment from the root chakra that is fully active to the crown chakra that expands and reaches immense spiritual heights.

The path of the Living Light includes numerous initiations. After each initiation, we take time to integrate the energy and become accustomed to the higher frequency. The initiations affect the body; consequently, there is a period of re-adjustment which can include deep healing. At first, our body may not be able to handle the higher frequency, and we may fall asleep or become drowsy during the practices. As we continue the spiritual work, we grow and integrate the frequency the initiation brought to us. Then, we can decide whether to go forward and open another etheric door through a subsequent initiation. For the ancient Egyptian practitioners, their whole life was a series of initiations and spiritual practice; they lived a sacred life.[22]

From Ascension to the First Mummy

Eons before the Golden Times of Ausir, the beings who lived on Earth were etheric and did not have the type of physical body we associate with human beings. They had wings of Light, similar to how the Neteru appear to us. They did not exit their life through the gate of death; they effortlessly ascended into their enlightened state and shining spirit body, and left the planet. It may be difficult for us to imagine what this type of existence would have been like.

Through time, humanity lost this direct access to ascension. During Zep Tepi, the ascension portal was only accessed by initiates who dedicated their life to ascending, through initiation, spiritual practice, and the opening of the heart, and who potentially had the understanding to follow it.

The exit door of ascension is accessed through enlightenment. When someone becomes enlightened, they have the opportunity to transform their body into a body of Light, instead of leaving the body behind at death. Thus, there is no physical death. In enlightenment, the body reflects the truth of the spirit, free from the conditioning. The enlightened consciousness can manifest itself without form, or in any form it wishes, for form is only a way to exist in a physical conditioned world.

As the world became more materialistic and conditioned, less people ascended and more went through the process of physical death. Today, in our world of Set, ascension is a rare occurrence. Perhaps in the caves of the Himalayas or the rainforests of Peru some enlightened masters are still able to find that path.

However, some highly evolved spiritual masters can embody the awakened heart-center and reach such profound levels of compassion and love that their body may not disintegrate at death. Or, if it does, it takes place so slowly over hundreds of years that it appears as if nothing is happening. The master moves to spirit, but their body retains the Light and love that they generated throughout their life. And the Light is not lost. The body continues to exude this pure vibration and is a gift for the community. The Light of the Master supports the Earth, even when the Master is gone.

In Atlantis, they tried to find a way to preserve the bodies of the most highly realized teachers and masters who were regarded as a precious resource for the society. Thus, the art of mummification was developed. The idea being that by embalming the body of these esteemed teachers, a spiritual connection with the consciousness of the deceased was available.

However, what began as a preservation practice for a few highly evolved spiritual teachers became widespread after the fall. First the priesthood wanted to be mummified, then the rulers, court officials, and eventually everyone wished to be embalmed. The spiritual significance of the mummification process was lost. It became part of the culture, and people believed that if it did not happen, the deceased would not find rest.

In the pharaonic times, especially in the middle and new kingdom, another belief emerged. The priesthood taught that since Ausir, who was regarded as the first mummy, was re-assembled by Iset and subsequently resurrected, a time may come when Iset, as the lady of compassion and HEKA, would revive any deceased person. The idea birthed the need to preserve the body. The deceased's vital organs were placed in four jars beside the body, in anticipation of Iset's appearance and the person's restoration to life.[23] In these later times, the teachings had lost their essence, and people became so attached to physical life that they did not wish to die. The reinterpretation of the resurrection myth, that death was a deep sleep until Iset awoke them, gave people false hope. They forgot that Iset offers one way of resurrection: that of spiritual awakening.

This was not simply a mummification of the body but also of the soul. In the same way that one should be careful when entering some Egyptian tombs, as the spirit of the deceased might still be there, discernment is also needed with regard to Egyptian mummies. Some of these bodies are energetically impure and carry unhealthy intrusions and energies. People may feel nauseous after walking through a room in a museum that has mummified bodies. Before you decide to be in their presence or connect with them, ask, "Is this beneficial for me?"

There are always exceptions to this, and this applies to the Egyptian mummies of the high priesthood, especially ones from the earlier time. Some of these mummified remains still exude the love of the person's spirit. Remember, though, that if you connect with them, you are calling them to you, and I recommend you do so with respect and with a pure intention for the highest good. Be aware that this is not something you do as a beginner.

Summary

The high initiates understood a teaching of ascension about the transformation of the body into its essence of Light. This door for leaving physical life was achievable through enlightenment and required a life dedicated to overcoming the conditioning and identification with the physical self. Initiations into HEKA and specific spiritual practices enabled the ancient practitioners to reach a higher understanding. They saw themselves as the tree of life, the resurrected Ausir, who awakens from the inert state of spiritual ignorance and brings awareness, stability, strength, and life-force energy to the self and the collective.

Spiritual Initiation

I once saw Iset with my physical eyes. She materialized next to an initiate whom I was guiding in a visualization. Iset showed herself as a woman kneeling with one wing pointing straight in front of her and the other towards the sky, exactly as she is depicted on many ancient Egyptian temple walls. Her entire body and wings were blue. The vibration of the energy was palpable.

In this practice, you visit the temple of Millions of Years, to meet Iset with the intention of receiving an initiation to open your spiritual path of the Living Light in accordance with the wishes of your infinite spirit and the highest good, to the degree that you are able.

Open your sacred space by welcoming Iset, Djehuti, the initiates of the Living Light who work for the highest good and the Light, and your Ba, your infinite spirit. Ask that a safe and protected space be created around you.

Lift the veil of time and space and find yourself in the Golden Times, in front of the temple of the Osirion. A priest approaches you holding a censer containing frankincense and myrrh. He wafts the smoke around you, clearing your body and mind from the energies of the world. Walk through the smoke and enter the temple.

You walk down a descending stone path which leads you into a room. Ask permission to enter and receive spiritual initiation into the Living Light, for the highest good and with a pure intention to serve all beings. If permission is granted, enter the room. A priest of Djehuti approaches and takes you through the chamber into another room with a black sarcophagus. Inside the sarcophagus are all your dismembered parts.

The priest speaks to you about the two types of dismemberment you have undergone:

- First, the challenges of life situations dismembered you. Your heart, like that of Ausir, was hurt many times and retreated into the underworld. The conditioned mind reigned as you took on the ways of the world.

- Second, a purification took place when you stepped onto your spiritual path. You began to dismember the conditioning and let go of the adopted beliefs and patterns that defined you and your way of life.

Looking at all the dismembered parts in the sarcophagus, invite the Divine consciousness to emerge from them. Say, "May I become whole once more. May I fully embody the spiritual being I am."

As a result, a ball of Light rises from the sarcophagus and flows into your heart-center. Reunite with your spirit and meditate for 10 minutes.

The priest of Djehuti takes you into the next chamber, where the ancestors of the Living Light wait. A highly realized ancestor welcomes you and asks if you wish to be a channel for the Living Light. If this is your wish, state your intention to be a pure channel and serve the highest good.

As a result of your intention, Iset merges with the ancestor and performs an initiation as you stand silently in this space. Iset may raise your vibration and offer you gifts of wisdom in the form of energy. You may or may not know what these gifts are. Stay in this space until the whole initiation is complete. Do not let your mind take you out of the process too soon.

After receiving the initiation and transference of Light, two priestesses representing Iset and Nebt-Het appear, one on either side of you. They take you out of the temple, and the initiates of the Living Light of past, present, and future, who work wholly and fully for the Light, welcome you into the community. Above you flies the Bennu bird, the phoenix, affirming a new beginning for yourself, humanity, and these sacred ways.

Connect to your root chakra and imagine etheric cords linking your root chakra and the Earth, anchoring you to the Earth. You become the tree of life that connects with the Earth and all the underworlds. Positive energy flows into you from the Earth and all these worlds. Inside of you, the Djed pillar rises, and your backbone is strengthened. Your crown is open, and the sky and upper realms share the Light of Source with you.

See yourself as the enlightened one. Intend that the Living Light that flows into your heart radiates out to all for the highest good. Meditate in this space for 10 minutes. After this, intend that the channeling of the energy stops.

Djehuti offers you a papyrus with a drawing of the tree of life. On one of the leaves he has written your name in golden ink. Djehuti thanks you for walking a path of service to the highest good. He offers you the Ankh, eternal life, and places protection around you.

Your initiation is complete; you have crossed the threshold and now walk this path in your own way. Take a moment to offer thanks to the Neteru and the ancestors for all you have received, including being a conduit for the Living Light. Give thanks to Iset for guiding you on this journey of this sacred book. And give thanks to yourself for your spiritual work. Slowly bring yourself back.

Close your sacred space by thanking all your spiritual helpers and guides. Ask that they seal and protect you, your space, and home before they go.

***

Note: An initiation is an intense etheric energy download. If possible, dedicate the rest of your day to self-care. Stay in a nurturing space and drink plenty of water as your body continues to adjust. You may experience physical releases such as a cold, nausea, and headaches, or feel tired. Paradoxically, you may feel elated or joyful. You may have a significant dream. Whatever happens, trust that it is exactly what you need.

Endnotes

21 The acacia is a thorny Egyptian tree. The word is Greek and means without malice.

22 An initiation into the Living Light is a sacred and powerful experience. This first initiation allows you to channel the energy. If you wish to walk the path of the Living Light, which is a big commitment, I recommend you attend, either in person or through a live online workshop, the Spiritual Path of Iset course. This course will offer you the initiation into the First Gate of Awareness and the spiritual practices that go with it. From there, you can walk the path at your own pace.

23 These four jars, known as the Canopic jars, symbolized the four elements and contained specific organs of the viscera.

Afterword

In 2006 Iset appeared in a vision and asked me to be her teacher. I could never have imagined the vast and profound body of spiritual wisdom teachings that would emerge through me —nor how these would be transmitted in the most concise, structured, and supportive way to help those who wish to walk the path of the ancient initiate.

Later, Iset offered me another vision. In Zep Tepi, we lived and worked as a harmonious community of spiritual practitioners, supported by the collective. We came together and practiced the teachings through ritual and ceremony. The temple was a living structure where we felt the presence of the Masters who preceded us and met the enlightened Neteru. It was like a star on the Earth, shining infinite Light beyond space and time. Together, the temples and sacred spaces in Egypt created a constellation of powerful etheric sites.

We no longer have the temples and sacred spaces, and my heart yearns for the paradise lost. And so Iset asked me to build this again. What has gone can be remade. Like the ancient initiates, we can raise the Djed pillar and resurrect the dead Ausir. Maybe one day a new temple of the Living Light will emerge.

Iset has said that, like Im-Hot-Tep, in order to manifest a new reality, we must become it. To build what we wish to see in the world, we must first develop it within ourselves. We must embody our Light. Even though there is no longer a living temple, every initiate of the Living Light is a sacred space, a star in the night sky, illuminating the darkness. Together, we can create a powerful constellation and spread the Light everywhere.

Iset says:

***

"You have been born at a time of transition between the eras of Set and Horan. Many times people wait for the cornerstone, but the foundation is of great importance. You are the foundation for the new reality to emerge. Each of you who wishes to walk the path of Light is precious. This lifetime offers you this choice. If you wish to take it, we, the Neteru, will assist you.

In this new reality, do not look for all-knowing masters; look for the person who has a heart of goodness and kindness, a sacred heart that radiates Divine love. Your inner work to clear the conditioning is so important. Without that, Set will always be with you, and your infinite potential will remain hidden. Open the ways through abiding the rule of Ma'at and living a sacred life of spiritual practice. Become the temple, the sacred space. Become the shift you wish to manifest in your life and see in the collective. This is the way of the initiate.

The Neteru have such respect and love for you. We surround you with our wings. We are helpers and mirrors. We open your center of awareness so that you can see clearly. Follow the path of Light and trust in the Light of your soul."

***

Thank you for journeying with me to the Golden Times of ancient Egypt. I hope that this sacred pilgrimage helped you rediscover many pearls of wisdom. The practices in the book can be repeated and become part of your daily life. You can develop a deeper relationship with the Neteru and with yourself. In the way of the old initiates, may I offer you a blessing:

"May you be blessed with Ankh-Wedja-Seneb — Eternal Life, Divine Strength, and Wellbeing."

Author Biography

Foteini Fotoula Adrimi, BA(Hons), MSc, is a director in the ISIS School of Holistic Health Ltd, a school of healing arts, spiritual development, and inner transformation. The School teaches the Path of the Living Light of HEKA, the spirituality of the Golden Times of ancient Egypt. Fotoula received these teachings through direct revelation from the Goddess Isis in 2006.

Fotoula's other passion is shamanism, which runs in her blood from her paternal side. She is an active member of the Global Shamanic Teachers network created by Sandra Ingerman and teaches shamanic practitioner courses, and introductory and advanced courses in classic and core shamanism and from her Greek heritage.

Originally an environmental town-planner and graduate of the Sorbonne Paris-IV, Fotoula, was initiated into the teachings of the Living Light and remembered the ancient wisdom from past lives in Egypt.

Fotoula has also brought forward two other key spiritual teachings: The Rays of Divine Consciousness practices, which transform our spiritual DNA into its primordial nature of oneness; and the Priestess of the Moon teachings, which support women to become spiritual celebrants and lead community ceremonies. All these teachings support personal and spiritual awakening through the power of unconditional love.

Since 1999, Fotoula has lived and worked in Scotland, UK. She has also taught in Greece, Germany, the Netherlands, and in China, online. She has led numerous spiritual pilgrimages to Egypt and sacred sites in the UK. Her first book, *The Golden Book of Wisdom: Ancient Spirituality and Shamanism for Modern Times*, an Amazon UK bestseller, is an epitome of spiritual learning, mysticism, and soul evolution.

www.theisisschoolofholistichealth.com

Previous Titles

The Golden Book of Wisdom: Ancient Spirituality and Shamanism for Modern Times

This book is a roadmap to spiritual awakening. Fotoula Adrimi — shamanic practitioner, healer, and teacher — combines her extensive shamanic experience with ancient esoteric knowledge. This book has inspired hundreds of people to find their own understanding of shamanic spirituality. For those who wish to make sense of their life, from a shamanic perspective, this book opens a door for deep realizations and awakening. The book includes 24 teachings about the physical and spiritual reality and how to journey in the in-between. Each teaching is explained through theory, stories, poetry, and real-life examples. The accompanying spiritual practices take the reader progressively into their own direct experience of soul evolution.

"A cornerstone for spiritual learning [...] exciting and illuminating [...] a must read for spiritual and shamanic practitioners." Foreword by Sandra Ingerman

Note to the Reader: Where Do I Go from Here?

Thank you for reading this book. If it has inspired you to walk the Path of HEKA and you would like to work with the Isis School of Holistic Health Ltd, we have much to offer you.

Initiations into the Living Light and sacred teachings: Since 2006, we have been teaching the Seven Gates of Awareness, and since 2022, Iset asked me to open the Initiation of the Nine Primordial Neteru. These teachings are shared mostly in person, or in live transmissions. The introductory course that offers the Initiation of the First Gate is the Spiritual Path of Iset, Part 1. For more information, please visit the website.

Live and pre-recorded webinars: Part One and Three of the book are shared through two Online Courses accessed through the website: Living Light One and Living Light Two take you deeper into the material, with key spiritual practices, teachings, and activations that are not in the book. There is also an introduction to the spirituality of ancient Egypt webinar.

Community support: For those who take initiation, there is a growing community of Iset initiates and a regular online circle, which Iset guides through me. We offer weekly transmissions of the Living Light, sacred journeys, and a monthly newsletter featuring a channeling from Iset.

Shamanism

My passion is classic shamanism. I have been teaching shamanic practitioners since 2012. I embody the shamanic path, also practiced by my ancestors. I incorporate some of the ancient Greek tradition and classic core and multi-cultural aspects of shamanism in my teachings. For more information on shamanic work, I recommend my other book: *The Golden Book of Wisdom: ancient spirituality and shamanism for modern times.*

Programs of Study

The ISIS School of Holistic Health Ltd offers six main teachings to support people's spiritual journey of awakening. Programs include:

- The Path of Isis: Mystery School of Ancient Egypt courses
- Shamanic Practitioner Training and workshops on shamanism
- The Rays of Divine Consciousness: Healing of the spiritual DNA
- The Priestess of the Moon: A spiritual celebrant program
- Meditation
- Past Life Regression Therapy, including Practitioner and Master Practitioner training

Book by Fi Sutherland

Coming Home: Awakening through the Stillness into the Living Light
ISBN: 9781999641023

Fi's inspirational memoir of her recovery from a near-death experience in Peru in 2009 guides readers in the awakening process through personal development, spirituality, and meditation. Fi emerged from a coma in the enlightened state of unconditional love and inner peace. In this blissful state, free from fear, she was fully present in each moment. The luminous experience strengthened Fi's resolve to follow her heart and help others to consciously achieve the awakened state.

Websites

The ISIS School of Holistic Health website includes information on all aspects of my work. The School was co-created in 2015 with Fi Sutherland and is the physical gateway into mystery teachings.

www.theisisschoolofholistichealth.com

and Facebook page:

www.facebook.com/theisisschoolofholistichealth

Healing Practitioners in the World is a community of practitioners who graduated from the Isis school and offer their professional services on a personal basis or in circles and courses. They do not teach the material but practice healing and hold events.

www.healingpractitionersintheworld.com

The Global Network of Shamanic Teachers is a community of shamanic teachers and practitioners. Everyone therein has been through a rigorous teacher training program, taught by Sandra Ingerman. The Author is an active member of this global network.

www.shamanicteachers.com

References

Adrimi, F. (2018). *The Golden Book of Wisdom: Ancient spirituality and shamanism for modern times*. Glasgow: The ISIS School of Holistic Health.

Allen, J.P. (2015). *The Ancient Egyptian Pyramid Texts* (2nd ed). Atlanta: SBL Press.

Almond, J. & Seddon, K. (2002). *The Book of Egyptian Ritual: Simple Rites and Blessings for Every Day*. London: Thorsons.

Armstrong, K. (2007). *The Great Transformation: The World in the Time of Buddha, Socrates, Confucius and Jeremiah*. Bloombsury: Atlantic Books.

Bauval, R. & Gilbert, A. (1994). *The Orion Mystery: Unlocking the Secrets of the Pyramids*. London: Arrow.

Blavatsky, H.P. (1982). *Isis Unveiled* (5th ed.). Los Angeles: The Theosophy Company. p. 159.

Budge, E.A.W. (1901). *The Book of the Dead Vol. I Chapters L–LXIV*. London: Kegan, Paul, Trench, Trubner & Co Ltd.

Budge, E.A.W. (1901). *The Book of the Dead Vol. II Chapters LXV–CLIX*. London: Kegan, Paul, Trench, Trubner & Co Ltd.

Budge, E.A.W. (1901). *The Book of the Dead Vol. III Chapters CLX–CXC*. London: Kegan, Paul, Trench, Trubner & Co Ltd.

Budge, E.A.W. (1987). *Egyptian Religion: Egyptian Ideas of the Future Life* (3rd ed.). London: Arkana.

Budge, E.A.W. (1987). *Egyptian Magic* (revised ed.). San Diego: The Book Tree.

Dee, J. (1998). *Chronicles of Ancient Egypt*. London: Collins and Brown.

Ingerman, S. (1991). *Soul Retrieval: Mending the Fragmented Self*. New York: HarperOne.

Ozanich, S. (2016). *Dr. John Sarno's Top 10 Healing Discoveries*. Warren: Silver Cord Records.

Seleem, R. (2001). *The Illustrated Egyptian Book of the Dead.* London: Godsfield Press.

Sutherland, F. (2020). *Coming Home: Awakening through the stillness into the living light.* Glasgow: The ISIS School of Holistic Health.

Glossary of Terms

Akhet: Neter, eternity aspect of the Living Light, symbolized as the endless horizon.

Amun: Neter, the hidden one.

Amun-Ra: Neter, the Light of creation that flows out of the abyss and creates all realms of existence.

Ammit: monster representing the hungry mind.

Ankh: eternal life, enlightenment.

Aten: Neter, manifestation of the Living Light as the spiritual and physical sun.

Atum: Neter, the source before light and the source after light, the sun of creation.

Ausir: Neter, Osiris in Greek, the energy of the pure heart.

Ba: Neter, Divine consciousness, the Eternal Spirit, the Creator.

Beings of Light: enlightened spirits.

Bennu: the phoenix or sky bird.

Central Sun: point of Creation, also called Ra.

Creatrix: an aspect of Mut, the great mother, who births the cosmos.

Djehuti (or Thoth): Neter, symbolizes the peaceful, wise elder, teacher of the sacred language and hieroglyphics.

Djed pillar: symbolized by the backbone, represents stability, strength, and a strong foundation.

Duat: the spiritual worlds of the Light.

Ennead: the nine Neteru which are relevant to the human journey — Atum, Shu, Tefnut, Nut, Geb, Iset, Ausir, Set-Horan, Nebt-Het.

Geb: Neter, the Earth.

HEKA: the Light of creation, invisible universal power that governs all.

Hat-Hor: Neter, meaning "House of Spirit," the Divine Mother of unconditional love, the cow Goddess.

Glossary of Terms

Horan (Horus in English): Neter, the spiritual warrior who overcomes the egoic mind.

Ib: the enlightened heart — the Ba in the body.

Im-Hot-Tep: meaning "He Who Comes in Peace," the chief engineer of the Living Light project.

Ipet: the energy of the Divine Mother Goddess, the mother of Ausir, all creation.

Ipet-Sut: known as Karnak Temple, "The Most Selected of Places," also, "The Mother Who Provides Everything for the People."

Iset (Isis in Greek): Neter, bestower of HEKA.

Iset-Sothis: Iset of Sirius, name used to identify Iset.

Iunu (Heliopolis in Greek): the city of the central sun of creation, near present day Cairo.

Ka: the etheric body, the double, the dream or astral body.

Khat: the physical body, or a person who is unaware of their Divine nature.

Khaibit: the personality and the ego, or conditioned mind.

Khem or Khemet: the land of Egypt.

Khnum: Neter, an expression of the Divine masculine aspect of the Creator.

Khonsu: Neter, the moon.

Living Light: the Light of the enlightened Self, Divine consciousness, the Living Sun.

Living Lotus: the primordial lotus flower.

Lotus: symbol of unconditional love and awakening.

Ma'at: Neter, the Divine principle of justice, order, and truth.

Mner: the Great Pyramid, the place of Ascension.

Mut: Neter, the great mother, the Divine feminine aspect of creation, the Divine womb that births the cosmos.

Na-u-net: Neter, the Divine feminine power of the abyss Nu.

Nebt-Het (Nephthys in Greek): Neter, the silent power of the unconscious.

Nekh-Bet: Neter, symbolized by the vulture, protects the crown chakra.

Neteru: the cosmic powers, later called the gods and goddesses of ancient Egypt by Egyptologists.

Nu: the unmanifested state of the abyss, which houses the primordial waters.

Nun: the Divine masculine power of the abyss Nu.

Nut: Neter, the sky.

Onpu (Anubis in Greek): Neter, protector of the sacred teachings. Onpu helps those who die pass to the spiritual worlds of the Light.

Pyramidion: the capstone of the pyramid.

Ptah: the creator, Neter of darkness.

Ra: Neter, the shining one.

Ra-Horakti: Horan rising like Ra on the horizon, a person at the point of enlightenment.

Sahu: the ascension body, also the name for the Orion constellation.

Sekhem: sacred fire, universal etheric energy.

Sekhmet: Neter, the destroyer of chaos, the protector of order.

Seshat: Neter, brings the wisdom of heaven to Earth, teacher of sacred geometry and architecture.

Set: Neter, the embodiment of the conditioned mind.

Shu: Neter, the air that creates the atmosphere and the cosmic winds of manifestation.

Sothis: mystical name of the Sirius star, known as the spiritual sun.

Sut: a reed found abundantly in the Nile.

Tef-Nut: Neter, the primordial waters, also the celestial waters.

Theo-dramas: plays that re-enact myths.

Utchat: Neter, the eye of Horan, the all-seeing eye.

Wad-Jet: Neter, symbolized by the cobra, protector in the physical world.

Wapwawet: another name for Onpu, meaning "The Opener of the Ways."

Zep Tepi: the initial or first time, or the Golden Times of ancient Egypt.

O-BOOKS

SPIRITUALITY

O is a symbol of the world, of oneness and unity; this eye represents knowledge and insight. We publish titles on general spirituality and living a spiritual life. We aim to inform and help you on your own journey in this life.
If you have enjoyed this book, why not tell other readers by posting a review on your preferred book site?

Recent bestsellers from O-Books are:

Heart of Tantric Sex
Diana Richardson
Revealing Eastern secrets of deep love and intimacy to Western couples.
Paperback: 978-1-90381-637-0 ebook: 978-1-84694-637-0

Crystal Prescriptions
The A-Z guide to over 1,200 symptoms and their healing crystals
Judy Hall
The first in the popular series of eight books, this handy little guide is packed as tight as a pill bottle with crystal remedies for ailments.
Paperback: 978-1-90504-740-6 ebook: 978-1-84694-629-5

Shine On
David Ditchfield and J.S. Jones
What if the after effects of a near-death experience were undeniable? What if a person could suddenly produce high-quality paintings of the afterlife, or if they acquired the ability to compose classical symphonies? Meet: David Ditchfield.
Paperback: 978-1-78904-365-5 ebook: 978-1-78904-366-2

The Way of Reiki
The Inner Teachings of Mikao Usui
Frans Stiene
The roadmap for deepening your understanding of the system of Reiki and rediscovering your True Self.
Paperback: 978-1-78535-665-0 ebook: 978-1-78535-744-2

You Are Not Your Thoughts
Frances Trussell
The journey to a mindful way of being, for those who want to truly know the power of mindfulness.
Paperback: 978-1-78535-816-6 ebook: 978-1-78535-817-3

The Mysteries of the Twelfth Astrological House
Fallen Angels
Carmen Turner-Schott, MSW, LISW
Everyone wants to know more about the most misunderstood house in astrology — the twelfth astrological house.
Paperback: 978-1-78099-343-0 ebook: 978-1-78099-344-7

WhatsApps from Heaven
Louise Hamlin
An account of a bereavement and the extraordinary signs — including WhatsApps — that a retired law lecturer received from her deceased husband.
Paperback: 978-1-78904-947-3 ebook: 978-1-78904-948-0

The Holistic Guide to Your Health & Wellbeing Today
Oliver Rolfe
A holistic guide to improving your complete health, both inside and out.
Paperback: 978-1-78535-392-5 ebook: 978-1-78535-393-2

Cool Sex
Diana Richardson and Wendy Doeleman
For deeply satisfying sex, the real secret is to reduce the heat, to cool down. Discover the empowerment and fulfilment of sex with loving mindfulness.
Paperback: 978-1-78904-351-8 ebook: 978-1-78904-352-5

Creating Real Happiness A to Z
Stephani Grace
Creating Real Happiness A to Z will help you understand the truth that you are not your ego (conditioned self).
Paperback: 978-1-78904-951-0 ebook: 978-1-78904-952-7

A Colourful Dose of Optimism
Jules Standish
It's time for us to look on the bright side, by boosting
our mood and lifting our spirit, both in
our interiors, as well as in our closet.
Paperback: 978-1-78904-927-5 ebook: 978-1-78904-928-2

Readers of ebooks can buy or view any of these bestsellers by clicking on the live link in the title. Most titles are published in paperback and as an ebook. Paperbacks are available in traditional bookshops. Both print and ebook formats are available online.

Find more titles and sign up to our readers' newsletter at
www.o-books.com

Follow O-Books on Facebook at **O-Books**

For video content, author interviews, and more, please subscribe to our YouTube channel:

O-BOOKS Presents

Follow us on social media for book news, promotions, and more:

Facebook: O-Books

Instagram: @o_books_mbs

X: @obooks

Tik Tok: @ObooksMBS

www.o-books.com